THE PSYCHO-THERAPEUTIC CONSPIRACY

A SERIES OF BOOKS
EDITED BY ROBERT LANGS, M.D.

THE FIRST ENCOUNTER: THE BEGINNINGS IN PSYCHOTHERAPY
William A. Console, M.D., Richard D. Simons, M.D., and
Mark Rubinstein, M.D.

PSYCHOANALYSIS OF CHARACTER DISORDERS
Peter L. Giovacchini, M.D.

TREATMENT OF PRIMITIVE MENTAL STATES
Peter L. Giovacchini, M.D.

A CLINICIAN'S GUIDE TO READING FREUD
Peter L. Giovacchini, M.D.

TECHNICAL FACTORS IN THE TREATMENT OF THE SEVERELY DISTURBED
PATIENT
Edited by Peter L. Giovacchini, M.D., and L. Bruce Boyer, M.D.

BETWEEN REALITY AND FANTASY: TRANSITIONAL OBJECTS AND
PHENOMENA
Edited by Simon Grolnick, M.D., and Leonard Barkin, M.D.,
with Werner Muensterberger, Ph.D.

SPLITTING AND PROJECTIVE IDENTIFICATION
James S. Grotstein, M.D.

EARLY DEVELOPMENT AND EDUCATION OF THE CHILD
Willi Hoffer, M.D.

STRESS RESPONSE SYNDROMES
Mardi J. Horowitz, M.D.

HYSTERICAL PERSONALITY
Edited by Mardi J. Horowitz, M.D.

BORDERLINE CONDITIONS AND PATHOLOGICAL NARCISSISM
Otto Kernberg, M.D.

OBJECT-RELATIONS THEORY AND CLINICAL PSYCHOANALYSIS
Otto Kernberg, M.D.

INTERNAL WORLD AND EXTERNAL REALITY
Otto Kernberg, M.D.

CHILDREN AND PARENTS: PSYCHOANALYTIC STUDIES IN DEVELOPMENT
Judith Kestenberg, M.D.

DIFFICULTIES IN THE ANALYTIC ENCOUNTER
John Klauber, M.D.

THE TECHNIQUE OF PSYCHOANALYTIC PSYCHOTHERAPY VOLS. I AND II
Robert Langs, M.D.

THE THERAPEUTIC INTERACTION 2 VOLS.
Robert Langs, M.D.

THE BIPERSONAL FIELD
Robert Langs, M.D.

THE THERAPEUTIC INTERACTION: A SYNTHESIS
Robert Langs, M.D.

TECHNIQUE IN TRANSITION
Robert Langs, M.D.

THE PSYCHO-THERAPEUTIC CONSPIRACY

ROBERT LANGS, M.D.

Jason Aronson, Inc.
New York and London

Library of Congress Cataloging in Publication Data

Langs, Robert J.
  The psychotherapeutic conspiracy.

  Bibliography: p. 321.
  Includes index.
  1. Psychotherapy. 2. Psychotherapist and patient.
I. Title. [DNLM: 1. Psychotherapy—History. 2. Psycho-
therapy—Methods. WM 420 L285p]
RC480.5.L354   616.89'14   81-20601
ISBN 0-87668-488-6   AACR2

Manufactured in the United States of America.

"Truth emerges more readily from error than from confusion."

Francis Bacon

CONTENTS

PREFACE

For the first 100 years of psychotherapy, the goal has been to understand the nature of emotional disturbance. However, as this book shows, the basic curative factor in today's multitude of psychotherapies is not the pursuit of the underlying truths of emotional disorders. To the contrary, therapists are offering patients a variety of fabrications and defenses designed to falsify and preclude the realization of the painful emotional truths that form the basis of mental suffering. Psychotherapy, be it psychoanalysis, crisis intervention, encounter group, or behavior modification, offers "cure" through lies and barriers, rather than through genuine insight.

The published material in the field of psychotherapy, discussed in the first section of this volume, is indeed cause for alarm. It provides us with every reason to believe there has been an unrecognized unconscious collusion between patients and therapists that is detrimental to the curative process while providing some measure of pathological satisfaction for both participants to treatment.

The sources and manifestations of this inevitably human conspiracy become clear when we turn, in the second part of the book, to the origins of modern-day psychotherapy and psychoanalysis—to the painful struggles of Sigmund Freud and his colleague, Josef Breuer, in their pioneering work with emotionally ill patients. A study of their writings shows that psychoanalysis and all of the forms of treatment derived from it began in part in a conspiratorial fashion. As yet, we have not recognized and resolved that conspiracy, nor have we fully understood its nature and causes.

The Interpretation of Dreams (Freud 1900) occupies a special place in this historical reconstruction, since there we find the tools necessary for defining the nature of unconscious or encoded communication. Derivative (encoded) messages are different from our usual way of thinking and functioning, and are the critical basis for emotional disturbance. They are also the most significant medium of meaningful exchange between patients and therapists. By developing an understanding of the attributes of unconscious communication, it becomes possible to comprehend the therapeutic conspiracy—past and present.

A new version of an old form of message decoding is also introduced in this section of the book. Patients' messages are decoded in light of the stimuli (triggers) that evoke them, and our understanding of emotional disorders and of interactions between patients and therapists is radically changed. Equipped with such means of understanding, the final section of this volume describes ways in which present-day therapeutic techniques offer "cure" without truth. Yet, it also defines the attributes of truth therapy—its great advantages and painful liabilities—the note on which this work concludes.

This book is not a pessimistic work. An understanding of the deep need for lie-barrier therapies, together with the explanation of truth therapy, offers much hope for better human understanding and for improved psychotherapeutic techniques. Those who are concerned with emotional illness—and whom among us does it not touch?—should find optimism and new direction in the ideas offered here.

The present volume is based on a series of previous studies of the therapeutic interaction and the techniques of psychotherapy carried out over a period of more than ten years. Though carefully documented, much of this work has generated controversy. This book is intended as a presentation of ideas and illustrations, and is not designed to provide detailed clinical evidence. The classical psychoanalytic literature on which it is based has been described in *The Therapeutic Interaction* (1976b) and in *Classics in Psychoanalytic Technique* (1981a). Its foundation in clinical experience and research is presented in *The Bipersonal Field* (1976a), *The Listening Process* (1978), *The Therapeutic Environment* (1979), *Interactions: The Realm of Transference and Countertransference* (1980), *Resistances and Interventions* (1981b), and *Psychotherapy: A Basic Text* (1982). Thus, the efforts reflected on these pages arise from an extensive body of literature and are a natural development of the author's clinical work.

This book develops a thorough critique of accepted and hallowed therapeutic practices. It does so in order to bring into perspective and disrepute questionable therapeutic work. In the main, however, it is an endeavor to understand how and why we have departed from the search for the truths of emotional illness. It is also an attempt to conceptualize the paradoxical therapeutic value of avoiding and falsifying these truths. Above all, this book proposes a more effective psychodynamic cure in terms of sound realizations rather than deceptions.

There is no intention here to impugn the motives of those practicioners involved with established procedures. Nor is the book designed to arbitrarily deride the clinical work of the therapeutic community. Rather, it is an attempt to create an informed profession and public who will be more accessible to sound forms of treatment. It is hoped that we will all use these new-found insights cautiously and wisely, and with all due humility. Let reasoned change prevail. But reasoned change there must be.

THE PSYCHO-THERAPEUTIC CONSPIRACY

PART I
PSYCHOTHERAPY TODAY

CHAPTER 1

A SENSE
OF CONSPIRACY

Psychotherapy is in a state of utter chaos. The signs are blatant and yet mostly ignored. It is an unfortunate tribute to the desperate defensive capacities of the human mind that there is so little outrage, so little concern.

There is, of course, the occasional outcry—the rare book that describes an apparently incompetent or openly destructive therapeutic experience, or the personal grief over an obviously failed treatment and the greater pain after the suicide of a psychotherapy patient. Large and small doubts and questions arise, but sooner or later they lose their intensity and fade away.

Excuses abound. There is always the patient's sickness to hold accountable, to blame. He or she was too sick, too determined to destroy a life, quite inaccessible to treatment. With that kind of a rejoinder in the offing, how is one to risk the challenge? How is one to substantiate criticisms and counterclaims? The doubts themselves are quickly viewed as signs of sickness in the doubter.

Psychotherapy deals with universal experiences such as disturbances in human emotions, communication, and understanding. Because the field involves experiences shared by everyone, many lay persons develop rather definite opinions about the nature of emotional illness. They even believe that they are in a position to evaluate the means by which such illness may best be ameliorated.

However, the ease of discourse is deceptive. The situation is something like believing you know a great deal about pneumonia because you've heard someone cough, taken his or her temperature, and seen a blood-stained sputum. Of course, you may know something of how to bring the patient's temperature down with aspirin, how to relieve the cough with an antitussive agent, and you can even provide tissues for the expectorant. The lack of understanding of the underlying processes may not prevent naive measures of this kind from proving helpful on occasion. Nonetheless, these simplistic ministrations are more likely to have little influence on the pneumonic process itself, and the patient may well die.

The problem with psychotherapeutic procedures is not as transparent, nor is it as unmistakably grim. In fact, the odds are reversed—naive measures often provide immediate relief. It is only on rare occasion that they fail blatantly and someone dies through suicide or murder. Direct and superficial therapies are inherently appealing, and their inadequacies are far from self-evident. In consequence, medical doctors were compelled to discover antibiotics, while psychotherapists continue to apply many of the treatment measures in common use in the 19th century.

Evaluation of any psychotherapeutic measure is further complicated by the fact that psychotherapy, like most everything in life, has a surface and depths. There are manifest happenings and transactions and deeper meanings, evident phenomena and their latent implications. Thus it is possible to study the therapeutic process only in terms of evident transactions or through a careful consideration of deeper and less apparent implications.

The surface or manifest happenings in the field of psychotherapy require only common sense to be understood. One must bear in mind, however, that direct and practical considerations are not always a sound measure of the most important implications (the depths or latent meanings) of a particular psychotherapeutic technique. Probing may reveal a level of experience of which the individuals concerned are not directly aware—either entirely within a particular individual or as one dimension of the interaction between two persons.

Let us begin with what appears to be the relatively simple definition of psychotherapy: the treatment of an emotional disorder by psychological means. This delineation is at once concise and entirely indefinite. Each key word raises a multitude of questions. What is treatment? What is an emotional disorder? What are psychological means? It would be virtually impossible to reach a consensus on any of the three key terms in this definition.

"Treatment" can involve virtually any procedure imaginable, and not a few that are beyond all common fantasy. In the name of psychotherapy, an individual may be offered anything from masturbation and sexual intercourse (hetero or homo, one-to-one or in groups) to a chance to spend time with someone who, in essence, will never touch him or her and who will also speak only on rare occasions.

"Emotional disorder" is another elusive term. There is evidence of an emotional component in all forms of physical illness. Some specific somatic syndromes, such as peptic ulcer and asthma, are based to a significant extent on some form of underlying emotional disturbance. There is also an enormous range of psychological symptoms, from anxiety and phobias to panic attacks and hallucinations. There are, in addition, individual quirks and signs of disturbance in a person's character structure and personality, and in his or her everyday way of relating to or avoiding others.

The use of psychological means to alleviate an emotional disorder can imply techniques as different as brainwashing and psychoanalysis. One might accept as psychotherapy any primarily nonphysical effort to alleviate an emotionally founded disorder; but then, what is one to do with the touch techniques used in psychotherapeutic modalities such as sex therapy, EST, and encounter groups, and even in psychoanalyses, where some measure of physical contact is sometimes deemed necessary for certain severely ill patients? On the other hand, since there are no specific criteria by which a psychotherapeutic experience could be clearly established, one could propose that the present broad definition is essentially meaningless. A situation of this kind reflects and invites unprincipled thinking and treatment measures.

Of course, to some extent the same criticism may be made of the definition of medicine—the science and art dealing with the maintenance of health and the prevention, alleviation, or cure of disease. However, the level of uncertainty is far greater in the field of psychotherapy than in the field of medicine. Whatever the common lack of clear delineation, the consequences of this uncertainty have been far more serious for the field of psychotherapy than for the field of physical medicine. Certainly, isolated instances of poor

medical practice exist, but questionable forms of psychotherapy
are far more pervasive and unrecognized than in any other branch
of the healing professions.

Let us return to the example of the person with a cough. On a
truly professional level, he can consult a medical doctor or a doctor
of osteopathy. On rare occasions, he might consider a chiropractor.
Among physicians, he could go to a general practitioner, an internist, or a specialist in pulmonary diseases. The selection, however, would not involve the anticipation of significantly different
recommendations; rather, it would stem from the natural question
of who could provide the most immediate and effective care for
the illness.

The therapeutic approach in most instances would include a
physical examination, x-rays, and perhaps some type of blood
work. Through these measures and a carefully elicited history, the
diagnosis would be made in relatively straightforward fashion. In
all likelihood, there would also be a relatively strong consensus
among the different practitioners. Treatment such as bed rest and
medication would be prescribed by all. And while the specific drug
might differ from one practitioner to another, the class of drugs
would in all likelihood be the same. Additional forms of therapy,
such as heat or massage, would be included only by selected practitioners, but their role in the cure would be relatively insubstantial.
For a cough, the patient might also consult a pharmacist, a nurse, a
physician's assistant, a drug-detail person, and sometimes even a
friend. However, advice from any of these individuals would involve evident risk in light of an obvious relative lack of expertise.
The likely compromise in total and definitive medical care would be
self-evident. In light of the inability of any of these persons to carry
out the proper tests, the dangers involved might be quite extensive.
Overall, then, in a situation with a physical symptom, the sound
options available to the patient are relatively few. While differences
in diagnosis and treatment may exist from one practitioner to
another, in most situations these would be minor.

In contrast, the patient with mental suffering has the good
fortune or grief to be able to choose from at least 300 forms of
psychotherapy. There is adaptational therapy, creative aggression therapy, art therapy, group therapy, selective awareness
therapy, biotherapy, catalyst therapy, cognitive therapy, emotional
common-sense therapy, computer therapy, crisis intervention, dance
therapy, depth therapy, direct psychoanalysis, electric shock

therapy, encounter therapy, existential–humanistic therapy, experiential analysis, conjoint family therapy, feeling therapy, feminine therapy, Gestalt therapy, holistic therapy, hypnotherapy, insight psychotherapy, interactional therapy, logo therapy, megavitamin therapy, mirror-image therapy, money therapy through financial counseling, music therapy, narcoanalysis, new identity process, preverbal therapy, pharmacotherapy, placebo therapy, play therapy, primal therapy, provocative therapy, psychedelic therapy, psychoanalysis, psychodrama, psychosurgery, radical therapy, rational-emotive therapy, reality therapy, realness therapy, rebirthing, relaxation training, role-acting therapy, role-playing therapy, self-psychotherapy, separation therapy, sex therapy, short-term therapy, soap opera therapy, social case work, supportive psychotherapy, systematic desensitization, T-groups, transcendental meditation, transpersonal psychotherapy, video psychotherapy, vita-Erg therapy, and writing therapy—to name just a few (Herink 1980). Psychoanalysis alone involves at least two dozen distinct forms of treatment—Adlerian, experiential, existential, Frommian, Freudian, classical, Kleinian, modern, Reichian, Reikian, Jungian, Sullivanian, Rankian, etcetera.

The practitioners of psychotherapy include physicians, psychologists, social workers, nurses, dance therapists, pastoral counselors, and an enormous number of individuals without any basic academic training whatsoever in areas related to emotional disorders and the techniques of psychotherapy. The situation is such that virtually any person in the United States who so chooses may put out a shingle and call himself or herself a psychotherapist. If someone is moved to consult with him or her, he or she is in practice.

A FIELD IN CHAOS

The particular therapist who does especially well or is particularly charismatic has, and generally exercises, full freedom to create a school of psychotherapy and teach the "new-found" techniques to others. The field is already overpopulated by a plethora of training programs, and many are given superficial credence by one or another of a host of accrediting bodies, each with a different set of ill-defined standards. Nonetheless, a training institute for psychotherapy may exist as an independent body and even obtain a state license without ever having to demonstrate that the techniques involved are credible or even the least bit effective.

Extravagant claims abound. A seething state of war prevails. Disputes within a particular faction lead to spin-off sub-schools. There are no kind words for alternative techniques. Occasionally a frontal attack is launched from one approach on the techniques of another. Most of the time, classical analysis is the butt of the assault. Often enough, the group under question simply ignores the threat as if it were not at all worth the effort of a rejoinder. A wide-spread fomenting discontent pervades the field and, in some ways, its clientele. The objecting factions and their objections are so diverse and fragmented that the disillusionment seldom crystalizes into a clear statement of objection and virtually never leads to effective action.

In all, schools of psychotherapy tend to be neatly insulated, well rationalized, and relatively impenetrable systems. Debates regarding therapeutic practice show little in the way of engagement. Under pressure, there is always the rejoinder that the other system is ridiculous, too deep, too superficial, or just plain "crap"—to use the language of Fritz Perls (1969) when he spoke of psychoanalysis.

Some therapists are out and out charlatans. Most, however, are quite dedicated and sincere in their efforts and beliefs. Still, there are no clear standards of technique and efficacy. Research into the effectiveness of various forms of psychotherapy is extremely crude and insubstantial. There are signs that anything may "cure" an emotional illness, though many things may actually harm the patient and exacerbate his or her symptoms. In many instances, the cure appears paradoxical in light of the openly hostile, attacking, demeaning, exploitative, or seductive qualities of the treatment procedures. Still, if relief comes, the rest is soon forgotten.

No single school of psychotherapy, not even psychoanalysis, has established a clear claim as the main voice of the profession and the optimal mode of cure. Privately, the members of each major form of psychotherapy believe they have the last word. They see themselves as the vanguard, or as the up-and-coming therapy of the future. Most therapists who adhere to a particular school are at a loss to understand why other healers do not break ranks and flock to their banner. Many groups plan missionary conferences and teaching programs to attract converts to their way of thinking and of doing therapy. And yet, because there is a notable percentage of therapists who shift their basic approach each year, the situation remains in a state of stalemate.

On the face of it, the absence of standards, the extraordinary promise of cure from practitioners of highly divergent techniques (compare electroshock with psychoanalysis, primal scream therapy with deconditioning), and the failure of any single therapeutic discipline to establish itself as the standard-bearer for the field, all point to a situation totally out of control. There is no clear or solid foundation or definitive methodology through which contradictory claims may be evaluated and the treatment experience understood in depth. Lacking any general sense of science, psychotherapists attempt to cover over their problems by terming their field an art. Clearly, something is entirely amiss.

It would seem, then, to be either inordinately dangerous or utterly pointless to take on the therapeutic establishment. When it comes to emotional disorders, reasoned exchanges are evidently impossible. Can a mere mortal challenge this army of gods? We have been so fearful of these deities and their tools, we have not dared to see the openness of their folly.

Here then lies the first of many conspiracies in psychotherapy: the willingness of patients and the public at large to sumbit to or accept without protest otherwise unmistakably destructive ministratrations. The variety of psychotherapeutic modalities lends support to the thesis that psychotherapy customers are rather indiscriminate consumers in their choice of therapy and therapists. It would not be surprising to discover that, contrary to popular belief and surface thinking, they actually have strong, latent needs to find the most compromised treatment situation possible and the worst practitioner available.

It is one of the great misfortunes of psychotherapy—and yet one of its great attractions—to have a client or customer who wishes as much for poor service or treatment as for good. Imagine being in a business where your customer clamors for a damaged product. How likely is it that you will give him or her a sound item (especially when it is cheaper and easier to produce the lesser piece)? The situation is virtually hopeless without careful scrutiny, especially when it is both more profitable and self-serving to offer the lesser product. Human nature, with its powerful, seemingly innate and biologically-founded defensive trends, leads most individuals in the direction of least resistance. And psychotherapists are, for better or worse, quite human. If patients want damaged services, damaged services they will get.

CHAPTER 2

AN UNCONSCIOUS COLLUSION

General impressions of a field such as psychotherapy are, of course, open to many uncertainties and biases. Each critique can be criticized, each evaluation subjected to rejoinder. Without definitive evidence (for the moment), those perspectives that are most cogent can only hope to touch a responsive chord in a sensitive reader, who may then readily accept the sense that they convey at face value, though all the while still keeping an open mind. An allusion to a single instance can be readily decried as a poor example, nonrepresentative, good reason for the existence of the other few hundred forms of therapy, or even simply ignored. In a way, however, every single written word and every therapeutic effort is the responsibility of the conditions of the field. Psychotherapists must be held accountable on some level for all that is done in the name of their profession. If the procedures involved have been clearly harmful to their patients, they should develop means by which to identify and eliminate the unwarranted practices.

The books on psychotherapy total a not so small multiple of the number of different schools extant today. They reach into the thousands. Attempting to sample the most popular and most frequently practiced techniques proves to be extremely frustrating and tedious. Each approach has its own rather idiosyncratic theory of emotional disorder, its own language and lingo, and its own set of rationalizations for its mode of practice. Illustrations tend to be poorly documented, with a minimal presentation of specific clinical data and virtually no sense of the therapist's interventions and the therapeutic interaction. More rarely, they are offered in such extreme detail that they become virtually incomprehensible.

This chapter does not develop a specific critique of the different forms of psychotherapy but, rather, a reasonable sense of what is happening in the field. In each example, one is dealing with dedicated therapists who have had the courage to dare to reveal themselves and the nature of their often highly personal work with their patients. Each of these excerpts involve procedures that they have, however crudely or inadequately, attempted to research and document. They have a strong rationale for their work and are deeply and sincerely committed to the practices they espouse. This material deserves our considerable respect, and criticisms should be tempered with the realization that these are the best possibilities we have been able to create in the first 100 years since the psychoanalytic revolution.

The sampling will help the reader to develop a more definitive sense of what takes place in the office of a psychotherapist, and will provide a substantial footing on which to begin a reappraisal of the field. Although we lack the tools for a detailed analysis of the nature of these therapeutic transactions, and especially of the conscious and unconscious interactions between patient and therapist, there are certain self-evident features of these vignettes that have not, as yet, been afforded the attention they deserve.

MODERN PSYCHOANALYSIS OR THE PARADIGMATIC TECHNIQUE

The first example involves the supervised case of a married male patient with a female therapist (Spotnitz and Meadow 1976, pp. 213 ff.). In one session, he describes how his wife is trying to push him into getting a better job. He has thoughts of divorcing her; he should get angry, but can't. He is angry and miserable about taking so long to grow up. He speaks of plunging a knife in his head and the therapist asks, "Why don't you do it?" The patient responds by refusing, and adds that he wants to grow up—that's what he is coming to therapy for.

In the next session, the patient indicates that he will be starting a job the next day. He is fearful that he will not have the right attitude, will not work hard, and will get fired. Then he would go downhill and be a bum, and he would *have* to shoot himself. The analyst asks what is wrong with that, and the patient says that he feels she is trying to destroy him, that she wants him to kill himself. The analyst then says that she doesn't want him to do that, she just wants him to say what comes to his mind (free associate). The patient responds that he does not want to die; he is mad at himself for not doing enough.

The nonprofessional but sensible reader might feel that there is something amiss in a therapist's asking a patient why he doesn't plunge a knife into his head or suggesting to a patient that there is nothing wrong in shooting himself. The nastiness and hostility, and even the murderous quality, seem self-evident. The patient is being goaded and provoked. However, the procedure is not the arbitrary product of the therapist's uncontrolled destructiveness. In fact, the supervisor (teacher) of this therapist actually felt that she was having difficulty in properly applying the provocative qualities of this particular approach, that she was not nearly aggressive enough.

The technique involved is said to be designed to direct the pathological narcissistic (self-directed) rage of a particular kind of patient away from himself or herself (where it is fixed and destroying the patient) and onto the therapist. The outward discharge of aggression—a variation on the abreactive (release) technique with which psychoanalysis began (see Part II)—is said to have a curative influence on the patient and his or her pathology.

Thus it was the therapist's statement that she did not want the patient to kill himself, only to free associate, that was seen in supervision as the basic technical error. The therapist was criticized by her supervisor because she had backed down from the more advisable style of intervening reflected in her earlier, however provocative, questions. The supervisor therefore proposed that his supervisee had a serious problem in handling her own aggressive impulses, and that this was interfering with a full application of the paradigmatic technique. The supervisee evidently accepted this evaluation and critique of her work and appears to have vowed to resolve her sadomasochistic problem in order to be a better therapist. Oddly enough, then, this therapist is asked to find a way to persistently attack her patient, and the suggestion is made by her supervisor that to work in a less hostile fashion reflects an emotional problem within the therapist—what is called *countertransference*.

The supervisee appears to have been strongly motivated to make some changes. Following the supervisory discussion, she had a dream of her patient that involved his impression that she was trying to destroy him. In one part of the dream, the patient gets off the couch and stands before her. The therapist is terrified that he will kill her. Her sense of the dream is that the attack would be sexual.

The next night, the therapist dreamed again. In her dream, a stranger takes the patient away from her in the midst of a session. The stranger then returns alone and tries to rape her. The therapist cries for help, but no one hears her. She wakes up in a state of terror.

These dreams were subsequently reported to the therapist's supervisor. They were understood to reflect the inner (intrapsychic) problems of the therapist, and apparently it was suggested that they involved pathological masochistic wishes—the *need* to be sexually attacked and raped. These wishes were said to be a factor in the therapist's difficulty in using the hostile but necessary techniques she was being taught. Her understanding of these dreams was then said to have freed her ability to utilize the proper approach to this patient.

In his session a week later, the patient says that he is feeling hopeless; there is nothing to do but kill himself. The analyst quickly asks why he doesn't do so now, and the patient says it would be painful. The analyst says that the patient could die without pain, but he states that he does not want to die. The therapist then asks why he can't die to please her. The patient responds that he has no such wish. His wife nags him about getting a better job, but he doesn't want to get one just to spite her. He gets mad when the therapist talks of his dying. How would she like it if he picked up the table and smashed it over her head? Would she like to die then?

This is an example of a psychoanalytic technique. The patient accepts this treatment effort despite his verbal protests and continues in therapy with the analyst. On the surface, the technique involves goading a patient toward killing himself. It is proposed, as noted, as a means of destroying what is called a narcissistic (self-attacking) defense by enabling the patient to put his feelings into words and to attack the analyst instead of himself. It is viewed as the preferred channel of cure for patients showing this type of severe narcissistic emotional disturbance.

For many individuals a technique of this kind would appear inherently destructive. When the patient says on the surface that he has not entered treatment in order to kill himself, he may himself well be commenting on the treatment process and objecting to its nature. If so, the patient is indeed divided: on the surface, he accepts this therapy and continues to work with the therapist, while on some other level, he is highly critical of the treatment procedures.

If the therapist's dreams are a clue, it may well be the *patient* who wishes to be attacked and raped, that he accepts the treatment procedure because it satisfies these highly pathological needs. When this gratification becomes excessive, the patient becomes directly furious at the therapist and lashes out at her.

If this is the case, this patient is participating in a psychotherapeutic conspiracy. The collusion involves a therapist who believes that she is offering a constructive form of treatment, even though there are indications that this is not at all the case, and a patient who on some level finds the treatment experience highly destructive and inadequate. (Note his comment that he gets mad at himself because he's not doing enough; in some encoded way, this could allude to an unconscious perception of the therapist.)

Still, because of some need to suffer, or due to other factors that have not as yet been identified, the patient remains in therapy despite his conscious and unconscious objections. The therapist herself continues to use these procedures despite the signs of doubt reflected in her dreams. Thus both patient and therapist appear to be quite divided in their attitudes toward this type of therapy. Because of this split (the contradictory needs and perceptions), which prevents responsive action, the treatment continues despite its highly questionable attributes.

The therapist's dreams help to clarify the nature of this psychotherapeutic conspiracy and are in some ways a highly poignant commentary on the field. Even without an elaborate dream analysis, it is evident that the dream was stimulated by both the treatment situation and the therapist's supervisory experience. The dream lends itself to several interpretations in this light. These formulations involve feelings and perceptions of the situation in which the therapist finds herself, that are not consciously and directly formulated and stated. The dream suggests an unconscious awareness within the therapist that there is indeed something highly destructive and sexual in the technique that she is using with this patient. Her fear that her patient will revenge himself on her may well be quite realistic. In dreaming that the patient gets off the couch, the therapist may be advising him—quite unconsciously—to leave treatment.

The second dream extends these impressions. In it, the therapist does indeed arrange for the patient to leave treatment, however temporarily. The image of rape may again represent the therapist's (self-) perception of how she is actually treating the patient. The therapist's own cry for help, which is heard by no one, may well allude to and convey the plight of many patients in psychotherapy today: through rare direct and, more often, indirect or encoded messages, they cry out for help when faced with a therapist who is being hurtful. As already suggested, these disguised pleas are seldom recognized and given the credence that is their due. On some level, the patient feels trapped in a terrifying situation from which there is no escape or relief. Remarkably few patients take flight from treatment despite a deep unconscious sense of this kind.

These dreams convey a sense of a therapist striving to perfect a technique that, on some unconscious level, she herself views as sexually and murderously assaultive. Because of a conscious belief and dedication to the paradigmatic technique that she is learning, this therapist is herself trapped in a destructive situation from which there is no evident escape. There are signs that she is terrified of what she is learning and yet lacks the resources and conscious insight to protest or do otherwise.

Although definitive data is certainly lacking, there are many reasons to believe that conflicts of this kind exist in virtually every therapist in the field today. In Part II of this volume, their existence is seen in both Josef Breuer and Sigmund Freud, the two founders of psychoanalysis. Because these conflicts go relatively unrecognized, therapists find it necessary to collude with their patients in order to work in a fashion that, on some level, both know to be flawed, although neither is capable of confronting the problem on a conscious basis.

These impressions find some support in an analysis of this dream in light of the therapist's supervisory experience. In general, the supervisors of psychotherapy have failed to provide the safeguards that the field requires. Instead, supervision has been an arena in which prospective therapists are rather rigidly taught (brainwashed?) the particular set of technical procedures that constitute the practices of the school of psychotherapy to which they are committed. In general, criticism of or disagreement with these procedures is met with considerable hostility and skepticism in the supervisor or teacher. Objections by trainees are seldom evaluated in light of their credibility; rather typically, they are viewed as a sign of problems in the student therapist, of unanalyzed countertransference. The student tends to meekly accept this criticism, however unjust, in order to obtain the supervisor's approval and to graduate from his or her training institute. This too is an unfortunate, though unconscious, conspiracy.

Since the dreams were prompted (triggered) by the supervisory discussion, it is not too far afield to speculate that they involve the supervisee's reactions to her supervisor. He had criticized the apologetic aspect of the therapist's work. He was critical of her inability to be more unrelentingly aggressive. In this light, the dream in which the therapist is terrified that her patient will kill her in some sexual fashion may be readily translated into a valid unconscious perception of, first, the very measures that the supervisor is advising the therapist to use, and second, the overall nature of the supervisor's directive to his supervisee. This implies that the supervisee experienced her supervisor as sexually hostile in his teachings. It seems evident that there is some measure of truth in this perception; it is difficult to suggest that the therapist is representing the situation in too extreme a fashion (to the extent that this is the case, however, there is some distortion in the supervisee's view of the supervisor, based on her own hostile and sexual fantasies).

The second dream lends itself to a far more convincing analysis of this kind. It does not seem too far amiss to suggest that the stranger who takes away the patient in the midst of his session with the therapist is the therapist's supervisor. In returning alone to the therapist, a situation comparable to supervision is created. There then follows an effort at rape, in response to which there is no one to hear the therapist's cry for help.

The cry for help is typical of supervisees and speaks strongly to the idea that the dream does indeed involve supervision. If so, the therapist is characterizing her teaching situation as a rape for which there is no recourse. In most supervisory situations, the supervisee is indeed at the mercy of the supervisor, who often lacks a sympathetic ear.

In all, whatever these dream images reflect of the patient's sadistic and masochistic, sexual and aggressive, difficulties, they also appear to provide a moving statement of a therapist's unconscious perceptions of her own work and of her supervisory experience. In both instances, despite signs of inner discontent and concern, the therapist proves to be incapable of conscious insight or action. Dividedness or splitting of this kind is indeed extremely common among psychotherapists. In a way, it is part of an *internal* psychotherapeutic conspiracy that few have found the means to resolve.

Psychotherapy trainees, whatever their professional qualifications, are strikingly poor therapists. They have chosen to become therapists for a mixture of reasons, some highly pathological and some enormously constructive. Attempting to do therapy, they are faced with such complicated communications from their patients and with such disturbing activations within themselves that it is virtually impossible for them to respond correctly and soundly on the spur of the moment.

In general, neophyte therapists, most of whom either are not as yet in personal treatment themselves, or who are in the opening phases of such therapy, tend to bring considerable turmoil into their therapeutic efforts. As a rule, it is only their sincere dedication and often their dogged determination to be helpful, however misguided the specific therapeutic measures, that offer a constructive note that is experienced by the patient. Much of the rest involves either being hurtful to the patient who does not do well or providing relief through some kind of dumping of the therapist's own disturbance into the patient, to which the patient responds paradoxically with improvement.

There is also in the work of such therapists a frequent shift to relatively manipulative techniques and to the uncertain cures effected in the various ways discussed earlier. On the whole, were it not that poor therapeutic work can often offer some type of paradoxical emotional relief to patients, trainees would have considerable pain and difficulty in learning this difficult art and science. After all, the blow to one's self-esteem in recognizing that he or she has been hurtful to a patient is enormous. It asks a great deal of a therapist to be honest in the appraisal and appreciation of his or her own therapeutic work and to tolerate the personal mortification that is an inevitable part of the learning experience. When a therapist has an emotional involvement as well, the grief is enormously increased. This, too, is a strong motive for conspiracy as an alternative to having to face and cope with extremely difficult realizations.

A sense of collusion is evident on all sides when it comes to treatment in the hands of trainees, most of it in the form of clinic psychotherapy. Many patients accept this type of therapy without the least question or doubt, as if it were the finest care in the world. An outside observer would detect abundant evidence of highly questionable practices, though neither patient nor therapist seems mindful. As a rule, a secretary rather than the therapist sets and collects the fee, and patients' charts are often scattered about and sometimes easily identified and read by passing strangers or other patients. Names of patients are called out for all to hear, and comments are made by clinic personnel that are obviously far too self-revealing, or which unnecessarily expose both patient and therapist alike.

Direct observation of sessions or the supervisory presentation by a therapist-in-training of his clinical work, often reveal the use of evidently poor techniques. At times, there is a strong sense of chaos, with hasty and disorganized interventions by a therapist who is under pressure from his or her client. Therapeutic inexperience breeds impulsive and poorly thought out interventions.

Here too, in most cases, there is nary a protest. Patients share anecdotes in clinic waiting rooms, and most of them virtually worship their therapists. Despite all sense of abuse and misuse, some of them even begin to feel and function better than they had before treatment started. Obvious difficulties are automatically ignored; the need to believe and idolize has a blinding function.

Surprisingly, there is evidence of similar denial, though in a different form, in those who supervise these fledgling therapists. Virtually nothing is written of the risks of treatment in inexperienced hands. The specific problems and massive difficulties in adequately mastering the proper techniques of psychotherapy have not been given sufficient consideration. Supervisors readily refer patients to their supervisees, even when evident problems remain in their work. Some of this may well arise because of the lack of definition in the supervisor's own therapeutic work. Some of it involves needing to believe as a supervisor that one has been helpful and successful with a supervisee. Some of it arises in having to be the beneficent provider. All of it helps to contribute to another psychotherapeutic conspiracy. These compromised treatment approaches serve therapists incapable of more arduous and insightful forms of work.

In keeping with these trends, many therapists think nothing of referring a patient to one or another clinic for psychotherapy, despite the fact that it is highly likely that the treating therapist will be relatively inexperienced. Many patients gladly attend such clinics, even if they actually have the funds for private psychotherapy. This denial of significant differences in levels of expertise, in capabilities as therapists, and in available potential to be constructively helpful or destructively damaging is especially striking in the field of psychotherapy. In most medical situations, patients are acutely aware of the value of seeing a well-trained physician, especially someone who has taken the time to become a specialist in a particular area. Yet even there, one often observes resistances in patients and family members against obtaining the best possible form of treatment for the individual who is ill. These unconscious obstacles exist in all situations; when it comes to psychotherapy, they are especially strong.

Similarly, both patients and therapists tend to ignore blatant differences in psychotherapeutic treatment approaches. The obvious discrepancies between cure through nudity and touching and cure through understanding are readily ignored. The difference between relief obtained by submitting to the overwhelming and intrusive pressures of a therapist and that obtained through self-realized insight derived from an unobtrusive and well chosen interpretation is similarly obliterated.

The basic denial of differences in likely outcome of treatment as a consequence of the level of training of a psychotherapist and of distinctly different treatment approaches offers strong evidence for the presence of a psychotherapeutic conspiracy. However, observations drawn from clinic supervisory work produce even more disquieting signs of collusion. Slowly—though it should have happened almost immediately—the realization develops that patients are willing to absorb and find relief through a wide range of clearly poor and destructive psychotherapeutic techniques. It requires several dramatic examples to overcome the surprise and shock of recognizing that in the midst of therapeutic chaos, some of these patients are actually functioning better than they had before therapy. Here is a challenge that defies understanding. Both supervisor and supervisee agree that the therapist has behaved quite badly and with great provocation. How is it possible that the patient improves under these conditions? In time, this book will provide some answers.

CHAPTER 3
OTHER CONSPIRACIES

Much has been written about Esalen, T-groups, antiestablishment groups, the humanistic movement, and the multiplicity of variations on psychotherapy that they have produced. Jane Howard, in her book, *Please Touch* (1970), describes her experiences with a variety of human potential movement therapeutic modalities. There is a powerful accent on disinhibition, surrendering controls, modifying usual interpersonal boundaries, giving up evident defenses, and the abandonment of all sense of privacy. These cures involve nudity and physical contact with other clients and with the therapist. Patients are goaded to let go, to spew out pent-up hostilities, to become vicious, and to destroy objects. Principles of ethics are invoked as a basis for prohibiting intercourse, though touching is encouraged. Laterday sex therapies, of course, show no such restraint. Intercourse with a surrogate, and perhaps some talk with a therapist, consistute the substance of such treatment.

In nude marathons and sensitivity-training workshops clothing is said to represent our mistrust of each other. The basis for this form of therapy is, "You were born nude, weren't you?" When emotions are felt, they are encouraged, pursued, and acted out on objects rather than people. Psychoanalysis had its origins in full body massages and in abreaction, in getting out so-called bottled up emotions. One hundred years later, they remain essentially unmodified and accepted forms of cure, though with modern-day touches.

Group members rant and rave about destructive figures in their past and present, and about people who are hateful, senseless, and who drove them crazy. In reading excerpts from all types of psychotherapy, themes of this kind emerge repeatedly. Virtually without exception—even in psychoanalysis—these communications are taken at face value. The bad other—though not the therapist—is accepted as the source of the patient's inner turmoil and pain. Exorcism is the cure. The past is attacked to cure the present.

As diverse experiences are accumulated, a common method and goal emerges. These psychotherapies appear to involve cure through discharge, by exorcism of the bad inner stuff, by abreaction, by attack. Still, a suspicion arises that other factors are at play. In light of the extraordinary power of these therapists and group leaders, is it possible that in some way these patients are also reacting to the immediate therapeutic experience? Could it be that the overbearing, goading, destructive figures whom these patients talk about from their pasts have something to do with the goading, destructive, relentless qualities of this type of therapeutic approach? Could these patients feel that their therapists are trying to drive them crazy? But if so, how could this bring them relief from their daily emotional suffering? Perhaps "getting well" is the only way to escape these overwhelmingly threatening therapists, the only way to survive the treatment.

Arthur Janov's (1970) primal scream therapy is a variation on this approach, a grand form of exorcism. The patient is subjected to personal and emotional isolation, and then to intense and often lengthy therapy sessions. Here, too, interventions are direct and goading. Patients are urged to dig deeper and to scream out. At times, they panic, become terrified of going crazy, and feel that they are disintegrating physically. This is all the better for the outcome. Janov states,

It is not the scream that is curative, in any case; it is the Pain. The scream is only one expression of the Pain. The Pain is the curative agent because it means that the person is feeling at last. At the moment that the patient feels hurt, the Pain disappears. The Neurotic has hurt because his body has been constantly set for the Pain. It was the tense apprehension that hurt (pp. 90–91).

Such are the rationales for psychotherapy.

There are far too many variations to touch all bases. Some forms of therapy combine this getting-it-all-out approach with efforts at explanation. Some ignore anything of which the patient is not immediately aware. Others try to probe deeper into evident patterns and generate explanations that take into account unconscious factors beyond the immediate awareness of the patient. In many, the therapist expresses openly his personal opinions, his feelings toward the patient, and even his dreams and life history. Depending on the paradigm, there is virtually no restraint on the therapist's communications and activities. For some, such as James McCartney (1966), psychoanalysis combined with genital contact, including sexual intercourse, is said to be a highly effective treatment modality.

Gestalt therapy is another treatment form in common use. It stresses immediate awareness and the experience of oneself and the moment, the here and now. It makes use of a wide variety of techniques in which the therapist is often quite active and involved. It stresses immediate feelings and enactments rather than analyzing.

In the hands of its founder, Frederick Perls (1969), Gestalt therapy involved the use of a hot seat on which a person in a group, who wanted to interact with the therapist, would sit. In his work, and in that reported by many others, there is a back-and-forth and bantering quality to the therapist's interventions. They tend to be rapid, challenging, and pressured. The patient is made to experience, feel, react, and enact. When the therapist spots something, feels something, infers something, he or she usually tells it outright to the patient. There is little time for reflection on either side.

In one situation, Linda, a member of a dream work seminar, reports a long dream about a lake drying up and porpoises who are in a circle in a religious ceremony. It's sad because they are dancing around the circle but the water is drying up. It's like a dying, and there are other details. At the end of the dream, when all the water dries up, Linda finds an old license plate at the bottom of the lake.

Perls quickly asks Linda to play the license plate, and when she
does, he prods her as to how she feels about it. He is certain it must
be of great importance. He then has her play the lake and discover
an existential message. He points out the contrast between the
artifacts found on the surface and shows how, as she goes deeper,
the apparent depth of the lake is actually fertility. He adds that
nature doesn't need a license plate to grow, and Linda feels she has
learned that she doesn't need permission to be creative.

John Enright (1975), in introducing Gestalt therapy, describes a
couple therapy in which the twosome is going over their problems
rather repetitiously and fruitlessly. The wife is staring past the
therapist quite fixedly. The therapist asks what she is looking at
and she states that it is the tape recorder. She is asked what she is
seeing, and she says it is just going round and round. The therapist
asks if anything else is going round and round, and the couple says
they seem to be.

In this last example, the therapist ignores the implications of the
fact that he is tape recording this marital therapy. He also accepts
at face value the patient's image of going round and round as
belonging to the couple alone. In no way does he consider the
possibility that he himself may be contributing to the sense of
empty circularity or that he, too, may be going round and round
with his clients. To do so would involve recognizing an encoded
message in the wife's communication. It would involve a type of
therapist-insight quite lacking in virtually all current therapeutic
efforts. It would also require that the therapist forego simplistic
thinking about others in favor of a far more complex form of
thinking about himself—and his clients as well. The human mind
prefers to simplify; it abhors complexities. This very natural tendency (which is sometimes quite protective) helps to support psychotherapeutic conspiracies in which the therapist's use of clichés
appears in some mysterious and hollow way to be the vehicle of
cure.

Gestalt therapy and its offshoots involve approaches to patients
that are highly manipulative. Clients are given advice, directives,
shown what they fail to see, and offered many pronouncements
that are based on the implicit belief that the therapist knows best
and sees best. The case material reported in the books on psychotherapy indicates that patients are more than ready to surrender

many of their human rights in the name of psychotherapy. They are prepared to forego any substantial sense of autonomy and independence, and to submit willingly to the pronouncements of their therapists. For their part, members of the mental healing profession appear to be more than willing to play God. Here, too, is another facet of the multi-faceted therapeutic conspiracy: the gains for the therapist appear to be self-evident, while those for the patient are more difficult to fathom. Perhaps individuals who seek psychotherapy have some kind of unconscious need to be abused and even punished. If so, they appear to have found professionals who are able to fulfill these wishes while believing they are acting in constructive fashion.

Albert Ellis, in his Rational-Emotive therapy, adopts a variation on Gestalt therapy that entails a let's-be-reasonable, direct, this-is-what-you're-missing approach to treatment. In principle, he suggests that patients can think themselves out of emotional disturbances and control their own destinies. On this basis, he has developed a highly active approach, with extensive pressures from the therapist designed to convince the patient that he or she is being irrational and need not be so. The conscious mind is assigned an omnipotence that is awesome. In contrast to the demeaning qualities of many of these treatment methods—and even though there is something demeaning about being goaded toward power and self-control—the approach used by Ellis is rationalized as a way of affording the patient direct control over his or her fate. As with many of the rationales for the various schools of psychotherapy, there is a clichéd and naive quality to this particular therapeutic philosophy. Simplistic credos appear to be in vogue at present.

In a book written by Ellis and a colleague, Robert Harper (1961), the authors describe the case of a patient they call Miss Marlo Long. When Marlo is jilted by a married man, she attempts suicide. The medical resident who pumps out her stomach quickly falls in love with her and they begin to date. Marlo is fearful that he too will soon jilt her. As she gets more involved, she becomes extremely jealous and possessive. Her resident boyfriend, Jake, induces her to take orthodox psychoanalysis, which focuses on an early pattern in which Marlo feared that her father would eventually reject her in favor of her older sister. While Marlo feels somewhat better as a result, her extreme jealousy and possessiveness continue. In disgust and despair, she terminates her psychoanalysis.

Jakes gets discouraged and starts to break up with her. Because of her suicidal tendencies, he decides to place her in a new therapy before he leaves. He therefore insists that she try a few sessions with Dr. Harper. After five visits, during which they work actively on her basic irrational thinking, Jake breaks off with Marlo and leaves her at her therapist's door.

During the session that quickly follows, Harper helps to quiet down his patient who then says she is ready to commit suicide. Harper tells her that this is her privilege, but then questions her as to why she planned to slit her throat when she could so nicely stick around and torture herself for another half-century or so. Marlo says she intends to do just that because no one can be trusted or depended upon—it's a phony deal.

Harper then attacks her thinking, questioning the conclusions she has drawn just because two lovers in a row have left her; it's a hell of a big conclusion from a pitifully small bit of evidence. When Marlo says that it's always the same, Harper tells her it's hogwash and wonders how she can believe such twaddle. He challenges her thinking, attempts to punch holes in it, and shows her that in some ways she herself has been a pain in the neck.

Later on, when Marlo says she can't trust anyone, Harper "relentlessly persists"—his words—that he can't see how two men in an entire lifetime stand for everyone. The two of them go back and forth like that for some time, eventually getting around to issues of how Marlo could begin to like herself. They also speak of the demands Marlo makes on her men and her inordinate need for approval. By the end of this hour, Marlo has a new sense of self-confidence, and within the year, she finds a new beau with whom she relates to quite realistically and with whom she is reported to now have a good marriage.

Here, the therapeutic approach appears to be that of chiding the patient and of talking her out of her seeming senselessness. In typical fashion, when the patient says that she can't trust anyone and mentions a phony deal, the therapist concentrates his reaction on her poor logic and external life. The possibility does not dawn on him that this patient may be expressing herself both directly and through a communication that contains a hidden or disguised (unconscious) message. It may well be that the phony deal reflects an unconscious perception within this patient of the phoniness of her therapist's interventions—in essence, of the existence of a therapeutic conspiracy.

Perhaps on some unconscious level this patient appreciates that his manipulativeness is in some sense fraudulent and renders him untrustworthy. In order to avoid such painful considerations, everything the patient says is taken at face value. The battle—and again, a struggle is in evidence—is won or lost on the surface. The patient and her life are the battlefield. At most, the therapist is a distant general directing and manipulating her armies. In some ways, he prefers to see himself as an innocent bystander offering coincidental advice. It is clearly self-serving for therapists to adopt such attitudes. Nonetheless, many patients accept these approaches, and some even afford them high praise.

There are many other forms of rational and cognitive psychotherapy in which therapists advise patients to make lists, to cope better, to be more realistic, to see evident absurdities in what they are thinking and doing, etcetera. Many of these efforts reduce complicated turmoil and emotions in patients who are faced with elaborate internal and external struggles to almost meaningless clichés. Perhaps it is the emptiness of the effort that proves curative in the face of chaotic meaning.

This type of cure extends into transactional analysis, a form of psychotherapy invented by Erich Berne (1961). Here, the fundamental interventions involve identifying three ego states or aspects of the self—the parent, the adult, and the child. Behaviors are reduced to parent behaviors, adult behaviors, and child behaviors, and conceptualized in terms of games, scripts, and relationships. The approach is direct and directive.

For example, a patient tells Dr. Berne that, like a little girl, she wants approval from her husband even though she rebels against what she has to do to get it, and that's also the way she used to feel with her father. When her parents separated the patient thought she could have kept her father, though some grown-up part of herself knew that she was acting like a little girl.

The therapist suggests that she might let the little girl out more, at least during her interviews, instead of trying to shut her in. With further material, the therapist then sets up a structural diagram showing the patient the mother she acts like, the grown-up part of herself, the little girl who wants approval, and the little girl who rebels. Later these are shown to represent the parent, the adult, the compliant child, and the rebellious child. Soon the patient is able to recognize when she behaves as the little girl and when she acts like the parent part. She is frightened by all of this, but shows improvement.

Transactional analysis also involves regression analysis. The therapist joins the patient in going back into the past while also remaining the adult observer. In one session, for example, the therapist begins by saying that he is five years old and has not yet been to school. The patient may choose his own age but must be under eight. The patient, who lost his father when he was two years old, quickly mentions his daddy is dead. The therapist says his own father is a doctor, and they soon exchange thoughts about deaths and funerals. The therapist questions how the patient's father can be in a cemetery and in heaven too. The patient is challenged in his belief that something came out of his father's mouth and went to heaven. The therapist doesn't see how the patient's daddy can be in two places. He asks what the father does up in the sky. The patient says that he sits beside Jesus and watches us. He then tells the therapist that he is funny looking and has a skinny face. The therapist finally says that the patient is crazy to believe his daddy can be in two places. The patient then says he wishes he had a real daddy and begins to weep. At that point the patient says he has had enough.

Since something different from usual, or dramatic, is taking place, the therapist believes that he has been helpful to the patient. Possible disguised messages that involve perceptions of the therapist and his techniques are ignored. Even the allusion to something coming out of the patient's father's mouth did not lead the therapist to wonder if the patient is referring on some encoded level to the therapeutic exchange. The patient's tearful expression of wishes that he had a *real* daddy could well be a disguised way of unconsciously indicating a wish for a true (noncollusive) therapist. Neither patient nor therapist senses this possibility at all.

The arbitrary quality of the interventions of the therapist is evident. There are really no rules of intervention for most forms of psychotherapy. There are instead vague and general principles, or the matter is left to the empathy and intuition of the therapist. Strange beliefs and fantasies in patients, reflections of underlying emotional illness, are simply challenged away. It soon becomes evident to the patient that it is dangerous and contrary to the therapist's wishes to maintain such illusions.

Still more telling is the ease with which the therapist tells the patient that he is crazy in his beliefs. This is a patently offensive statement, which soon brings the patient to tears. Still, the very fact that the patient has experienced an emotion—even though it may well have been the result of having been hurt by the therapist—leads to the arbitrary and unanalyzed conclusion that a positive therapeutic experience is taking place. It appears that it is possible for a therapist to say or do virtually anything whatsoever in the name of psychotherapy and to have it accepted by his or her patients. Once more, one must suspect the presence of collusion. And once again, one must wonder if one factor is a need by patients to be threatened and even condemned by their therapists.

Our sample of psychotherapies has moved from those that entirely involve action and reaction, to those that entail a mixture of action and words, and will now go on to those treatment modalities that are mainly word-oriented. Typical among these approaches are psychoanalysis and psychoanalytic psychotherapy. In these situations, patients are asked to say whatever comes to mind, to free associate. With many frequent and noticeable exceptions, the therapist will mainly listen and respond from time to time with comments. However, excerpts from these treatment modalities indicate that many therapists are quite active when using these therapeutic paradigms and that the existence of the extremely passive and relatively silent psychoanalyst is quickly fading from our midst.

The main vehicle of cure in the psychoanalytic forms of treatment is that of interpretation—making something previously unconscious for the patient, conscious and part of his or her direct awareness. To oversimplify, this intervention is, in general, utilized whenever a previously unrecognized pattern of behavior on the part of the patient is detected by the analyst, or when a daydream or fantasy of which the patient is apparently unaware seems to be evident in his or her associations. The therapist then endeavors to explain to the patient the nature of this unconscious element or factor. The theory states that it is this same hidden or unconscious determinant that has created and sustained the patient's emotional disorder. The focus is on the patient's inner fantasy life, past and present, including contributions from pathogenic childhood experiences. It is proposed that once the patient has a conscious awareness of the detrimental influences of which he or she had previously been unaware, the patient is then able to use his or her conscious insight to recognize the irrationality involved. The patient thereby gives up his or her symptoms, which are sustained by these unconscious factors.

There are today many therapies that claim to be psychoanalytic in nature. While they share some beliefs in common, they are in the main highly distinctive; each involves a theoretical position that calls into question and often negates the other forms of psychoanalytic treatment. In each instance the therapist purports to seek out and identify the hidden mental, intrapsychic truths that account for the emotional disturbance in his or her patients. That these truths are stated quite differently in the view of one group of therapists as compared to another, and often enough even among therapists who share the same persuasion, has caused discomfort for some members of the profession; mostly, this troublesome situation has been ignored.

Are there, then, many different truths to the underlying nature of an emotional illness? Or is it possible that there is but one basic truth, and that other beliefs constitute deceptions or fictions, or at best, secondary truths of little consequence? In time, answers to these compelling questions will be offered.

It is well to realize, however, that there are some therapists who profess no interest whatsoever in the underlying basis or truths that pertain to a patient's emotional illness. Therapists who make use of conditioning or deconditioning, or of shock therapy, have little interest in listening to and understanding their patients. Instead, they invoke assaultive or training procedures designed to change a patient's symptoms and behaviors without insight. Nonetheless, a vast majority of therapists, including many who make use of drugs, electroshock, and conditioning paradigms, do make an effort to listen to and at least superficially comprehend the nature of what the patient says. Most of this understanding is quite superficial, even though patients usually come to feel that they have widened their understanding of themselves. Any sense of apparent (even transparent) new knowledge, regardless of its source or validity, appears to elate both patients and therapists.

When relief comes, there is little inclination on either side to investigate its basis.

The psychoanalyst, above all, attempts to search out the hidden inner truths on which emotional disorders are founded. While his or her quest for these deeper realizations is decried by other therapists and belittled by many as useless, absurd, and even insufficient, psychoanalysts themselves believe that the ideal cure of an emotional disturbance must be founded on a maximum degree of self-understanding. Most present-day analysts are not at all troubled by the existence of some two dozen or more schools of psychoanalysis, each believing that their particular definition of inner truth is valid and exclusively the last word in emotional disturbance. In time, serious consideration will be given to these conflicting ideologies, but for the moment, we simply want to sample a psychoanalytic interpretation—the basis of a psychoanalytic cure.

For this purpose, we turn to a monograph published by The New York Psychoanalytic Institute, the first Freudian training center in the United States (Waldhorn 1967). The material is taken from a study group of senior psychoanalysts and involves an investigation of the place of the dream in psychoanalysis. The session was reported by one of the psychoanalysts in attendance.

The patient is a 30-year-old woman writer in her second year of analysis. She has a multiplicity of symptoms, including depression, poor self-esteem, and poor relationships with men. It is formulated that the patient is acting out basically Oedipal relationships with men in a manner that is highly sadomasochistic. Her material has been interpreted as revealing intense incorporative wishes toward her father and underlying feelings of emptiness and worthlessness.

In the weeks prior to the dream that the group studied, the patient worked over a new relationship with a man, John. She had fantasies that he was in love with her and that they would soon be married. There was little evidence that this was the case. John had been away and did not write to the patient. He was supposed to return a few days before the night of the dream that was reported to the analyst and then to the group.

In the dream, the patient has cancer of the breast and a woman doctor says it will have to be removed. She says there will be after-effects that the patient will feel in her neck. The patient has a friend who has had the operation. She is scared and panicked and wonders how she can get away and not have it done.

The patient offers many associations to this dream. She thinks it has to do with feeling incomplete and needing union with a man to make herself so. She connects this to her concerns about John and then thinks about being afraid of scorpions.

The patient has a second dream in which she is at her sister's wedding. Her relatives are there, including an aunt. There is a cupboard filled with watches or chains that the aunt has received from the patient's uncle. There are watches and rings and jewels in rows. She takes one out and shows it around. Her uncle says it is expensive, and he goes on exaggerating the cost and value. There are aunts and uncles that the patient does not like and feels ashamed of. They are her mother's friends, and she doesn't like her friends seeing them. Her sister is supposed to go away, and the next day she will come back. There is a drawing done by one of the patient's friends, and then she can't remember.

The patient offers further associations. She had awoken in a restless state and wasn't able to work in the morning. She called a girlfriend who suggested she call John. The patient called John and he made excuses, but they then made a date.

The analyst asks for associations to the business about the doctor. The patient says that in the dream she is matronly and stern. The patient wonders how a man could make love to her if she were missing a breast. She would be terribly self-conscious. She thinks of a woman who was all cut to pieces by cancer, but she is not anxious. She must have a strong constitution. The patient can see the line of the cutting. There seems to be no question of a biopsy first and she wants to run away.

The analyst then asks about the part in the dream about the neck. The patient responds that sometimes she makes a wrong movement and her neck muscles can hurt. It is a vulnerable area and she feels self-conscious. Her neck is an asset, since it gives her a classic look. She thinks also of whiplash.

Here the analyst asks the patient if her mention of self-consciousness reminds her of her recent descriptions of how terrible she felt before she had any breast development. The patient asks the anlayst if he thinks the fact that John didn't call her made her reexperience her feelings of inadequacy; they may still be present.

The analyst then offers an interpretation to the effect that the patient seems to be reminded of that time in her life when she felt inadequate and unsatisfactory, and this leads her to wish that she could have something added to her to make her feel better. The same need is now dealt with by wishing for the growth of her breast, and this idea is expressed when she dreams of something growing inside of her. But in some way this involves a forbidden or dangerous wish, and that part of the idea is expressed by visualizing it as a cancer of the breast. The punishment for the patient's wish and the undoing of the wish are expressed by the threat of the breast being cut off. The analyst adds that it is interesting that a woman seems to be the one who says this has to be done. He and the patient had seen this same idea in the patient's desire to make herself become pregnant when she felt she was threatened with the loss of Bob and had the same sort of panicky feeling of inadequacy. In addition, this whole business tends to make her think of herself as an undeveloped child again. Whenever she feels that a man might be abandoning her, she feels very inadequate, immature, underdeveloped and lacking in something, and she desperately feels that she must get him reattached to her.

The patient responds that she had not thought of herself as underdeveloped and recognizes that she has modest breast development. She doesn't feel uncomfortable in a bikini and feels attractive. When she draws, there are many breast-like forms, but there are no vaginas. There are many penis forms such as she drew in a sketch that she has shown to her analyst. The patient feels better after the session.

For many, this particular interpretation is overly long and confusing. The patient's dream can be seen as being so lengthy as to lose all sense of meaning, and viewed as a form of resistance—i.e., as a reflection of opposition to the therapeutic procedures. It seems likely that most readers would find both the patient's material and the analyst's interpretation extremely convoluted and confusing.

Further, the patient's response itself does not suggest confirmation of the intervention. In fact, the patient seems to contradict the analyst, and eventually she alludes to showing him a sketch she drew. (This particular reference is to a modification in the usual ground rules of analysis, an area we will consider later on.) This suggests a form of inappropriate contact, and may well be an encoded commentary on the interpretation. It also seems likely the analyst was taking notes (the material is reported in great detail). If so, the patient's response to the intervention is in part an encoded allusion to her sense that *the therapist* is sketching *her* by taking notes that others will see. Here too, collusion is in the air.

For the moment, it is well to formulate some impression as to how this particular interpretation might bring about symptom relief for this patient. Is it based on an inner sense of confusion within the patient that obscures her more anxiety-provoking concerns? Is it founded instead on some type of perception of the therapist's need to exhibit his prowess, much as the patient was allowed to show the therapist her sketch? The allusion to penises may touch upon the phallic-exhibitionistic (and sexualized) qualities of both acts. Unfortunately, it is also possible that the interpretation was relatively incomprehensible to the patient. On this basis, the patient might feel somewhat better in knowing that her terrible emotional secrets are safe from the analyst and that he does not fathom their more threatening aspects. Perhaps too the intervention is experienced as theoretical and clichéd, and its fanciful form of meaninglessness gives the patient her sense of relief.

Finally, we should leave room for the possibility that the patient felt relief because in some mysterious way she better understood herself after the analyst's interpretation. Even though she did not validate or extend any of his comments and disputed much of what she was able to remember, perhaps she found a measure of understanding in the analyst's comment that she was unable to put into words. Such a suggestion, however, defies all scientific principles and all elements of clear validation, which would require some direct or indirect sign of newly-won understanding. It proposes that patients may feel better in psychotherapy through insights of which they are entirely unaware or for which they show no indication even indirectly. These are entirely self-contradictory statements.

On the whole, therapists have ignored issues of validation and have not developed definitive signs of new insight in their patients. With few exceptions they have tended to assume that their interpretations must indeed be inherently correct and of benefit to their clients. Those patients who fail to improve are seen as resistant and as having some need to suffer or to defeat the analyst. The possibility of outright error in the form of an elaborate interpretation is seldom considered.

For the moment, then, this material suggests the possibility that one form of psychoanalytic conspiracy involves the offer by a psychoanalyst of an essentially meaningless interpretation that is then accepted by a patient who does so unconsciously because he or she feels that his or her disturbing emotional secrets are safely sealed off from the therapist and treatment process. Elaborate psychoanalytic interpretations, filled as they are at times with vivid primitive imagery, can be viewed unconsciously by a patient as a highly exhibitionistic act, which then justifies the patient's own pathological exhibitionistic tendencies. In principle, if the therapist behaves in some disturbed fashion comparable to the disturbance from which a patient suffers, the patient may then feel reassured and somewhat improved.

Of course, room must be left for the possibility that psychoanalysis (or one of the other forms of therapy that have been illustrated in this chapter) is not at all conspiratorial, but serves the patient truthfully, wisely, and almost entirely. However, the superficial analysis of each of these excerpts does not appear to substantiate such a position. Instead, each of the vignettes has suggested some form of unconscious collusion and has involved techniques with evident flaws. Some appear to be downright destructive, while others appear almost meaningless. There are, indeed, a number of different but interrelated unconscious conspiracies between patients and therapists designed to sustain the use of highly questionable treatment approaches.

CHAPTER 4
WHERE LIES THE PROBLEM?

According to some representative psychotherapeutic techniques, an emotional disorder may be cured by sexual intercourse with someone outside of therapy, with a surrogate selected by the therapist, or with the therapist; by proper instruction in sexual and masturbatory techniques; by disrobing in front of others, including the therapist; by bathing and touching others; by patients telling each other what they think and feel about both themselves and their fellow group members; by being isolated to the point of disorganization and screaming; by losing control and raging and berating others; by destroying objects; by being told what to think and feel; by being told what is rational and irrational, right and wrong, wise and foolish; by enacting a variety of games, dramas, and roles; by dancing, singing, and writing; by focusing on how one thinks and feels at the moment; by remembering the past; by talking and understanding; by taking drugs; by making lists and following rules; by being told one is crazy or stupid; by learning how to talk oneself out of one's madness; and by being told to kill oneself—to name just a few of the methods.

One must come to the conclusion that this is some type of collective insanity. There is no conceivable way in which most of these incredibly divergent techniques can be justified or accepted. Some of the measures used by therapists are an assault on human sensibility and integrity. Some reflect a belief that a lack of interpersonal boundaries, a complete loss of control, and the absence of principles and decency are the royal roads to mental health. Others presuppose that complicated psychological pronouncements will do the job.

Nevertheless, there are literally millions of psychotherapy patients. Some, of course, become disillusioned in one or another form of treatment. The vast majority, however, tend to idealize their therapists and the modes of therapy they use. They return session after session for a treatment experience that would appear to any outside observer to be an horrendous assault or a waste of time. They believe deeply in the rationalizations and justifications offered by their therapists for the things they do. If there is evidence that therapists collectively have created a form of madness, then patients collectively have come to share in the madness and to idolize their perpetrators.

Are we dealing with a sham, a hoax? Probably not. There is, as noted, reason to believe that the vast majority of therapists are sincerely committed to the therapeutic procedures they use. Clearly, if it were otherwise, they have hundreds of alternative measures to adopt. They are doing their best, however senselessly.

How did all of this come about? What can be done about it? Why has it happened? What does it mean?

These are serious and compelling questions. They lead us to wonder: does the problem lie with therapists? Is there something about people who chose this particular profession that has led to this particular calamity? If not consciously and deliberately, do therapists have some unrecognized and unconscious need to exploit the public? Are they trying to protect themselves from something they cannot handle? Are they for some reason fearful of the emotional truths for which they seem to design endless procedures to avoid? Have they been far more self-serving than acting in the interests of their patients? Are they the unwitting victims of their own emotional difficulties as they influence their choice of profession and treatment approach?

Then too, are patients to be held accountable for the state of the field? Without their knowing it, are they seeking out procedures that will exploit, abuse, and seduce them? Do they have some unrecognized unconscious needs for this kind of treatment? If they were more rational and even simply more sensible, would they really tolerate most of the therapeutic practices in existence today? Or is there some powerful hidden and unconscious wish that attracts them to these highly questionable approaches to their emotional illnesses? Have therapists indeed correctly understood their unconscious needs, so that patients themselves have helped to create the market for these types of treatment procedures? Do they too fear the underlying truths of their emotional sicknesses and wish mainly to avoid these realizations? In sum, do they unwittingly seek out the role of victim in collusion with their unwitting victimizers?

If not entirely in therapists or patients, does the cause lie in the nature of emotional disorders? Is there something about this particular group of human dysfunctions that is essentially unmanageable for all concerned? Are there qualities to the hidden or unconscious basis for emotional sickness that are so terrifying that most individuals, whether patients or therapists, prefer to avoid them at all costs? Are we dealing with nightmares no one dares dream, let alone grasp and understand? More broadly, then, is there something about the clear understanding and treatment of these emotional disturbances that is so dreadful that the natural inclination on all sides is avoidance and flight?

As specific answers to these questions are proposed, the reader will discover that the burden falls to all three: therapist, patient, and the nature of emotional disorders. As the underlying factors in emotional suffering are explored, the inevitability of what has transpired will be appreciated. There is indeed much that is terrifying at the heart of an emotional disturbance. So much so that collusion is indeed far more attractive than a controlled, direct, and honest search. Still, this type of misalliance is not without its cost. Perhaps as one comes to understand the situation more clearly, one will find that many of the fears are quite unfounded. If this were not the case, one would have to simply settle for one's limitations as a human being in dealing with one's emotional disturbances. In a sense, this is the pessimistic philosophy that underlies most present forms of psychotherapy. To discover otherwise, then, carries with it a strong sense of hope and optimism.

CHAPTER 5

THE DISCOVERY OF THE THERAPEUTIC CONSPIRACY

The conspiracy has not gone undetected. There have been signs of discontent among patients and therapists. There are indeed therapists who have from time to time raised very telling questions regarding the efficacy of most treatment procedures. There are some who have questioned each of the important schools of psychotherapy on serious and thoughtful grounds. On the whole, however, the nature of the problem has not been comprehended as it influences each of the various modes of treatment, nor has it been possible to arrive at a broadly applicable solution.

The most thoughtful of these critics have themselves been psychoanalysts. Since psychoanalysis strives to arrive at both conscious and unconscious truths, and attempts to take into account both surface and deeper phenomena, it alone appears to be the discipline from which the answers can emerge. With sympathy and compassion for all concerned, it is the psychoanalyst who is most likely to find the means of encompassing with understanding these extremely divergent treatment approaches.

Few psychoanalysts have made this kind of attempt, but a handful have from time to time raised questions regarding the psychoanalytic approach itself. Taking as their cue Freud's unrelenting search for the truth of a patient's emotional disturbance, they have tried to probe deeper into the treatment process than their predecessors. They have questioned the value of a treatment procedure that studies, in virtual isolation, the inner mind of the patient with a striking disregard for the patient's interaction with the analyst and for the analyst's contributions to the patient's therapeutic experience. Their work suggests a need to understand not only the unconscious mental processes of the patient, but also those of the therapist and the unconsicous transactions between the analyst and patient in the therapeutic experience itself. By widening the field of direct and especially indirect observation, many surprising findings emerge. It is on this basis that the psychotherapeutic conspiracy was eventually defined and understood.

To cite a few salient examples, several psychoanalysts in Europe, mostly in Great Britain, stressed from the 1930s onward the importance of relationships with others (so-called object relationships), including those between the patient and therapist. In this way they extended Freud's initial intrapsychic focus into the realm of relatedness. Ronald Fairbairn, Melanie Klein, Harry Guntrip, and D. W. Winnicott were chief among this group of analysts. In the United States, interest in object relationships, and more particularly in the interaction between the patient and therapist, lagged behind. Harold Searles, a psychoanalyst in Washington, D.C., almost entirely on his own pioneered psychoanalytic studies of the unconscious communicative interaction that characterizes the treatment experience. By implication, his work has called into question the less dynamically interactional approaches of other psychoanalysts and of those who use far less insightful treatment methods.

It is these psychoanalytic writings that form the heritage of this book. Little by little, they have suggested that the painful secrets that patients and therapists have conspired to avoid are not only within the unconscious mind of the patient, but also in the hidden recesses of the mind of the therapist. With both parties to treatment motivated for defense, the discovery of the hidden truths that account for the psychotherapeutic conspiracy (and for the patient's emotional disturbance as well) has been difficult to accomplish.

It is not surprising, then, to learn that the identification of the psychotherapeutic conspiracy occurred only in a small measure through insight into the difficulties of one therapist's personal therapeutic endeavors and personal experience as a psychoanalytic patient, and more so through a careful study in supervision of the work of other therapists. In this respect, the discovery and delineation of collusion in psychotherapy can claim an important historical antecedent. It was in large measure through Sigmund Freud's analysis of material presented to him by his colleague and mentor, Josef Breuer, as it pertained to Anna O., the first patient to be treated with Breuer's cathartic method, that Freud eventually came to discover transference (most broadly, the importance of the relationship of the patient to the therapist, though not the reverse) and the psychoanalytic method itself.

It has required 20 years of supervisory work to generate these current discoveries. Interacting with direct observations of patients and the unfolding of an interpersonal-intrapsychic theory of both the treatment experience and emotional disturbance, the detachment of a supervisor studying the therapeutic experience offered by student therapists to unknown patients proved to be indispensable. (It is impossible to learn how to do psychotherapy without such supervisory help.) However, insight emerged only because these student therapists would present the details of their therapeutic exchanges in strict sequence. This permitted not only observation and formulation, but also prediction and validation. It embedded the supervisory work in interactional considerations. New understanding soon followed.

A critical step toward understanding the situation involves the realization that the answer to these questions lies in the patient's communications to the therapist during the sessions involved. This particular resource had gone unrecognized for many years because the relevant communications are indirect (or latent). The manifest responses from the patient are accepting and filled with gratitude, despite the evident hurts, but contained in these manifest communications are encoded messages that unconsciously reveal the patient as not at all appreciative. Thus, unconsciously, the patient fully realizes the destructiveness involved. The key to unraveling the psychotherapeutic conspiracy lies not so much in the understanding derived from direct formulations by a therapist or supervisor, but in decoding the hidden messages contained in the patient's material. It is the unconscious wisdom of the patient (which unfortunately, he or she is unable to render conscious and make use of directly), that provides the key means through which the psychotherapeutic conspiracy may eventually be identified and understood.

Several striking supervisory experiences brought home these crucial realizations. What actually happened is presented here by combining several clinical experiences into one and by heavily disguising the actual happenings as well. However, the essential qualities of the therapeutic transactions have not been significantly modified.

This is a book of illustration and example rather than one of scientific documentation. Since it is intended for a broad readership, the privacy of the patients involved must be protected at all costs. Nevertheless, the substance of these therapeutic experiences is preserved. The vignettes used in this volume, although partly fiction, faithfully reflect what actually happens between patients and therapists.

A CLINICAL VIGNETTE

The patient is a young woman in once-weekly psychotherapy with a trainee at a clinic. The issue of his training status was never directly mentioned by patient or therapist. The woman's concern involved severe episodes of depression and a very poor marriage situation.

For reasons that are not relevant for the moment, the patient repeatedly fell ill physically in the course of her therapy. She would call her therapist, often at the last minute, and cancel her sessions for two or three weeks at a time. The therapist reacted with anger and complaints. He tried to confront the patient with the ways in which the canceled hours disrupted the therapy. He even threatened her with termination. Still, his best efforts failed to change the pattern.

Throughout, the patient seemed to ignore the therapist's barbs and complaints. She would speak with impassioned pain of the woes of her marriage and of how she felt trapped in a hopeless relationship with her husband. She blamed many of their difficulties on her mother-in-law. Her husband was so attached to his sick mother that he spent more time at his parents' home than at his own. It was as if, the patient said, the two of them were conspiring to destroy her marriage. His mother, she went on, is especially hateful. She'd like nothing better than to see the patient out of the picture. The trouble is, sometimes she's real nice and concerned, but then she suddenly turns against the patient with a vengeance. It's like she's trying to drive her crazy.

The therapist, with whatever seeming wisdom, used this material to show the patient what he called her "narcissistic vulnerability"— the ease with which she allowed others to hurt her. He tried to show her too just how paranoid and suspicious she was. After all, he pointed out, her mother-in-law was a sick woman and in need of her son's care. Hypersensitivities of this kind were exactly what created her depression and misery in the first place.

The next day, the patient called her therapist to once more cancel a session. She indicated that she was ill with a fever. She had seen her internist, who had diagnosed the early stages of pneumonia. At his wits end, the therapist became suspicious. How could she become physically ill so quickly? Was she lying to him? He decided to check out her story. He got into his car and drove to the patient's house. He rang her doorbell and her mother answered. The patient was indeed ill in bed with a raging fever. Oddly enough, the patient was well and present for her session the following week.

This material was presented in a teaching conference. At this juncture, the presenter was interrupted to discuss the evident paranoid problem in the therapist. In sobering fashion, we confronted the subject of unresolved emotional problems in psychotherapists. With considerable discomfort of our own, we agreed that his behavior reflected an unfortunate basic mistrust of the patient and a terrible loss of control. We expected the patient would be enraged and possibly even ready to terminate her treatment. We were completely surprised by what actually happened.

The patient entered her session all smiles. "I have never felt better," she began. "I have had the most marvelous insight. It suddenly dawned on me that my husband is the one who is sick and paranoid, not me. He needs his mother because he is totally unable to handle the least bit of stress. He needs to treat me like a helpless child because he himself is such an idiot. He has absolutely no faith in me. He runs off to his mother and then believes I'm trying to get rid of him so I can have an affair. There I was lying in bed fighting pneumonia and he pops up at the house out of nowhere, searching the closets for some man he imagines to exist. He's such a fool. Him, the college graduate, and me with a high school education. Now I have to stay with him to help him get to be just a little less crazy. Maybe if he grows up just a bit I could leave him. Realizing just how sick he is made me feel a lot better about myself. I think his problems with his mother have warped his mind. He pretends to go over there to help her, but I've seen him in action. He treats her like dirt. He's a hypocrite. Sometimes I think I married him to be his victim."

Not a word was said about the therapist's visit to the patient's home. Instead, the patient's perceptions and feelings were played out in her relationship with her husband. However, this patient's hidden message contained a *displacement*—a shift from the therapist to the husband. Through disguised and displaced messages, she very accurately identified the therapist's sickness and paranoia, his need for treatment, and even the source of some of his problems in an early destructive relationship with his own mother (which he frankly admitted to us when we discussed this session). With considerable feeling and concern, the patient indicates her unconscious decision to stick with her therapist until she can help him to change. While this is admirable and caring, it is also perhaps indicative of a fateful, self-destructive attraction to destructive men. This patient may well have had a self-harmful and masochistic need to be abused by others. Her reaction to the therapist is therefore one of a likely mixture of healthy and sick responses. As for her sense of relief, this is an example of a *cure by nefarious comparison*, and it shows us how patients, in the face of blatantly destructive acts by their therapists, may mobilize their own resources and thereby obtain relief from their mental suffering.

Before the incident of the visit by the therapist to the patient's home, the patient had been speaking of a kind of collusion between her husband and mother-in-law designed to destroy her marriage and to drive her crazy. Communications of this kind often state something directly in one area that applies to another area. The mechanism of *displacement* is in operation, and it is put to frequent defensive use by patients and therapists alike.

It seems likely, then, that the patient is representing in disguised form (through the use of displacement) a highly sensitive unconscious perception of the therapist and his supervisor. Clinic patients are clinic-wise and are well aware on some level that their therapists are trainees and under supervision. They also rightly sense that their therapists are as highly vulnerable in this respect as the patients themselves.

As a result, in this particular instance, rather than directly confronting the therapist with his destructive attitudes and the ways in which he was unwittingly attempting to destroy the treatment process and to drive his patient crazy, the patient found an indirect means of communicating these impressions. To the extent that her husband and mother-in-law were indeed unconsciously colluding to hurt the patient, the outside situation lent itself quite readily as a *vehicle for encoded (disguised) communication* about the therapist in the associations of the patient. If the outside collusion was essentially a product of the patient's imagination, one would have a more unfortunate situation in which the therapist's unconscious hurtful behaviors were distorting the patient's perceptions of and responses to her spouse and mother-in-law as well.

In either case, on a communicative level, the encoded message would be identical: The patient is attempting to let the therapist know her perceptions of a psychotherapeutic conspiracy that involves herself, the therapist, and a supervisor. Most pointedly, in her statement that she may well be the willing victim, the patient reveals her unconscious wisdom in recognizing, however indirectly, her own participation in the therapeutic conspiracy at hand. There appears to be a compliance on both sides, each based on a separate set of pathological needs. The wishes involved are so powerful that there is virtually no direct recognition of the collusion in response to the therapist's openly destructive and suspicious behavior.

This vignette offers clues as to the basis for the patient's participation in a therapeutic conspiracy of this kind. There is evidence that the patient has within herself an unconscious need to suffer at the hands of a man. Patients who are plagued with conscious and unconscious guilt and needs for punishment are attracted to and accept the ministrations of highly destructive therapists as a way of seeking relief from their "sins," real and imagined. Then too there is the patient's evident relief in realizing that one's therapist is in important ways sicker than the patient. The vulnerabilities and errant ways of destructive therapists therefore have a paradoxical way of reassuring a patient that his or her illness and guilt is not so terrible after all. Patients appear to be drawn to these uninsightful ways of obtaining symptom relief, approaches that characteristically avoid the identification of painful unconscious truths.

In the session under consideration, the patient had more to say that is related to the psychotherapeutic conspiracy: her associations implicitly linked her husband to her father. When she was in her teens, her father forbade her to date. He sometimes followed her when she went out in the evening. If he discovered her with a young

man, he went into a rage and locked her in her room. At this point,
the therapist intervened. He told the patient that she was furious
with her husband because he reminded her of her father. She chose
to ignore her husband's loving feelings toward her and his sincere
worries about her fidelity. He reminded the patient that she herself
had actually had an affair early in her marriage—her husband had
reason to worry. Her underlying rage at her father led her to distort
her view of her husband. She also used his behavior as a way of
trying to deny her own suspiciousness.

The patient began to cry. "My father never understood me," she
sobbed. "He always sided with my mother against me. He was
crazy, I tell you, not me. He was always after me. Learning how to
handle him taught me a lot. His spying on me fired up my imagination. That's how I began writing those mystery stories. It's one of
the few successes I've had in my life. He couldn't take that away
from me. Neither can you."

"There, you see," responded the therapist. "Now you think I
want to harm you. You take your feelings toward your father and
bring them to me. He hurt you, so you imagine I must want to hurt
you as well."

With that the patient became hysterical and stopped talking. She
cancelled the next session because she was physically ill again, this
time with a bladder infection. But then again, she returned to
therapy the following week. The "treatment," as it is called, moved
on from there.

The therapist went from one intervention to another, confident
that he was right in what he had to say, even though the patient did
not support his comments on a conscious level (and certainly not
indirectly or unconsciously). Most therapists tend to have undue
confidence in the validity of their interventions and seldom question themselves in the face of repudiation by the patient. Many
therapists, as seen here, have a tendency to press on with their ideas
and impressions, bowling over the patient, as it were, in a somewhat assaultive fashion. All too often, patients return for more.

An understanding of displacement helps one to reinterpret this
material, especially as it sheds light on the patient's unconscious
perception of and involvement in a therapeutic conspiracy. In the
first part of these additional associations, the patient is clearly
linking the therapist's unwarranted visit to her home to her father's
destructive suspiciousness, and the two behaviors are indeed quite

comparable. It would therefore appear that the patient continues in this type of therapy because of some type of unconscious need to reexperience a rather sick and suffering relationship with her father. Psychotherapeutic conspiracies, then, may well be designed in part to permit this type of pathological and unrecognized repetition. Together, patients and therapists live out the disturbing aspects of the patient's (and therapist's) past life and its unresolved residues within his or her mind.

The therapist's intervention seems to have been intrusive, accusatory, and hostile. It was self-serving in that it set aside his own questionable behavior with the patient and the possible encoded meanings of the patient's material as it pertained to her unconscious perception of him. The truth in the patient's communications appeared to concern her unconscious perceptions of the therapist and her responses to his interventions. The interpretation that this material involves the patient and her husband is an attempt to generate a substitute for these truths, a form of fiction or a lie-barrier directed defensively to seal off the more chaotic underlying actualities as they relate to the therapist and therapeutic interaction.

In substance, then, the intervention was assaultive, unsympathetic and devoid of true understanding. Once again, the patient appears to have perceived these qualities in the therapist's effort. With the further use of displacement, the patient speaks of how her father never understood her and how he sided with her mother against her. These are apt, though encoded, characterizations of the therapist's intervention. With some justification, the patient sees this type of work as reflecting a kind of craziness and pursuit.

At this point the patient indicates how she is able to obtain something constructive from the therapist's hurtful efforts; why she has gone along with a therapeutic conspiracy in which the past is relived rather than its modus operandi understood, why she accepts a treatment situation in which she is spied on and attacked verbally; why she continues with a therapist who claims to offer her understanding even when his work serves mainly as a vehicle for his own attacks on the patient; why she stays with a therapist who uses words as a vehicle for action and assault rather than for insight. The answer, again through displacement, is that learning how to handle an assaultive and crazy person (father or therapist) has helped her to grow and mature, to cope better. These traumatic relationships have stimulated her creativity and prodded her into being productive. One of the reasons for the existence of psycho-therapeutic conspiracies is related to the fact that human beings respond at times to trauma and adversity with highly adaptive and innovative reactions. Stress is often the mother of growth. When the maturational burst appears, neither patient nor therapist bothers to look carefully at its sources.

Thus the patient's participation in a psychotherapeutic con-spiracy may be motivated by the fear of emotional truths and by self-destructive tendencies on the one hand, and yet on the other, by a paradoxical need to find a stimulus for development in a hurtful therapeutic experience. Quite unconsciously, a therapist who is fearful of dealing with emotional truths may generate hurt-ful interventions that on some unconscious level are based on an appreciation of the type of stimuli that may prod the patient toward a constructive response. Thus, in addition to the hurtful self-serving needs within therapists that lead them to participate in this type of collusion, there may also be unconscious wishes to help the patient develop and grow in this peculiar fashion. The risk is, of course, that the prodding will be overdone, that the constructive aspects of the conspiracy will collapse, and that the patient will be left with trauma and regression, a worsening of the clinical picture.

There are many forms and dimensions to the psychotherapeutic conspiracy. Therapists who propose to impart sound understand-ing are drawn to the collusion based on both destructive and constructive pathological needs that misguide them in their efforts. Patients who profess to wish to get well by understanding them-selves engage in these misalliances for defensive purposes, fearing the truth of their illnesses because of a need for punishment and to remain sick, and yet with the wish to become well in some paradoxical and uninsightful manner. Since the conspiracy is so strongly motivated by the unconscious needs of both patients and therapists, it has been especially difficult to identify and resolve.

There is often a powerful match between the unconscious needs of the two participants to the treatment situation. A guilt-ridden, self-destructive (masochistic), depressed patient will unconsciously and unwittingly accept a conspiracy in which the therapist satisfies his or her destructive and sadistic needs to a degree that would be self-evident to any impartial observer. Both the masochism of the patient and the sadism of the therapist are thereby satisfied, sometimes with resultant symptom relief for the patient (and even the therapist).

Another dimension of the conspiracy is the patient's acceptance of the therapist's proposal that he or she alone is the sick member of the therapeutic twosome and that the therapist, by contrast, is quite healthy. In itself, the idea that the patient is ill and the therapist is healthy need not be conspiratorial. However, it becomes so when the patient actually functions quite well and adaptively on a conscious or unconscious level and reveals a considerable capacity for sound unconscious functioning. It is collusive to neglect the strengths of the patient, however unconscious they may be.

Similarly, it is conspiratorial to deny the actual reflections of sickness in the therapist as revealed in his or her mistaken silences and interventions. It is the therapist's responsibility to express his or her strengths consciously and manifestly through immediate interventions. If these are disturbed, the therapist's unconscious strengths are of little value to the patient. As shall be seen, the definition of the assigned as compared to the actual roles of each member of the therapeutic dyad, especially in regard to who it is that is functioning as patient and therapist, is an important source of conspiratorial interaction between patients and therapists. Patients often function unconsciously as therapists, and therapists as patients.

Conspiracy may be one of victim and victimizer. It may be a means by which both patient and therapist evade painful truths, to the relief of both. As the clinical vignette presented in this chapter demonstrates, it may be that the conspiracy entails a treatment situation with a mixture of constructive and destructive qualities that is the best either patient and therapist can generate.

Then too, while professing to seek truth and understanding, the psychotherapeutic conspirators may accept lies or fictions, or even statements of truths that are actually used in a false manner. The therapist's statement that the patient, because of her experiences with her father, mistakenly imagines that he, the therapist, wishes to hurt her, is an example of such a lie. In truth, this therapist has in fact been hurtful to the patient, and if anything, he has behaved just like her father. No distortion, transference, or fantasy is involved. Instead, there is a sound unconscious perception by the patient that she dares not state directly to her therapist. The fiction, however, spares both parties to therapy a measure of anxiety and pain.

In order to recognize the psychotherapeutic conspiracy, the details of each therapeutic interaction are needed. General descriptions are inherently false and deceptive. The specifics are required in order to identify the patient's unconscious or encoded responses and messages. One simply cannot rely on the conscious or direct reactions of the patient. The patient's unconscious communications are far more trustworthy.

Cure, then, may result from the therapist's failure to understand. Cure may also come through paradoxical reactions to a therapist's assaultive behaviors. All the while, the patient may unconsciously know the terrible truths of the underlying therapeutic conspiracy. It is one of the remarkable capabilities of the human mind to divide its knowledge, understanding, and perceptions into those that are conscious and those that are unconscious. This split is often merciful and spares much pain. At other times, it places the individual in highly self-destructive situations that are accepted on the surface, though their detrimental qualities may be sensed unconsciously. However, the very mental mechanisms that protect a person from being overwhelmed emotionally and enable him or her to cope are the same ones that divide the self and create mental illness.

CHAPTER 6
AVOIDING THE CONSEQUENCES OF CURE

In the name of gaining mental health, a therapist may do almost whatever he or she pleases with a patient. The therapist may express manifestly an intention to heal through insight and understanding, while in actuality offering something far different. He or she may even profess to cure through highly dramatic and traumatic techniques in a fashion fully accepted by the patient, even though common sense would call for outrage.

In the psychotherapeutic conspiracy, lies are offered in the guise of truth. Truths are offered in a way that enables them to function as lies. Truth and understanding are discarded altogether. Protective fictions are substituted for underlying chaotic truths. Words are used for action and discharge rather than as a means of control, binding, and understanding. In the name of cure-through-understanding, relief through certain misunderstanding is offered.

The therapist functions unconsciously as a patient; the patient functions unconsciously as the therapist. While stating that he or she will cure the patient, the therapist attempts unconsciously to cure himself or herself instead. While indicating that he or she wishes to be cured, the patient unconsciously attempts to cure the therapist in his or her place.

There are distinct advantages to both patient and therapist in accepting their manifest roles and yet functioning unconsciously in rather different fashion. The patient finds immediate relief in recognizing that while he or she enters therapy with certain emotional complaints, the treatment process soon focuses unconsciously on the expressed illness of the therapist. By having his or her sickness set aside, the patient feels an immediate sense of comfort. Quite willingly (though without direct awareness), the designated patient becomes the functional therapist. A particular form of conspiratorial cure involves situations in which therapists unconsciously benefit from the unconscious ministrations of their patients. (It must be stressed that this involves the therapist's ways of expressing his or her pathology of which he or she is unaware, and the patient's therapeutic measures are carried out without awareness and through encoded and displaced communications.)

The therapist is afforded the honored position of the healer. Nevertheless, the therapist engages in a sanctioned technique through which important aspects of his or her own psychopathology are expressed. While consciously and seriously dedicated to the cure of the patient, the therapist unconsciously becomes involved in the cure of his or her own emotional ills. The primary benefit to the therapist may be considerable, though much depends on whether he or she is eventually able to consciously recognize the actual state of affairs. Even without doing so, the therapist may nonetheless find considerable emotional relief.

Thus the therapist states that he or she will work with the patient's communications, while all the while imposing his or her own thoughts, feelings, and fantasies. The therapist indicates that he or she will interpret the meaning of the patient's material and identify the patient's own unconscious and hidden messages; instead, he or she uses his or her own fabrications and fictional systems to cover over and avoid the underlying truths in the patient's communicative expressions.

Both parties to treatment tend to accept the concept that the therapist knows best, especially when it comes to what is healthy or sick, real or imagined, curative or hurtful. Quite often, though, the therapist decides that a particular image from the patient is a product of his or her imagination when it is actually quite in tune with reality. Then too, statements from patients that are accepted as realistic are actually, on more careful analysis, products of their imaginations (fantasies).

In the psychotherapeutic conspiracy, the therapist takes his or her own statements to the patient at face value. The therapist believes that what he or she says is intended as meant and that all that is meant has been communicated. His or her messages are manifest and direct, and there is a strong denial of the existence of unconscious messages and hidden meanings and functions. On the other hand, the patient's expressions are seldom accepted as such. They are often seen as containing hidden and encoded messages. The patient says one thing but means another. In all, the accepted collusion states that the therapist says what he or she means to say and says no more, while the patient almost never says what he or she means, and always means more than he or she has said.

To sum up, in the psychotherapeutic conspiracy between patients and therapists, it is the therapist who is the main perpetrator of harm and distortion. The patient is the willing victim. The conspiracy is largely unconscious, outside of the awareness of both participants. Adorned with sincere wishes by therapists to help their patients, the cure—if it does occur—is by collusion and victimization or traumatic stimulation for growth.

At the heart of the therapeutic conspiracy is a deep and abiding dread of the underlying truths of the patient's neurosis and of the emotional illness of the therapist as well. The realizations involved seem so dreadful and dangerous that relief through virtually any other means is preferred by patients and therapists alike. Collusion and conspiracy are therefore inevitable.

The nature of the psychotherapeutic conspiracy may already make considerable sense to the reader, but part of it may appear dubious and ill-defined. To fully appreciate the nature of the psychotherapeutic conspiracy, one needs a sense of the history of the psychotherapeutic movement, an understanding of the nature of an emotional illness, and a simple means of comprehending communication outside of awareness—unconscious communication. Only then can one have a full sense of the therapeutic process in all of its variations.

With this type of background insight in hand, one can then return to the details of the psychotherapeutic conspiracy in a position to far better formulate the contributions of the patient and

therapist, and of the emotional disturbance they hope to solve, to
the collusion existing between the partners to treatment. The pre-
ceding chapters have presented an introduction to the nature of the
psychotherapeutic conspiracy. The following chapters provide the
means through which this remarkable state of affairs may be fully
understood.

PART II
PSYCHOTHERAPY YESTERDAY

CHAPTER 7

THE FIRST THERAPEUTIC CONSPIRACY: BREUER AND ANNA O.

Statements of historical analysis are always a mixture of facts and interpretation. As a rule, one approaches a particular aspect of history with a singular goal in mind and selects and formulates in keeping with one's purpose. However, one accepts the rules of historical analysis that preclude the distortion of actual known facts. So long as the basis on which the historical theme is developed is stated, inconsequential but necessary omissions can be accepted. The goal is to reconstruct and recount a segment of history with a fairness and perceptiveness that holds to the truth of the situation while providing fresh insight into the past and present.

Prior to the 1880s, there was virtually no concept of the meaningful nature of emotional illnesses. Emotional disorders were believed to be a concomitant of physical disturbances of the brain and hereditary disorders of the nervous system. Correspondingly, the crude therapeutic measures available emphasized physical relief and efforts to suggest away disturbing emotional symptoms.

Virtually every form of present-day psychotherapy, and especially those that profess to understand factors in a patient's neurosis, have their origins in the work of Josef

Breuer with his patient, Anna O. Breuer's efforts were soon shared with Sigmund Freud, his student and colleague (though publication of Breuer's work was delayed some dozen years for reasons to be discussed later on). The main questions here are: Did dynamic psychotherapy show any signs of conspiracy at the time of its remarkable origination? If so, what was the nature of this collusion and what were its sources? Is it possible to understand present-day psychotherapeutic conspiracies in light of their beginnings?

The presentation and discussion of the case of Anna O. will therefore concentrate on those facts and inferences that illuminate the theme of psychotherapeutic conspiracy. From time to time, other aspects of this therapeutic experience will be noted. Nonetheless, their role will not be stressed or fully discussed. The result will be a rather biased consideration, though with full respect to the other dimensions of the discovery of insightful forms of therapy.

The work of Breuer with Anna O. contained within it the origins of such matters as the conflict theory of neurosis, the nature of unconscious mental contents and functions as they influence an emotional disturbance, the understanding of the nature of hysterical emotional symptoms, and a host of insights into the therapeutic process. The positive contributions of psychoanalysis and its pioneers are firmly established. Perhaps too much so; possibly to the point where they have blinded us to their more questionable efforts and errors. Thus the consideration of conspiracy must include a full appreciation for both its inevitability and for the many marvelous and constructive, nonconspiring aspects of the therapeutic procedures involved.

With good reason, we are inherently fascinated by origins. Our own beginnings involve our most personal secrets, facts, wishes, and dreams. They are the stuff from which myths are made. The origins of every important individual, and of every critical social and political movement, contain within them deeply important messages and implications. By unraveling the secrets of birth, we learn much about the nature of humankind. We gain a tool that may help us control our future and destiny, personal and social.

Often, an analysis of origins shows how the seeds of the future are sown in its very beginnings. Once the breakthrough has been established, a rather typical process unfolds. On the one hand, the new ideas and therapeutic procedures are solidified and eventually ossified to a point of reification and immutability. On the other hand, some measure of continued evolution and revision takes place. The die-hards stay with the safety of the long-standing, well-worn theory and techniques. Others who are more adventurous evolve and change the technique to a point where they split off from the mainstream. If the technique and theory also pose some noticeable measure of threat for those who make use of them, splinter groups are inevitable. Each new group refutes and adopts selected aspects of the basic position.

The true evolution of a basic psychotherapeutic theory and technique is most difficult. Much of the original position remains fixed and becomes so vital to those who embrace it that further change is experienced as cataclysmic. Thus lack of change, sameness, the need to split off deviants (mutants), and difficulty in adopting significant internal alterations are characteristic of therapeutic movements such as psychoanalysis.

Many of the difficulties in this evolutionary process arise because the movement under study was created out of conspiracy, designed to conspire, and required a secret unrecognized allegiance among its followers lest the truth be known. A false foundation is simply unable to support a growing structure. It must extrude challenges that contain unrecognized truths, since it is unable to meet and handle them. Thus our subject is the origin of a highly attractive, yet extremely threatening, basically false treatment modality, which has nonetheless spawned a highly viable and truthful theory of personality and development. Later on, this particular paradox will be examined, and the flaws in the theory will be defined. For now, the question is just how much of the adult existed in the seedling of the child. The answer lies in the origins of present-day psychotherapy.

In December 1880, Josef Breuer, a physician and internist, was called to the home of a 21-year-old woman by the name of Bertha Pappenheim. Thirteen difficult years later, in 1893, when Breuer wrote up the case for publication (Breuer and Freud 1893–1895) he used the pseudonym Anna O. for his patient. Here too she will be referred to by the name by which she is known in the psychoanalytic literature.

Although the landmark book in which she is described, which Breuer coauthored with Sigmund Freud, was entitled *Studies on*

Hysteria (1893–1895), most observers agree that Anna O. was suffering from a psychotic illness—and Breuer too referred to her in these terms. She experienced an abundance of symptoms, ranging from a psychogenic cough to a variety of occular disturbances, paralyses, contractions, anesthesias, language disorders, muteness, and altered states of consciousness—what she called her "clouds." She also hallucinated and was suicidal.

At the time, there was, as noted, little in the way of therapy available to Anna O. There were rest homes, sanatoria, and various types of hydrotherapy and massage. Forms of electroshock already existed, as did sedatives and morphine. Personal isolation and care by a companion were possible. Some use had also been made of hypnosis, though entirely as a means of subjecting the patient to a variety of therapeutic suggestions. (In the main, these suggestions involved cajoling the patient to recognize the unreality of his or her illness, to relax and feel well, or more directly, to give up his or her symptoms.)

Not surprisingly, many patients became well with these therapies. Some, of course, became hopelessly insane and nonfunctional; yet others gave up their symptoms and led useful lives. This in itself suggests the presence of a wide range of psychotherapeutic conspiracies, though at the time therapists made little claim to understanding the nature of their patients' emotional illnesses. They tended to acknowledge the limitations of their efforts and to be gratified if the patient became well—no matter how this was accomplished. Perhaps the situation best suggests the resourcefulness of emotionally disturbed patients, who may, under selected but difficultly defined conditions, find means of resolving their symptoms in the face of entirely inadequate therapeutic procedures.

By now, it may be equally unsurprising to realize that virtually all of these primitive methods of cure or relief (the latter is the more accurate term) are still in active use this very day. Many of the treatment modalities described in the first part of this volume owe their heritage to these 19th century therapeutic techniques. These include sex therapy and nude marathons, as shall soon be seen.

At the time of his consultations with Anna O., Josef Breuer had made use of one or another of the therapeutic modalities available in his work with patients whose illnesses appeared to be psychologically founded. While many physicians felt that the use of hypnosis was dangerous, and that it could even make a healthy

individual into a neurotic hysteric, Breuer nonetheless was evidently
adept at hypnotic techniques. Prior to his work with Anna O.,
however, in keeping with the fashion of the times, he used this
procedure entirely as a means of enforcing directly curative suggestions.

When Breuer first visited Anna O., she was already quite ill and
confined to bed. Her father, whom she had nursed for some time,
was in the throes of dying from a lung abscess. The family, however,
was quite well off and able to afford the services of Dr. Breuer, who
had an excellent reputation as a clinician. At the time, Breuer was
about to turn thirty-nine.

By his own description, Breuer found his sick patient to be a
highly sympathetic, intellectually vital, extremely imaginative
young woman. It was evident he found her attractive. For what
appears to be both scientific and personal reasons, Breuer adopted
a rather intensive treatment approach. Anna O. was noticeably
verbal, even though at times she became mute or spoke only in
English. It could hardly be coincidental that no one in her immediate surroundings but Breuer could understand and converse with
her in this language. Indeed, this is perhaps a first sign of a conspiracy between the twosome.

The details of Breuer's initial therapeutic efforts are unclear. It is
entirely possible that he recommended baths, and he may have mas-
saged her, though he does not mention doing so in his case report.
He did, however, feed his patient, and there is evidence he treated
her with morphine. He most certainly must have examined her physically, and other types of nonsexual physical contact were quite
common at the time between patients and physicians, including
those who were attempting to treat an emotional illness.

It seems likely that Anna O. regaled Breuer with vivid and imaginative descriptions of her hallucinations, delusions, and other products of her imagination. She was prone to create stories and fairy
tales, and in later years wrote at least one play and several other
pieces. Alternating between clouds or absences (fugue states or
altered states of consciousness) and the waking state, Anna O. said a
great deal to Breuer. The latter was soon able to realize that if his
patient, while in an altered state, described in some detail the
hallucinations that she had experienced during her absences, she
would wake up with a clear mind and in a calm and cheerful state.
Also, during her absences she appeared to attempt to recreate

situations and episodes that had tormented her. Often, they involved highly imaginative stories, many of which concerned a girl anxiously sitting by a sick-bed. The absences soon extended into a state of auto-hypnosis. Breuer found that he could offer Anna O. considerable relief as long as he permitted her to vent her experiences under hypnosis. He soon began to visit his patient on a daily basis, and later on he saw her as a rule twice each day.

Because of her suicidal impulses, Anna O. was transferred to a country house where she could remain on the first floor rather than on the third. Breuer was no longer able to see her with the same regularity. He was, however, able to visit her during certain evenings, and he would then take advantage of her hypnotic state by relieving her of the imaginary products that had accumulated since his last visit. Anna O. would assure herself that it was Breuer who was by her side by carefully feeling his hands. She would then, sometimes with a struggle, describe her hallucinatory and other imaginary experiences to Breuer. The patient herself, using English words, spoke of this as a "talking cure" and as "chimney sweeping."

In all, the treatment continued until June 1882. Under the guidance of his patient—and she very much led the way—Breuer soon discovered that a series of meaningful experiences, many of them highly traumatic and disturbing, lay beneath each of her symptoms. Remarkably, if under hypnosis he could coax his patient to recall all of the occasions on which she had experienced a particular symptom, the disturbance then disappeared. This involved an excruciatingly detailed process that relied heavily upon Anna O.'s remarkable memory and Josef Breuer's equally remarkable intense interest and concern. (He recorded the proceedings in great detail only to later apparently destroy this material.)

The discovery of the relief the patient obtained through recollection is described by Breuer as having taken place accidentally and through his observation of spontaneous utterances from his patient. The first instance of this cure greatly surprised him. It occurred during what must have been the summer of 1881. Anna O. had suddenly found it impossible to drink liquids. The symptom proved difficult to resolve. Then, one day while under hypnosis, she spoke of an English lady-companion whom she disliked. With a strong sense of disgust, she described going into the lady's room and observing a little dog drinking out of a glass. The patient had said nothing and had held back her considerable sense of anger. Once the anger had been released under hypnosis, the patient was able to drink a large quantity of water without any difficulty. The symptom never returned.

Thus the talking cure, the cure by chimney sweeping, the cure by talking away symptoms, found its origins. Breuer soon took to deliberately exploring the sources and memories to which each particular symptom the patient experienced could be related. Guided by the genius of his patient, and brilliantly perceptive in his own right, Josef Breuer was the first known physician to listen to the wild ravings of an emotionally ill (psychotic) patient and to find they contained hidden meaning. He was the first physician to attempt to trace these meanings into the patient's recent life, though not into her childhood. The discovery of hidden meanings beneath paralyses, facial ticks, and the like was a monumental breakthrough. The development of a means of cure by having the patient describe and vent or abreact the feelings connected with experiences and their implications was even more staggering.

At the request of his patient, Breuer terminated the treatment of Anna O. in June of 1882, quite close to the anniversary of his patient's transfer to the country house the year before. By then, most of her symptoms had been alleviated. Breuer himself (Breuer and Freud 1893–1895) described his patient as quite well, though he did add that it was considerable time before she regained her mental balance entirely. "Since then," his final comment went, "she has enjoyed complete health" (p. 41).

Later historians, including Freud, tell us that Breuer's description of Anna O.'s mental health was in some ways rather inaccurate. It was in a sense an historical statement that violated the canon of accurate reporting of events. It may well have been that at the immediate moment of termination, Breuer's patient had mobilized her resources and had appeared relatively intact. On the other hand, there are signs that Breuer distorted historical truth to some extent. Thus there is evidence that Anna O. spent time in mental health sanatoria quite soon after, and for some time subsequent to, her treatment by Breuer (Ellenberger 1970). She required therapy for an addiction to morphine to which Breuer had apparently contributed. Despite all of this, Anna O. went on to become the founder of the social work movement in Germany, the director of a home for wayward children, and a champion of unwed mothers and maligned women. There are indications too that she had little use for psychoanalysis, the treatment modality that she herself had helped to create. Her latter life appears to have been a mixture of high level functioning and emotionally protective behaviors, a combination not unlike the attributes of her treatment with Breuer.

According to the case report, Anna O.'s cure reached its fulfillment when, in her last session, she reproduced a terrifying hallucination that she had experienced while nursing her father. She had awoken during the night in great anxiety about her ward, who had a high fever. She was in the country and expecting the arrival of a surgeon from Vienna who was to operate. Her mother had absented herself, and Anna was sitting at her father's bedside with her right arm over the back of a chair. She fell into a waking dream and saw a black snake coming toward her father from the wall to bite him. When she tried to keep the snake off, her arms became paralyzed. When she looked at her fingers, they turned into little snakes with death's heads. When the snake vanished, she was terrified and tried to pray, but language failed her. She was finally able to think of some children's verses in English and then prayed in that language. The whistle of the train bringing the surgeon broke the spell.

It was this scene that Anna O. created on the final day of her treatment with Breuer. As a sign of cure, upon this particular occasion she was able to respond to the danger by speaking and praying in German. It was in this context that Breuer then reported that she was free subsequently from the innumberable disturbances that she had previously exhibited.

This brief description, the first case ever treated with a psychotherapeutic approach designed to develop insight into the basis for a patient's emotional disturbance, demonstrates Josef Breuer's unique ability to listen to his patient and to permit her to direct the unfolding of the treatment experience—an approach with some heritage in the work of earlier mesmerizers and hypnotists (Ellenberger 1970). It appears that Anna O. had the conscious wisdom to appreciate the nature of the cure that she required. In response, her physician had the perceptiveness to follow her directives and to elaborate upon her leads. This is indeed a fine beginning to the line of insight-oriented psychotherapies that have unfolded with Breuer's cure by abreaction and recollection as their fountainhead. On the face of it, the situation appears ingeniously creative and successful in all innocence. It may well be, however, that a more careful scrutiny will reveal far more. It may well extend the initial suspicion that a psychotherapeutic conspiracy was in part also in play.

Breuer began his discussion of the case by indicating that he had suppressed quite a number of interesting details. He saw Anna O.'s illness as determined by a monotonous family life to which she had responded with the constant activity of her imagination. Her habit of daydreaming had laid the foundation for a dissociation of her mental personality and the ultimate development of hallucinatory absences because of the patient's anxiety and dread. Breuer made much of the patient's two states of consciousness—waking and altered—and of the manner in which her absences were a *conditione seconde*, the critical, vulnerable mental state within which her illness unfolded.

As for the disappearance of her symptoms, Breuer agreed with his patient that she had talked them away. He distinguished this process from the use of suggestion and stressed the release of strangulated affects—abreaction. He also specifically stated that "The element of sexuality was astonishingly undeveloped in her. The patient, whose life became known to me to an extent to which one person's life is seldom known to another, had never been in love; and in all the enormous number of hallucinations which occurred during her illness that element of mental life never emerged" (Breuer and Freud 1893-1895, pp. 21-22).

On the face of it, then, this is an important chapter in the history of psychotherapy. It involves an eminent Viennese physician and a young woman plagued with emotional symptoms. The patient, through some type of inexplicable wisdom, both quite directly and by implication, led her physician into an entirely new mode of treatment: the talking cure. Both the patient's genius and the physician's wisdom in listening to and taking seriously his patient's guidelines are to be commended. When she was allowed to talk, and once Breuer decided to listen, the patient was able to reveal that emotional symptoms had hidden roots and sources. These tended to be concentrated in recent though earlier traumatic experiences. In a stroke, the hidden or unconscious basis of emotional illness and its roots in earlier traumas were discovered. These were momentous findings indeed.

There was more. Much was made of unexpressed or strangulated emotions, affects whose release had been blocked at the time of the trauma. Under hypnosis, it proved possible to recreate and to have the patient reexperience these terrifying moments and to foster the release of the pent-up feelings. With the discovery that the patient's symptoms disappeared once this process had been completed, there was every reason to believe that a new era of psychotherapy had begun.

There were also, as noted, important breakthroughs regarding the conception of the nature of emotional illness. With the focus on strangulated affects, it was proposed that hysterical or emotional paralyses and other somatic symptoms occurred because the affects had been converted through some mysterious process into the somatic symptom. This process of *conversion* became the key to what was perhaps the first sensible theory of how a physical symptom could develop on the basis of a psychological disturbance. Then too, the role of an altered state of consciousness in creating a vulnerability to emotional symptoms, and more specifically an interference in the experience or discharge of affects, was also proposed.

This much of the story already suggests some interesting historical perspectives. This particular form of hypnotherapy is in extensive use to this very day. Techniques for abreaction, such as those involved in Janov's primal scream therapy, also abound. It is inviting to believe that abreaction, the release of strangulated emotions and feelings, is in itself curative. By implication, this would mean that individuals prone to fits of rage and emotional upheaval-discharge should be the healthiest souls among us. This is a dubious conclusion at best.

The talking cure, of course, is also still very much in our midst. Breuer's cathartic method is the direct antecedent of Freud's method of psychoanalysis. An endless variety of talking cures have emerged from the two sources. Some of them quite clearly bear a strong resemblance of the techniques used by Breuer: a mixture of abreac-

tion, tracing out historical antecedents, reenactments of past traumas, role-playing, and a heavy measure of reassurance, persuasion,
and sundry side remarks, including the feeding and direct caring
for patients, and often some measure of physical contact. There is
sometimes as well a sharing of some type of secret or special
language, in a manner not unlike the private exchanges between
Anna O. and Breuer that took place in English and in the private
theatre the two created together.

As for signs of collusion, there is only small cause for suspicion.
Anna O. often recognized only Breuer, and as already noted, there
were periods when she spoke only in English, a language that Breuer
alone understood. She refused the ministrations of other physicians, including a consultant mentioned by Breuer who turned out
to be the famous physician Krafft-Ebbing. There were times when
Anna O. acknowledged the existence of only her physician and
would eat only if he fed her.

To stretch matters just a bit further, one might question Breuer's
motives in seeing his patient not only daily, but for long periods of
time on a twice-a-day basis. By all standards of medical practice,
then and now, he spent an extraordinary amount of time with his
patient. For her part, Anna O. responded in a manner that clearly
intrigued and fascinated her physician. She developed a mode of
cure that closely bound him to her. With the early signs of its
success, Breuer became even more committed to the intensive
treatment of his patient.

It seems fair to say, then, that there was some measure of
collusion between Anna O. and Breuer in which the patient led her
willing physician to a mode of cure that kept him close at hand. In
addition, there is every reason to believe that Anna O. knew on
some level the inadequacies of the treatment practices of her time.
Her creation of the talking cure, and of the cure by tracing out
antecedents and releasing affects, was motivated by a sincere and
deep need to be well in some lasting fashion.

On his side, Breuer was an extremely dedicated physician. He
had a bent for research and had already contributed significantly to
the medical literature. To this day, physicians speak of the Hering-
Breuer pulmonary reflex, which is one aspect of our breathing
mechanism. Clearly, Breuer was a physician interested in new
perspectives. He was able to quickly sense that he was involved

with a patient who could lead him toward new horizons. His pursuit of the talking cure and his commitment to his patient follow naturally from these positive inclinations.

Whatever their collusion, whatever motivated Anna O. and Breuer to engage in such a unique and intensive personal involvement, each was commited to an important and legitimate pursuit. The sense one has that Anna O. got something more than the cure of her symptoms and Breuer something more than a new theory and treatment of emotional illness, takes nothing away from their combined contribution to medicine and psychotherapy. Great discoveries are often fueled in part by unconscious and sometimes pathological needs that take little away from such discoveries' creativity and importance.

To persist a bit further, one should examine the two most striking hallucinatory phenomena reported by Anna O. in her work with Breuer. Interestingly, the first of these was the initial occasion on which Breuer observed that the recall and verbal utterance of the conditions under which a symptom first occurred actually led to the disappearance of the disturbance. The second is the last hallucination described by Anna O. to Breuer—at least as far as the published case is concerned.

The first instance involves Anna O.'s refusal to drink water. As mentioned earlier, this was traced to her discovery that her English lady-companion's dog had drunk water from a glass in her room. Speaking English was strongly associated with Breuer, so we may suspect that in some hidden and encoded fashion, this particular hallucination may well have had some connection with Anna O.'s relationship to Breuer. In this context, it is noteworthy that virtually nothing was said by Breuer of his relationship or interaction with his patient. The talking cure involved events in the life of Anna O. and symptoms—objects of study such as hallucinations and paralyses. The relationship between patient and physician was afforded no consideration at all. It is as if Breuer was studying and dissecting a section of lung tissue under a microscope. He was probing and investigating, and supposedly responding in a detached and scientific manner. There was little or no sense of interaction, of interplay of emotions, of reaction to the highly personal, private, and sometimes overwhelmingly terrifying hallucinations and to the other experiences that Anna O. described to Breuer.

There is indeed an unreal quality to the case report, a quality that persists in the description of many psychotherapies to this very day. Certainly, putting the relationship between patient and therapist to the side, affording it no consideration whatsoever, is extremely common at present. In fact, there are those who feel that to do otherwise is quite absurd. Some of this derives from the medical model of emotional illness and the effort to treat an emotional symptom much like a segment of diseased tissue.

One must remember, however, that it was Anna O. who created the talking cure to realize, first, that a psychotherapist is dealing with a whole human being filled with emotions and responsiveness and, second, that the patient has an enormous impact upon the therapist whether the therapist wishes to recognize it or not. Through this perspective, one may detect a rather striking kind of conspiracy: the avoidance of the relationship between the patient and physician or therapist by both parties to treatment. In the case report, Breuer refers to the way in which Anna O. ignored the presence of her consultant. He calls this a negative hallucination and states it was broken only when the consultant had blown smoke in her face. Anna O. suddenly saw the stranger in front of her, rushed to the door of the room in which she was being seen in order to take away the key, and fell unconscious to the ground.

In some sense, Anna O. seems to have responded to Breuer's presence through the development of a more subtle type of negative hallucination. But then too Breuer treated his patient in part as if she herself did not exist. One might even speculate that Anna O.'s reaction to the imposing presence of the consultant carried with it the dramatized message: to be aware of the presence of a therapist is totally overwhelming and impossible.

Could it be, then, that both Anna O. and Breuer very much needed not to be fully aware of the other person and of the nature of their interaction? Could it be that such an awareness would have been too problematic for them both? And can these questions be applied as well to a collusion between present-day patients and therapists to deny both the full existence of each other, and the impact each is having upon the other?

In the memory of the dog drinking from the glass, there are strong affects of disgust and anger. The image is dirty and repulsive, and there is a sense of dangerous contamination. Anna O. refused to swallow water because it was associated with a dog drinking from the same glass. What underlying meaning could account for Anna O.'s reaction? What sort of substance could be involved?

Following the thinking of Breuer, any idea that it could pertain to something sexual is out of the question. Sexuality was said to be astonishingly undeveloped in this patient. And yet, the image of the dog lapping water from a glass has strong symbolic sexual qualities. It quite easily lends itself to images related to sexual intercourse and cunnilingus. Although one must be cautious in making appraisals of this kind, this communication offers a first hint of inner or unconscious sexual fantasies within Anna O. that may have been conveyed only in disguised form. Based upon the recently acquired knowledge that our *perceptions* of other persons are also encoded, the possibility exists that the same hallucinatory communication contains an encoded sexual image of Breuer.

Thus it is possible that the experiences Anna O. described while under hypnosis did in some way and on some level entail communications relevant to her relationship and interaction with her physician. While both participants unwittingly conspired to some degree to consciously deny the existence of that relationship, Anna O. could not help but express her fantasies and perceptions in some form. In addition, to the extent that this particular hallucination did indeed contain unconscious sexual implications, there is evidence that sexuality may have been strongly repressed by this patient but might not have been especially underdeveloped. It therefore follows that in this respect, there may well have been some type of unconscious collusion on both sides designed to set sexuality to the side. This collusion and personal need may have led to a form of denial that produced that particular statement from the pen of Josef Breuer. Once again, there is considerable evidence that this kind of collusion and denial exists between many psychotherapeutic partners to this very day.

The final memory and hallucination reported by Anna O. to Josef Breuer involved, as may be recalled, a scene where she was caring for her father, hallucinated a snake moving toward his bed, experienced a paralysis of her arm, and saw snakes with death's heads where her fingers should have been. Anna O. then experienced an inability to pray in German, though she did utter a prayer of protection in English.

What can be said of this final communication of patient to physician? A number of later writers have commented upon the hostility of Anna O. toward her father reflected in her inability to fend off the snake. Others have pointed to the symbolic meaning of the snake, a typical encoded representation of the penis. The suggestion is made that Anna O. harbored guilt-ridden sexual fantasies toward her father that were the cause of considerable anxiety and conflict. Some have even suggested that the hallucination represented Anna O.'s own wish for a penis, a theme that connects to her evident frustrations over the restrictions that befell her because she was a woman.

The snake hallucination therefore speaks again for unconscious and repressed sexuality within Anna O. It points to the possibility of either sexual fantasies and wishes or sexual perceptions of her physician, or both. The latter could well have been based on some of the actual implicit (unconscious) qualities of the ministrations of this physician; though in addition there may have been a measure of misinterpretation or sexualization by the patient. As a final report, then, the hallucination may well have been Anna O.'s last attempt to work over with her physician some type of intrapsychic and/or interpersonal sexual conflict. In part out of their naivete, and in part through unconscious collusion, this possibility was entirely ignored by both individuals.

In addition, the same material may be thought of as having some bearing on other aspects of the relationship between Breuer and Anna O., especially in light of its emergence on the final day of treatment. After all, the image involves a caretaker and her patient. The treatment relationship has rather similar properties. Strikingly, however, the caretaker, instead of carrying out her protective functions, failed to guard the sick person from the danger at hand. On the surface, the threat was that of an attack by a snake or, as already noted, symbolically it may well have been sexual in nature. What more could all of this mean?

If one simply proposes that the important mechanisms of displacement (from the relationship with Breuer to that which Anna O. had with her father, and from the present to the past) and symbolic representation produced this manifest message as an encoded communication, a number of likely speculations follow. The hallucination may well suggest Anna O.'s conscious or, more likely, unconscious perception that Breuer had actually failed to deal adequately with the greatest danger faced by his patient for the moment, her illness. While it may well be that Anna O. felt quite well on one level, on another she apparently sensed that something had gone awry.

This formulation challenges the statement made by Breuer that Anna O. was relieved of all of her symptoms and raises the possibility that a patient may get well in the face of failed psychotherapeutic efforts and, further, that therapists sometimes misperceive the results of their labors and present them in far too favorable a light. With Anna O. this last possibility may well have been the case. Historians (Ellenberger 1970) have revealed that Anna O. was hospitalized soon after completing her therapy with Breuer and on several subsequent occasions. Nonetheless, at the time of termination, the patient may have shown much in the way of symptom alleviation. It is difficult to entirely resolve this question, though some form of collusion is in evidence.

Another feature of the hallucination suggests additional implications. Anna O., the caretaker, experienced the danger of the snake in two ways: as coming toward her father and as part of herself— her fingers. In a sense, this implies a danger to both the sick person and the caretaker. One possible meaning is that in this encoded fashion Anna O. was trying to indicate her perception that both she and her physician were in some ways dealing with comparable dangers, and that in some important and sick ways they were quite alike. The threat in all likelihood was that of frightening sexual impulses and wishes. Thus the patient appears to have been suggesting that both of them had expressed in some symbolic or more direct form highly charged sexual impulses and fantasies that neither could adequately manage. To put this a bit differently, the source of the sexual anxiety appears to lie both within the caretaker and the patient.

Apparently, it was Anna O.'s decision to terminate her therapy. Later reports (Jones 1953) suggest the possibility that Breuer too may have pressed for an end of the treatment. In either case, it may be speculated that both patient and therapist felt overwhelmed by sexual and aggressive impulses, fantasies, and perceptions of each other to a point where they felt that termination was the only recourse. This is, of course, a collusive action, strongly designed to seal off a sense of mutual inner turmoil and interpersonal anxieties.

Both patient and therapist had a strong investment in this conspiratorial act that in all likelihood brought both of them some measure of immediate relief. Needless to say, this type of collusive and defensive termination is still a common phenomenon in the broad world of psychotherapy.

This case affords the reader the opportunity to experience the kinds of overwhelming threats that motivate both patients and therapists alike toward shared collusive actions and defenses. Without the advantage of a sense of distance and an understanding of the forces at play, there are few alternatives. The disadvantages are self-evident, while the gains are more than understandable. The very human sources of psychotherapeutic conspiracy are indeed in evidence in these origins and involve problems that to this day most therapists have quite unfortunately failed to master.

Based on this case report from *Studies on Hysteria*, then, one is left with the impression that Josef Breuer and Anna O. opened the door to a variety of psychotherapeutic methods on the basis of an intriguing combination of healthy and unhealthy motives and efforts. The patient wished to get well in some more substantial sense than possible with the forms of therapy in use at the time, none of which were investigative, based on efforts at understanding, or genetic. The physician wished to cure his very sick patient and was no doubt dissatisfied with the means available to him at the moment. With an eye toward improving these methods of cure and with a bent toward research and discovery, Josef Breuer was more than ready to respond to Anna O.'s suggestion of the talking cure.

There appear to be several collusive aspects to this remarkable discovery. There are suggestions that both Anna O. and Breuer had a special interest and involvement in the relationship they had developed. There are Anna O.'s total avoidance manifestly of any allusions to sexuality and Breuer's conclusion that it was essentially nonexistant in his patient. There are evident symbols of sexual contamination and threat, with indications that they pertained to the relationship between the patient and therapist. These clues point to a bilateral collusion to avoid all possible direct expressions of sexuality and even latent or hidden sexual elements especially as they pertained to their relationship. This deeper collusion was bolstered by the evident avoidance of any consideration whatsoever of what was happening between them or within either participant to this remarkable therapeutic experience. Finally, the encoded messages from Anna O. suggest that the treatment procedure was more a failure than a success, not surprising for a first and pioneering effort. These signals were ignored by both parties, as were the signs of an overwhelming sense of sexual danger that appeared to be eroding the therapeutic relationship. In response and through collusion, the patient apparently became well and terminated the treatment. For the moment, Anna O. had her cure and Josef Breuer his abreactive method.

There is a strong sense, however, that all of these levels of collusion were absolutely necessary for the continuation of this therapeutic experience. In evidence, there is the moment when Anna O. acknowledged the presence of the consultant who forcefully imposed his existence upon her. Strikingly, the patient went to remove a key. Could this imply that something quite crucial needed to be ignored or removed? In any case, the patient collapsed into unconsciousness, overwhelmed by the realization of the existence of the consulting doctor.

While Breuer himself showed no sign of this kind of total vulnerability to the realization of his patient's existence, his avoidance of their relationship seems highly protective. After all, this patient was revealing to him her deepest and innermost secrets. One senses considerable danger in treating them as communications from a human being with whom a physician is intensely involved. The danger appears virtually overwhelming if one considers that these secrets in some way actually involved valid encoded perceptions of the physician himself. There was a great need for both patient and therapist alike to defend against realizations of threatening impulses in the physician of which he himself was quite unaware.

It appears, then, that the first psychotherapeutic collusion was highly human, greatly protective, founded upon blatant defensive denial (negative hallucinations) and repression (avoidance of activated inner fantasies), and necessary on both sides for the continuation of the treatment. Since neither patient nor therapist understood or seemed capable of mastering the highly threatening material that began to emerge as Breuer modified his patient's defenses, collusive action appears to have been the only alternative for the moment. Further, the protective aspects of the conspiracy enabled the abreactive therapeutic process to go on for some time and to provide the patient with some measure of symptom relief.

These are indeed strange conditions for a talking cure. Still, this type of cure had been avoided for centuries. It is still avoided in many circles at this very time. However, massive and unconscious collusion of this kind takes place only in response to truly over-whelming anxiety and danger. The secrets of mental illness are unlocked only at great risk to both patient and therapist alike. There seems to be good reason for both individuals to wish to avoid these risks and to go about the process of cure or relief in some other way.

It would appear too that Breuer cured Anna O. through a curious mixture of unlocking some of the encoded or unconscious meanings of her emotional illness, while in no way detecting the deeper meanings of what he had unleashed. This was a cure with-out full understanding. And yet, it was by no means a cure through total avoidance and obliteration. Something happened, and it may well have been therapeutic, when Breuer and Anna O. cooperated to the point where she was able to reveal the secrets of her illness in disguised form. Both took the effort no further. Still, a first step had been made.

CHAPTER 8

DEEPER SOURCES OF COLLUSION

As Breuer warned, case reports, like history recounted, are selective. One makes observations, develops interpretations, and plays back what happened in a way that supports one's hypotheses. One then develops and extends the technique of psychotherapy based on one's theory. In its own way, the mode of therapy seems to reaffirm the emerging theory of emotional disorder. Closed circles of this kind are difficult to break. They form the basis for the most dubious theories and practices of psychotherapy.

Upon completing the apparently successful—though in reality quite incomplete or perhaps failed—treatment of Anna O., Breuer did nothing to announce his unique findings and treatment modality, so far as is known. There is no indication that he presented a paper to any medical group. It is quite clear he made no effort to publish a paper based on his experience.

While some later writers (Sulloway 1979) think it likely that Breuer discussed his experience with a number of colleagues, there is strong reason to believe otherwise. Almost everything personal that is known about this celebrated patient and physician has come from sources other than Breuer himself. Virtually all that follows here comes from Freud and Ernest Jones (1953), Freud's first major biographer. And even Freud did not recount much of this tale until after the death of his esteemed colleague. Then, too, a notable portion of Freud's recollections reveal a striking measure of forgetfulness on his part, and there is at least one important report that was without doubt in error. There is a sense again that one is dealing with disturbing and forbidden transactions. There is an aura of anxiety surrounding these origins that led to secrecy and misinformation.

It seems likely that Breuer, who had completed the treatment of Anna O. in June of 1882, said nothing of his experience to anyone until he confided in his junior colleague, Freud, in November of 1882. The date is marked by a letter from Freud to his fiancé, later his wife, Martha Bernays (Jones 1953). A second letter, written in July of 1883, indicates that Breuer then fell silent on the subject until this later date (Jones 1953), when he appears to have told (confessed?) all. Subsequently, and mostly because of continual prodding by Freud, Breuer elaborated upon his experiences with his patient. He made use of notes, which he later destroyed, since he indicated clearly in 1894, when he finally recorded some of the details of this case for posterity, that his writings were based on recollection alone.

There is strong evidence that both Breuer and Freud were dealing with a highly charged subject. There is the sense of the unspeakable, of taboos, and of avoidance and fear. For Breuer, Freud was a close colleague and confidant, and yet he said nothing of his experiences with Anna O. for five months. He was reluctant to pursue the matter, despite a sense shared by both himself and Freud that his clinical findings had major implications both for the theory of emotional disorders and for the advancement of psychotherapeutic procedures. It must be remembered yet again that, prior to Breuer's efforts to achieve cure through recollection and discharge of affect, all that was available to psychotherapists was quite crude and extremely limited in value. Freud himself remarked on the abundance of neurotics in Vienna, relative to the smaller number of patients suffering from clearly organic neurological disorders. There was a powerful need for more effective treatment methods.

In all, Breuer's handling of this information was highly conflicted. At first he concealed everything, then he spoke only of a portion of his observations. Later he revealed even more, but then was reluctant to pursue the matter further. As the years passed,

Freud virtually begged his mentor to report his findings in a
scientific paper; Breuer adamantly refused. He staunchly maintained his position even when Freud offered to serve as coauthor.
Surely, these are highly uncharacteristic attitudes in a physician
dedicated to science and discovery, already successful in carrying
out and reporting such pursuits, and committed to the advancement of treatment modalities. Something very powerful must have
been at work.

Freud too showed considerable hesitation and uncertainty in
regard to Breuer's technique and findings, doing so in a somewhat
different fashion from his colleague. The available biographical
material on Freud indicates that over the following 40-year period,
he tended to forget significant portions of Breuer's tale. This alter-
nation between remembering and forgetting also characterized
Freud's attitude toward his own monumental discovery or invention
of transference—the manner in which a patient makes a false
connection between attitudes and feelings toward an earlier figure
in his or her life and the treating physician.

The long delay between Breuer's description of his new hypnotic
technique and Freud's own decision to use it in his own practice is
also striking. While still a student, Freud had been especially
interested in a public exhibition of hypnosis given by the magnetist
Hansen. In 1885, Freud observed the practice of hypnotherapy, constituted mainly by the use of hypnotic suggestions designed to wipe
away a patient's hysterical symptoms. At the time, he studied
hypnosis with the famous French physician Charcot, through a
special grant that took Freud to Paris. He translated one of Charcot's
books into German, and himself wrote on the subject. Yet all the
while, though a champion for the cause of hypnosis, Freud did not
use it in his own medical practice at this time.

For reasons that are not known, Freud did finally begin to use
this technique in December of 1887. However, it was still another
18 months before he shifted from the use of hypnotic suggestion to
Breuer's more compelling and exploratory cathartic method. Even
then, the hypnotic work was combined with direct suggestions,
therapeutic baths, and total body massages performed directly by
Freud himself (perhaps the first clandestine form of sex therapy).
Later on, as is well known, Freud eventually gave up hypnosis,
shifted to a technique that combined physical pressure on the
forehead with free association, and ultimately arrived at the use of

free association alone, with the patient reclining on a couch and facing away from the analyst. (Some of the reasons for this transition will be explored in later sections of this book.)

When individuals including patients, physicians, and psychoanalysts are in close contact, they are vulnerable to unconscious conspiracy. Some are even open to deliberate collusion and dishonesty. Having identified the signs of trouble in both Breuer and Freud, one must turn to their sources and to the manner in which they rooted the origins of psychoanalysis and of most later-day psychotherapies, in a form of conspiracy between patient and therapist.

Breuer's great secret in the treatment of Anna O. was first revealed by Freud in 1932 in a letter to Stefan Zweig (Jones 1953), who had written about Anna O. erroneously. In the letter, Freud emphasized that Breuer's patient had never, as reported, confessed to suppressing certain experiences of a sexual nature while sitting at her father's sickbed. Freud then went on to say that what really happened with Breuer's patient was something that he was able to guess later on, long after he had broken with Breuer (somewhere around 1897).

Freud described suddenly remembering something that Breuer had once told him in another context before they had begun to collaborate, something that he had never repeated. It involved the evening of the day when all of Anna O.'s symptoms had been disposed of for the moment and the treatment terminated. Breuer was summoned to the patient again and found her confused and writhing with abdominal cramps. When he asked her what was wrong, she replied, "Now Dr. B.'s child is coming!"

Freud stated that at this moment Breuer held in his hand the key that would have opened the "door to the Mothers," but lamented that Breuer had let it drop. Instead, the physician was seized by what Freud described as conventional horror, and he had taken flight, abandoning the patient to a colleague. It was after this that the patient was placed in a sanitorium and had to struggle to regain her health.

Freud added that he was so convinced of this reconstruction that he had published it somewhere. Breuer's younger daughter read this piece and asked her father about it shortly before his death in 1925. Breuer is said to have confirmed Freud's version at that time.

Ernest Jones (1953), in the first volume of his biography of

Freud, reports what he terms a fuller account of the situation given
to him by Freud personally. There, Breuer is described as being so
engrossed with Anna O. that his wife became bored at listening to
no other topic, and ultimately quite jealous, unhappy, and morose.
It was Breuer, Jones reports, who decided to bring the treatment to
an end, citing the patient's improvement as his rationale. There
followed that night the hysterical childbirth or pseudocyesis that
required the hypnotic termination of the phantom pregnancy that
Anna O. had been developing invisibly in response to Breuer's
ministrations. Breuer is said to have calmed down his patient by
hypnotizing her and then to have fled the house in a cold sweat.
The next day he is supposed to have left with his wife for Venice to
spend a second honeymoon, which is said to have resulted in the
conception of a daughter.

This last detail is most definitely in error. There is no record that
the Breuers visited Venice at that time. Further, Breuer's youngest
child, a daughter, was born in March of 1882, some three months
before the termination of Anna O.'s treatment. The child, whose
name was Dora (a pseudonym that Freud later chose for the
patient involved in his first description of a dream analysis and
fragment of an analytic experience), was actually conceived in June
of 1881, around the time when Anna O. was transferred to her
country house. It is entirely likely that Anna O. knew of the
pregnancy of Breuer's wife either through reports from her physician or from direct observation, or both. The influence of this
pregnancy on the course of her therapy, and on its termination,
received no consideration in the writings of Breuer and Freud or in
virtually all that has been written of this important historical
sequence later on.

There must have been compelling motives for Breuer to have
concealed a significant experience of this kind. Freud's letter to
Zweig implies that Breuer had never reported the incident directly
to his colleague, and suggests that Breuer had recounted some type
of fictional story, perhaps about another physician, whose meaning
Freud had been able to decipher. However, one may question
whether Freud was dealing entirely with a reconstruction based
on indirect communications from Breuer; perhaps the incident was
conveyed in more direct form after all. In any case, there is every
reason to believe that Freud's report is basically accurate.

It is well known that Freud, as noted above, attempted repeatedly to pressure his colleague into reporting the case of Anna O. Based on the information available to him, Jones indicates that Freud was aware of an important source of Breuer's reluctance. His colleague therefore must have described a critical experience of some kind that prompted Freud to lessen his insistence. The matter remained quite unresolved until Freud found an ingenious solution.

Through the researches of a French psychoanalyst, Leon Chertok (1968), this particular conversation can be dated as having occurred sometime in 1892. It involved a frightening experience that Freud himself had with a patient and that he eventually told to and analyzed for his colleague. The incident appears to have happened sometime between 1889 and 1891, most likely not too long before Freud described it to Breuer. The untoward event involved a highly cooperative woman patient with whom hypnosis had effected marvelous results. Using the cathartic method, Freud had been relieving his patient of both her mental suffering and her attacks of pain by tracing them back to their origins. However, as she emerged from the hypnotic state on one occasion, she threw her arms around Freud's neck. In writing of this experience, Freud later stated the following:

I was modest enough not to attribute the event to my own irresistible personal attraction, and I felt that I had now grasped the nature of the mysterious element that was at work behind hypnotism. In order to exclude it, or at all events to isolate it, it was necessary to abandon hypnotism (Freud 1925, p. 27).

The mysterious element was not only some type of erotic stirrings in the patient, but also specifically the presence of a displacement or transference that, according to Freud, interposed a third figure drawn from the patient's childhood between the therapist and the patient. At the heart of this thesis was Freud's belief that the patient's attraction to him as a therapist had in no way been stimulated by his behaviors, technical or otherwise, and were basically misdirected toward him as the therapist. The correct target was some figure in the patient's past toward whom the patient had experienced sexual wishes; their arousal through the hypnotic experience was coincidental to the fact that memories from the past had been mobilized. Set to the side were such possibilities as the likelihood that the patient with whom Freud had this experience had been seen in her home and might have received full-body massages from Freud, who may well have had at the very least some other form of physical contact with her as her therapist, such as pressing on her forehead.

In a stroke, then, Freud had invented a concept of monumental importance. Because of inner needs within the patient, her feelings, fantasies, and impulses were transferred from the past onto the present with the therapist. Transference involved a mistaken or false connection, a *mésalliance*, as Freud termed it. It had nothing whatsoever to do with the present, the person of the therapist, or his or her behaviors. It arose internally from within the patient under the conditions of hypnosis or psychoanalysis, and was essentially unfounded and unrelated to current realities.

On the face of it, there is every reason to believe that something is not quite right here. Something does not ring true. There is a sense of falsification or denial, and of invention. After all, a study of Freud's techniques of therapy at this time reveal many highly charged, manifestly or latently seductive qualities. These attributes are disregarded through the idea of transference. The therapist is entirely exonerated of any contribution to the patient's arousal. Transference appears to be a very handy defense for the therapist, a strong form of self-protection.

When the patient agrees to the transference formulation—one that ignores entirely the therapist's participation in an interaction with the patient—the foundation is laid for a most compelling conspiracy. In actuality, this is the very basis for the most critical element in the psychoanalytic conspiracy that exists at present between patients and analysts. In unreal fashion, the therapist is viewed as a foil or kind of blank screen onto which the patient projects or enacts his or her sexual and other entirely unfounded and distorted feelings. In a sense, the therapist is pure and contributes nothing to the patient's experience. The patient is impure, sick, and entirely accountable.

Clearly, this is a most interesting therapeutic arrangement and form of collusion. Once again, its attraction for therapists is self-evident, while that for patients is more mysterious. And yet, one must be starting to sense that patients are more than prepared to accept fully the burdens of sickness and even misbehavior that exist in a psychotherapeutic interaction. They are willing to be dumped into, and dumped into they are.

Freud conveyed the proposition of transference as the explanation for his patient's unexpected seductive behavior to Breuer early in 1892. Reassured, Breuer finally agreed to publish his work with Anna O. in a paper and book to be written conjointly with Freud, who would add four cases of his own. The result was a preliminary communication, published in 1893, and the volume *Studies on Hysteria*, published in May of 1895. After considerable struggle, much of it studded with a variety of psychotherapeutic conspiracies, the psychoanalytic movement and the thrust toward insightful forms of psychotherapy were born.

There are a few additional pieces of relevant information regarding the actual events that surrounded the treatment of Anna O. Bertha Pappenheim was known to Martha Bernays, Freud's wife. In an early letter to Martha, at a time when Freud was still engaged to her, he described Breuer's recounting of the treatment experience. In his first letter to Martha on the subject, Freud referred to Bertha Pappenheim by name, stating that she was part of a lengthy discussion with Breuer on moral insanity, nervous diseases, and strange case histories. Freud added that Breuer then became rather personal and intimate, and told Freud things about his wife and children that Freud was not to repeat until after he was married to Martha.

In another letter cited by Jones (1953), dated October 1883, Freud is reported to have fully described the childbirth experience and the problems between Breuer and his wife resulting from Breuer's preoccupation with his patient, Anna O. Martha is said to have identified herself with Breuer's wife and stated that she hoped the same thing would not ever happen to her. Freud said that she was quite vain in supposing that other women would fall in love with *her husband*, adding, "For that to happen, one has to be a Breuer" —this from a letter dated November 11, 1883.

It appears that Freud had some form of clear knowledge of Breuer's difficulties with Anna O. He is quoted by Jones as indicating an awareness of strong countertransference difficulties in Breuer regarding his patient. The term countertransference as used here implies personal difficulties within the therapist in his relationship with the patient.

In the letter to Zweig, Freud's allusion to Breuer's holding the key that would have opened the door to the Mothers must have referred to unlocking the secret of transference. The reference to the mothers is drawn from Goethe's *Faust*, Part II, Act 1, and was known to Breuer, who referred to it in his discussion of Anna O. in *Studies on Hysteria* (Breuer and Freud 1893-95). The mothers are Goddesses who dwell below in an internal void without space, place, or time. Mephistophles sends Faust to them to be instructed in knowledge of the essence of beauty and the means of evoking models of beauty. They are part of the higher secrets and to speak of them is nothing but embarrassment. Mephistopheles hands Faust the key to the mothers, which glows and shines. The words, "the mothers," hits Faust like a stroke; they are words he does not want to hear. Breuer, in his allusion to the mothers, spoke of descent into the mothers as a way of referring to an exploration of the depths. At the time, he was discussing the efforts to get to the roots of seemingly irrational psychological symptoms. Breuer stated that a feeling of oppression is bound to accompany all such efforts (Pollack 1968).

For Freud, then, the ultimate secret in psychoanalysis was transference. It was Breuer who had been bold and ingenious enough to probe into the underlying factors in hysterical symptoms. In a sense, he had stirred gods that were at once awesome and beauteous. Freud, as an observer of Breuer and Anna O. recounted, evidently saw as the basis for the patient's reaction to Breuer her involvement with her father. In Freud's thinking, Breuer had done nothing to justify his patient's fantasy of impregnation. The experience, as Freud reassured his colleague, had entirely different origins.

Breuer seems to have been sufficiently convinced to permit the publication of his work with Anna O., though there is no mention whatsoever of the final incident. Oddly enough, at the time when *Studies on Hysteria* was being translated for the *Standard Edition*, the official rendition of Freud's work in English, Freud is said to have pointed to the place in the text where Breuer wrote that his patient was now free from the innumerable disturbances that she had previously exhibited, and that afterwards she left Vienna and traveled for a while. Freud indicated that there was a hiatus in the text, though he did not state its contents.

Earlier, in 1914, while writing on the history of the psychoanalytic movement, Freud himself made note of the evident sexual symbolism in Anna O.'s hallucination of the snake and the stiffening and paralysis of her arm. He therefore raised questions regarding Breuer's denial of any sexual factor in her illness. There Freud stated that Breuer had developed a very suggestive rapport with his patient, which he would today call transference. Freud then added that he had strong reasons to suspect that after all her symptoms had been relieved, Breuer must have discovered from further indications the sexual motivation of this transference, though the universal nature of this unexpected phenomenon escaped him. As a result, "As though confronted by an 'untoward event', he broke off all further investigation." Freud added that Breuer never said this to him in so many words, but that Breuer had told him enough at different times to justify this reconstruction of what had happened.

In the early 1890s, when Breuer and Freud were studying their hysterical cases together, Breuer called Freud in for a consultation regarding an hysterical woman patient. Freud listened to Breuer's description of the case and suggested that her symptoms were typical products of a fantasied pregnancy. Without saying a word, Breuer took up his hat and stick and hurriedly left the patient's house. For Freud, the implication was that the recurrence of the old situation was too much for his colleague to handle.

CHAPTER 9

THE SEVERAL LEVELS OF CONSPIRACY

History is at times a selective recounting and falsification of the past. Omissions, alterations, and uncertainties seem inevitable. Secrets are kept and burried with their keepers.

Reconstructing what transpired between Breuer and Anna O. is a case in point. Granted the gifts that existed in both of them, there is considerable evidence of additional conspiratorial, hidden motives in both. These contributed as much, and perhaps even more, to the discovery of psychoanalysis than did their most unimpeachable wishes and efforts.

There is every reason to believe that Anna O. experienced an enormous need for a very special relationship with her physician. For his part, Breuer seems to have been quite taken and infatuated with his patient, who bore his dead mother's name. It is impossible to know precisely the extent to which these feelings and needs on both sides extended into loving and even sexual feelings. Whatever was conscious, there is little doubt that there was a tremendous unconscious involvement and attachment, much of it extending well beyond the usual and clear boundaries of the relationship between patient and therapist.

Some of the background of these extraordinary needs is known. Anna O. was apparently intensely involved with her father. Her own emotional illness began during his eventually fatal sickness. She was his devoted nurse and suffered her most terrifying hallucination while caring for him. At the time of his illness, she devoted all of her time to caring for her father. It seems evident that Anna O. was seeking a replacement for the father whom she was losing and eventually lost. But beyond that, Bertha Pappenheim was the third of four children. The second child, a girl, died at the age of two of cholera, four years before Bertha was born. The older sister died of consumption at the age of 17 when Bertha was eight. A brother 18 months her junior survived.

The death of Anna O.'s two siblings must have left its mark. There is reason to believe that Anna O. suffered from a form of survivor guilt, which undoubtedly was mobilized and intensified with the pending loss of her father. She may well have experienced an overwhelming need to work over her responses to these losses in some meaningful fashion. Certainly there was nothing collusive there.

Other needs are also in evidence. Anna O.'s vulnerability to loss seems to have intensified her need for a replacement figure. She herself may have believed that she was a replacement for the sister who had died before her birth. The wish then was to reenact with Breuer the replacement of one person with another. Here are preliminary signs of hidden collusive wishes.

Another response to major loss is the wish to modify usual relationship boundaries. All human beings feel vulnerable in the face of the finality of death. A common means of attempting to deny its inevitability is to become involved in a forbidden relationship, one that modifies the usual rules and limits of society and decorum. Then too, involvement in this kind of relationship may also be an unconscious means of seeking out punishment for unresolved guilt. As for Breuer, Freud's letter to his fiancé Martha Bernays suggests that his colleague, despite statements in his own autobiography to the contrary (Cranefield 1958), may have been unhappy with aspects of his marriage. At the time he first met his young patient, Breuer was about to turn forty. He was either already in the midst of, or would soon have to deal with, some form of mid-life crisis. He was faced as well with the burdens and problems of having five children between the years 1869 and 1882.

Breuer's mother, Bertha, died during the birth of his brother when Josef was between the ages of three and four. He was brought up by his father and a woman relative. His father, a teacher, was his first mentor. The two were quite close. When Breuer was 23 or 24, his brother died of tuberculosis, an illness of the lungs much like that which proved fateful to the father of Anna O. When Breuer was 30 years of age, his father died.

There is evidence, then, that Breuer found in Anna O. a replacement for his mother whose first name was identical to his patient's—Bertha. The cathartic method enabled Breuer to achieve an intimacy with his patient of a kind never realized before. The sense of fusion and of undoing loss must have been considerable. The special way in which Breuer and Anna O. spoke only in English, the way in which Anna O. would permit herself to be fed only by Breuer, the hypnotic experience itself, and the twice daily ministrations provided a sense of closeness with distinctly special qualities. The experience was well designed to create the illusion of bringing back his mother from the grave. Thus the cathartic technique may well have gratified deep longings within Breuer to be reunited with his lost parent.

It is possible that on some conscious or unconscious level, Anna O. sensed some of these collusive needs in her physician. The fantasied pseudocyesis speaks to this point. Based on a reading of Freud's writings and early case histories, it is clear that therapists tended in those early years to reveal a great deal of themselves and their personal lives to their patients. It therefore seems likely that Anna O. was aware of these traumatic aspects of Breuer's life, as well as the pregnancy of Breuer's wife and birth of Breuer's last child. Breuer's father had lived in Pressburg, the home of Anna O.'s father.

In this light, the hidden meanings of the false pregnancy take on a number of unconscious implications of rather striking proportions. Many of these touch upon unconsciously perceived aspects of collusion between Anna O. and Breuer. Thus it may be proposed that the false pregnancy reveals an unconscious perception of Breuer's wish to be involved with his patient sexually and to impregnate her on some level. It is entirely possible, of course, that Anna O. herself also entertained such wishes, and that the extended treatment experience was designed unconsciously and collusively to gratify these desires in both participants. The pseudocyesis also appears to contain an encoded message that reveals a devastatingly destructive unconscious perception of Breuer as someone who impregnates and destroys (murders). A powerful reprimand would be implied such as, "Through this treatment, Josef Breuer, you have impregnated and destroyed me as your mother was impregnated and destroyed by your father (or you or her physician). Indeed, look at what you have done to me and abandoned me to."

With these as the "rewards" for an attempt at insightful therapy, there is a powerful motive for unconscious collusion between patients and therapists. The implication is quite clear: the therapist who dares to tamper with a patient's defenses, and who dares to expose that patient's most private and intimate secrets, must be prepared to confront on some level the most terrifying aspects of his or her own past life and current inner mental world. Because we all share so much of the human condition, this type of experience is inevitable. This is another dimension of the terrifying underlying truths aroused in the course of a psychotherapeutic experience, which motivates patients and therapists alike to conspire to avoid such realizations. Paradoxically, the very conspiracy itself may on some level be a reenactment of a piece of childhood collusion in the lives of patient and therapist alike. It is certainly no small wonder that Josef Breuer, faced with this type of powerfully enacted communication, took flight from the psychotherapeutic scene. Faced with moments of stress and crisis of this very type, there are many present-day psychotherapists who abruptly terminate a treatment experience and even give up the practice of psychotherapy altogether.

To sum up, there is every reason to believe that, for conscious and unconscious reasons, there was a strong mutual attraction between Breuer and Anna O. This measure of love and involvement was a prime contributor to the evolution of the talking cure. The conspiracy between them was designed to maintain a belief in the purity of the motives of both patient and therapist as a way of concealing the underlying erotic feeling and fantasies. In this way, the search to understand emotional illness and to alleviate its effects through verbal exchanges was born in part out of pathological need and pathological repair, whatever other factors may have been involved.

How did Anna O. deal with the undoubtedly unspoken collusion between herself and Breuer? Since the love element was powerful but had to be kept secret, she found indirect ways of attracting his exclusive attention and of experiencing a special relationship with

him. Anna O. was undoubtedly a woman highly sensitive to hidden
or encoded messages. It seems likely that she realized in some way
that her physician was vulnerable to an excessive involvement with
her. His over-interest sparked her own quest to find a means of
capturing and maintaining his attention. The laborious qualities of
the cathartic method, the signs of disturbance in the morning and
again at night that brought Breuer to her home twice daily, and the
fascinating structure of her daydreams and symptoms were all
designed on one level, quite unconsciously, to capture the devotion
of her physician. Anna O.'s illness was as much the product of her
wish to engage the attention and ministrations of her physician as
it was the result of her own inner sickness and pathological past.
Mental illness itself is not infrequently unconsciously created as a
means of establishing a mode of relatedness with another individual
and a therapeutic or other type of conspiracy.

Anna O. was apparently quick to recognize that all mention of
love and sexuality was forbidden by her physician. In keeping with
the qualities of denial reflected in Breuer's own autobiographical
statements, sexual feelings and fantasies were to be precluded
entirely. If Anna O. wished to keep Breuer close to her side, she
dare not speak directly of sexual matters. This is another form
of collusion quite common in present-day treatment situations.
Many therapists, through direct and indirect cues, let their patients know those topics that are open for exploration and those
that are not. Patients who transgress these restrictions tend to
be treated rather badly by their therapists. The material that a
patient communicates in psychotherapy is as much determined by
the therapist's attitudes and interventions as it is by the patient's
own internal needs. At times of extreme collusion, the therapist
becomes the main determinant of the patient's conscious and unconscious expressions.

While the conscious mind can suppress, the unconscious mind
will speak its piece one way or another, usually through explicitly
encoded communications. Anna O. called the talking cure "chimney sweeping." As Freud himself pointed out, chimney sweeping is
thought to bring good luck because it symbolically represents
sexual intercourse, the man inside the woman. As already noted,
snakes are well-known phallic symbols, and the image of a dog
lapping water from a woman's glass readily conjures up sexual
implications. These allusions provide clues of underlying, repressed

sexuality within Anna O., involving her own fantasies as well as unconscious perceptions of Breuer. They appear to be part of the sexual undercurrent of the relationship between Breuer and his patient which they both colluded to suppress and deny.

These speculations are, of course, further borne out in Anna O.'s experience of the false pregnancy and delivery. Freud reports that her very words were to the effect that she was delivering Breuer's child. In that afterthought there could no longer be any denial of sexuality.

Many analysts have taken the pseudocyesis as a sign of transference, a false connection between wishes directed toward Anna O.'s father that were displaced and carried over mistakenly to her physician, Breuer. The central unconscious fantasy is said to be the wish to have a child with her father, the culmination of the Oedipal constellation. Analytic commentators on this case typically believe that whatever disturbed Anna O.'s relationship with Breuer was also based mainly on the patient's pathological transference. Breuer's failure to actually cure his patient is thus thought to be the result of unresolved transference fantasies.

The sense of the situation becomes somewhat different when one recognizes the pervasive conspiracy that existed between Breuer and Anna O. There is strong evidence of actual erotic involvement, however muted, on the part of Breuer toward his patient. He appears to have been obsessed with her presence and her problems. It interfered with his marriage. He may have been in love with her. He may well have wished, consciously or unconsciously, to have a child with her. In this light, Anna O.'s pseudocyesis appears to have reflected a highly preceptive reading of the conscious, and especially unconscious, mind of her physician. It was her way of expressing a realization of the unspoken sexual involvement that actually existed between herself and her physician. To call this "transference" and imply that it was based entirely on sick fantasies, and that it had no basis in the reality of the relationship with Breuer, is in itself a major form of conspiracy. It is, as noted, the most characteristic conspiracy developed by psychoanalysts in their work with their patients.

It is most important to realize that the conspiratorial use of the concept of transference was not a form of collusion that Breuer adopted with Anna O. He himself did not write of the topic in his discussion of the case, nor did he have the capacity to invent or conceive of that particular possibility. Throughout, Breuer simply disregarded his relationship with Anna O., and he totally ignored the pseudocyesis with which his patient confronted him.

It seems likely that Breuer realized on some level that he had in reality become overinvolved with his patient. Rather than denying that he had stimulated the pseudocyesis, he may well have been repulsed by the effects of his somehow communicated wishes toward his patient. He may well have sensed and eventually been repulsed by his romantic feelings toward Anna O. This could account for his flight from the patient.

It remains unclear as to who actually terminated Anna O.'s treatment, she or her physician. If it were the patient, Breuer may well have felt frustrated and disappointed, and he could easily have communicated some of his underlying feelings toward his patient in far less disguised fashion. If it were Breuer himself who decided to end the treatment, given our later knowledge that his patient in reality was still quite sick, one would have to judge this decision as a reflection of his fears that his feelings toward his patient were getting out of control. It may well be that the sexual element of their relationship was somehow coming more into the open.

For Breuer, the possibility of an actual sexual interlude may well have been quite real and quite terrifying. Unable to manage his own burgeoning inner feelings and impulses, and faced with a patient still open and receptive, he may well have taken flight as his only protection and recourse. Unable to invoke the concept of transference, and therefore unable to deny and pretend he was entirely uninvolved with his patient, abandoning the treatment seems to have been Breuer's only option. In present-day treatment situations, this type of measure is not uncommon. Given this plight, there are other therapists who simply give in to their inappropriate wishes and make sexual contact with their often willing clients. These are, of course, various types of collusive resolution to an unfinished psychotherapeutic experience.

The first collusion between Breuer and Anna O. was to engage in therapy as a cover for, and secret expression of, a mutual attraction and perhaps love. Whatever sincere wishes existed on both sides to relieve Anna O. of her suffering, there was also the wish to maintain a collusive form of involvement that would gratify pathological needs in both physician and patient. Anna O. had a nonsexual form of sexual involvement, a replacement for her father and perhaps even her dead sisters, and an opportunity to be admired under conditions that would probably preclude sexual consummation or marriage.

In later life, Anna O. never married, though she became the director of a home for oprhaned children and championed the cause of wayward women who were being exploited for prostitution and other purposes by male white slavers. As reflected in an occasional recorded remark, she had little use for psychoanalysis. The themes of her life are in keeping with the conjectures that have been made here regarding the unconscious threads in her relationship with Josef Breuer. Sexual consummation was never achieved, and the patient devoted herself to women who were being exploited sexually by men. The powerful and repetitive qualities of this devotion suggest a strong and dramatic input from the treatment experience with Breuer. While there will always be a question of how openly and directly Breuer's attraction and erotic feelings toward his patient were expressed, there can be little doubt that they formed a major undercurrent to the treatment experience.

Of course, in keeping with the level of thinking at the time, Breuer made no effort to understand the unconscious collusion between himself and his patient. The focus was on Anna O.'s symptoms and their sources within her psyche and in her recent past life. The relationship was obliterated and denied. The conspiracy designed to leave out the personal interaction between patient and therapist was maintained almost to the very end. It was Anna O. who dared to break the silence. Her pseudocyesis contained the final and most crucial message to her physician: "You and I have been involved very deeply and it has been highly sexual as well. You must do something about our relationship if I am to be cured." Breuer's hypnotic suggestion that the pregnancy did not exist could hardly have solved the problem. This may well be why his patient suffered greatly in the years that followed her treatment with him.

Many forms of present-day psychotherapy conspire to ignore the relationship between the patient and therapist. They pretend that nothing is happening between them. Instead the therapist proposes that whatever is going on in this area is either totally irrelevant or, at the very least, inconsequential for the patient's symptoms or for the treatment process. Since nothing is happening, there is almost no need to state that whatever is not going on certainly is not sexual, nor is it inappropriately aggressive. There are no fantasies within the patient toward the therapist and no perceptions of the therapist, conscious or unconscious. While the degree of denial is massive, its use is extremely common. The vast majority of psycho-therapies touched on in the first section of this book adopt some form of this particular position. Breuer's collusion with Anna O., the first psychotherapy patient, has provided them a heritage that they carry forward to this very day.

The experience of Breuer with Anna O. tells something again of the unfortunate necessity for this type of collusion. If it can be maintained, the treatment can continue with a focus entirely divorced from the therapeutic relationship. The conscious and unconscious happenings between patient and therapist can be ignored. The patient is the sick one; the therapist is healthy. By offering pseudo-insights, direct advice, ways of listing, provocative efforts at catharsis, and whatever, the patient may feel some symp-tomatic relief. Some of this derives from the defensive avoidance of the disturbing interaction with the therapist; some of it from the blaming and implicit attack on the patient. Providing punishment for the inevitable measure of conscious and especially unconscious guilt that exists in each human being and in each patient will sometimes have distinctly therapeutic effects.

This type of collusion and denial is vital for patients and therapists who cannot tolerate the open expression of sexual and aggressive fantasies and perceptions, especially as they apply to the other member of the therapeutic dyad. The threatening and sometimes primitive fantasies that exist in the minds of patients and therapists alike, mobilized by the unique qualities of the therapeutic situation and experience, are of such terrifying proportions that they must be avoided at all costs. If they can be sufficiently obliterated, the defensive collusion may indeed provide the patient with a measure of symptom relief. Likewise, the obliteration of frightening qualities and tendencies seen in those to whom one can relate is also often a source of an immediate sense of relief.

Josef Breuer dared to disturb the defenses of one of his hysterical patients. He dared to unleash some of the meanings encoded, hidden, and bound up in her symptoms. He dared to descend into the mothers. Certainly, there are signs that this descent evoked guilt within him related to fantasies of his own mother, whom he lost early in childhood. But more universally, he dared to probe the secrets of the human mind. What he found was somehow terrifying. At some point, the unfolding got out of hand. The dangers and possibilities were so real, his only recourse was flight.

To this day, countless therapists dread the contents of the unconscious part of the mind. They dread the highly sensitive perceptions patients have of them unconsciously and the ways in which their own innermost secrets are revealed in how they work with their patients. They fear too the primitive qualities of their patient's own inner mental life and imagination. They create misalliances with their patients designed to exclude all such realizations in their transactions and communications. At times, it is of considerable relief to patients to pretend they no longer unconsciously perceive seductiveness in their therapists, or to pretend that they are no longer experiencing the influence of primitive and terrifying fantasies. So long as the denial holds, symptom relief may be in the offing.

For Breuer and Anna O., the truth of their sexual collusion was so disturbing, neither dared utter a word about it. Anna O. dared not speak of sexuality at all, a point made explicit by Breuer at the beginning of his case report. Breuer himself dared not report the pseudocyesis, lest the secret be revealed for the world to see. The case report was falsified to protect the innocent and the victims of their own discovery.

All of this helps to explain why Breuer would not publish his work with Anna O. His conflicts over the collusion and the secrets he had to safeguard interfered with the advancement of the science and art of psychotherapy. Psychotherapeutic conspiracies are, on the whole, quite stultifying. They lead therapists to have the need, consciously and unconsciously, to protect themselves at all costs. Not infrequently, a major price is to be paid in the form of a lack of progress in the field. Further, as noted before, treatment procedures that are founded upon unconscious collusion cannot tolerate an assault by the truth. Collusions imply fictions and lies, deceptions that then must be maintained at all costs.

It may well be that some sense of guilt in Breuer prompted him to tell Freud about the treatment and to offer his colleague a thinly disguised version of the actual circumstances of the termination. One can well imagine the conflict experienced by this great scientist and physician: on the one hand, the realization that he had discovered a major new technique for the treatment of emotional disorders, and on the other, the anxiety of revealing how the entire situation, the technique itself, got quite out of hand and proved to be unmanageable.

For Breuer, it appears that the sexual issues were quite real. He did not treat them as his patient's unrealistic fantasies and figments of imagination. In appreciating in some way their realistic aspects, he was being faithful to the truth of the situation. There is a sense that both patient and therapist were experiencing enormous difficulty in maintaining boundaries and decorum. Some type of catastrophe seemed inevitable. Flight was the only recourse.

During the late 1880s, Pierre Janet in France began to report a hypnotic technique that involved the tracing out of the antecedents of a particular symptom. Freud kept encouraging and even goading Breuer into publishing his own experience with this method. Primacy is extremely important to scientists, as well as most others. Freud's frustration with Breuer must have grown with each month and year. Of course, we already know that Freud himself was reluctant to use this technique. We may suspect that he too sensed its terrifying potential. It is a matter of record that he chose to treat his first patient with whom he used Breuer's cathartic method in a sanitorium rather than in her home.

Freud's use of the cathartic method and his willingness to use his own case material must have encouraged Breuer to publish his work with Anna O. In each of Freud's cases, the underlying sexual thread was quite prominent in connection with the patient's symptoms. Much of Freud's discussion involved the role of unconscious sexual factors in the etiology of hysteria. Oddly enough, Breuer himself spoke quite specifically of the sexual roots of hysteria. Anna O., however, was proposed as the exception.

One may speculate that Breuer felt a peculiar sense of relief when Freud, sometime around 1890, told Breuer of his own misadventure. For Freud, it was impossible to conceive that a physician could lose control sexually on any level when it came to his or her relationship with a patient. While perturbed, he was clearly not terrified by his patient's amorous behavior to the point of taking flight, at least not physical flight. Instead, he immediately decided that her behavior could have nothing to do with his own personal attractiveness or, for that matter, with anything whatsoever that he had done. To account for it, he proposed an entirely different source: the patient's earlier love for her father or some other comparable figure, mistakenly transferred onto Freud as the therapist. In all, the therapist was seen merely as a player being used for the enactment of the patient's drama.

With this as his mental protection, a psychic form of flight, Freud was able to remain an analyst and to tolerate the behaviors and revelations of his patients. Lacking this particular false explanation and defense, Breuer had no choice but to soon give up his short-lived career as a psychotherapist. It is not without meaning that the world's first insight-oriented therapist treated only one patient with the cathartic method, even though he evidently made some abortive attempts with others as well.

The total picture presents another striking paradox. In many ways these early psychotherapeutic conspiracies interfered with the progress of each specific treatment situation and with the development of the field. On the other hand, the psychotherapeutic conspiracy that was based on the concept of transference enabled Freud to create the field of psychoanalysis and to extensively explore and map out the features of the unconscious mind. Then too the conspiracy that developed between Breuer and Anna O. contributed significantly to the creation of the cathartic method and to the extension of this treatment experience for a year-and-a-half. Thus, while ultimately limiting and self-defeating, psychotherapeutic conspiracies are not without their salutory effects.

Although Breuer was unable to fully embrace Freud's concept of transference, it seems likely that he was able to make some use of the intellectual defense offered by Freud against his own sense of threat caused by a real involvement with the patient. The ten years that passed between the termination of the actual treatment experience and Freud's renewed efforts at publication must also have provided Breuer with a sense of distance that lessened his anxiety and guilt. His yearnings for scientific credit, and his wish to contribute meaningfully to the field of medicine and psychiatry, must also have been factors.

Still, even in the publication of *Studies on Hysteria*, there was collusion between Breuer and Freud. It is more than evident that Freud knew that Breuer's case report was incomplete on at least one extremely significant point. As we know, he took the trouble to point this out to the translator of the *Standard Edition* of his works into English. He alluded to it in his writings on a number of occasions and ultimately spoke of it quite openly to both Zweig and Jones. He also suspected the presence of countertransferences in his colleague and recognized the hidden sexual symbolic meanings in the productions of Anna O. And yet, knowing all of this, he agreed to the publication of *Studies on Hysteria* despite these important omissions. Something collusive was clearly at work.

Every step of the way in the treatment process with Anna O. and Breuer's flight from the therapy, and in the publication of the case report, conscious and unconscious conspiracy played a notable part. Origins of this kind indicate the unmistakably powerful threat confronted by anyone who chooses to unravel the emotional secrets of the human mind. It is a dangerous undertaking. Those who carry it out generally do not fare very well. They require protection at most any cost, even if it means glaring omissions and falsifications; even if it means hurting the patient in some way. Still, for many, to do otherwise would mean courting disaster.

Breuer himself provides the epitaph to this discussion. In a letter written to Auguste Forel in 1907 he wrote that he had learned a great deal from Anna O., including,

. . . that it was impossible for a "general practitioner" to treat a case of that kind without bringing his activities and mode of life completely to an end. I vowed at that time I would *not* go through such an ordeal again. . . . The case of Anna O., which was the *germ-cell* of the whole of psycho-analysis, proves that a fairly severe case of hysteria can develop, flourish, and be resolved without having a sexual basis. I confess that the plunging into sexuality in theory and practice is not to my taste. But what have my taste and my feeling about what is seemly and what is unseemly to do with the question of what is true? (Cranefield 1958, pp. 319–320, emphasis added).

CHAPTER 10

FREUD AS CONSPIRATOR

At the beginning of his medical career, Sigmund Freud worked as both a neurologist and a psychotherapist. Freud made a number of early original contributions to the medical literature, as had Breuer. His main areas of expertise involved the study of paralyses in children, aphasia (the inability to understand words and to speak properly), and the anesthetic properties of cocaine.

Freud's interests gradually shifted toward emotional rather than neurologic disorders. Initially he made use of electroshock, direct suggestion, hydrotherapy, and his own application of body massages. While his mind puzzled over the mysterious basis for emotional symptoms such as hallucinations, delusions, paralyses, anxiety attacks, and obessions, his techniques were in no way investigative.

The idea that emotionally founded symptoms had underlying meaning was vaguely in the air. In the mid-1880s, when Freud studied hypnosis, two aspects of this procedure were especially prominent. The first was that suggestions made by a hypnotist when a subject was under hypnosis were especially powerful and effective. This implied that hypnotic suggestion therapy would be more efficacious than suggestion therapy carried out while the patient was in the waking state.

The second observation involved the manner in which master hypnotists such as Charcot could, upon suggestion, actually produce hysterical symptoms such as paralyses and anesthesias. This convinced Freud and others of the underlying psychological basis for such disturbances. In addition, there was the convincing use of posthypnotic suggestions, through which the hypnotist arranged for his subject to carry out complex and often bizarre behaviors once he or she was no longer in the hypnotic state. An individual carrying out such actions had no conscious awareness of their source in the hypnotist's suggestions. He or she would tend to rationalize or explain away the most peculiar deeds. For Freud, this implied that there could be motives for human behavior that were outside of awareness.

A critical link was still missing. The realization had not yet developed that hysterical and other symptoms were not only psychologically based, but also contained within them encoded messages. For example, an hysterical paralysis might contain the message, "I want to strike you dead with my fist and must prevent myself from doing so." Or it might be a way of saying through body language, "I want to masturbate, but must not do so." Such symptoms would later be seen as complex messages of this kind, containing both the threatening or forbidden impulse and the defense or protective measure directed against it. For the moment, it was one thing for a master hypnotist to suggest a symptom to a patient, and quite another matter to conceptualize that patients unconsciously created these symptoms out of anxiety and conflict, and as means of communication—a way of expressing inner or unconscious messages.

Still lacking too was the equally important realization that if a therapist were to listen wisely to his or her patient, the patient could in some way convey these same encoded messages in what was said to the therapist. The notion that patients in some way unconsciously could and wished to express and reveal the underlying meanings of their emotional disorders was quite unknown. Once Freud began to sense this possibility, his initial approach was based on a belief that the patient, if prodded, could reveal these secrets directly. Either through direct pursuit by the analyst or by his or her pointing out an obstacle to such immediate awareness, Freud felt that the patient could uncover or arrive at ideas he or she was suppressing directly or repressing unconsciously.

This approach contains a critical issue that is a central concern in this book. As we have seen, many therapists either deny the existence of unconscious thoughts and fantasies or believe that they are of little relevance to emotional illness. Others feel that whatever effects these mental processes which take place outside of the direct awareness of the patient might have, they are of no importance in the treatment of emotional disturbance. These attitudes would characterize the vast majority of psychotherapists at work today. They would also characterize the totality of psychotherapists at work in the 19th century. In no other field of medicine or science have matters of this kind stood at such a total standstill. Again, this suggests that the nature of the beast, the factors in emotional illness, resist progress and endanger those who dare to probe.

Still, some therapists are convinced that emotional disorders are founded in large or small measure on disturbances in unconscious thinking and feeling. Many believe that the key to neurosis lies with disruptive inner fantasies or daydreams that are operating outside of the awareness of the patient. More recently, there are those who have added to this factor the role of disturbing perceptions of others, especially the therapist, that are experienced unconsciously and communicated, in turn, in encoded form outside of the awareness of the perceiver. Whatever the other factors in emotional illness (e.g., hereditary trends, familial and cultural influence, etcetera), these two unconscious elements are especially central to the understanding of seemingly irrational and illogical, unrealistic emotional symptoms; they are at the center of an emotional disturbance, while the other factors are contributory but more peripheral.

It was on the basis of this theory of neurosis that the effort to understand and master these hidden fantasies and perceptions, which express themselves in disguised or encoded form, became a critical factor in helping a patient to achieve the alleviation of his or her symptoms on an insightful basis. The theory proposes that emotional illness arises from pathological inner fantasies that disturb relatedness and cause conflicts, and then result in symptom formation. Similarly, a disruptive unconscious perception of another person may be taken in and detrimentally influence a patient's emotional balance.

In the first situation, the therapist's goal is to render the unconscious fantasy conscious, so the patient is able to examine and modify the unrealistic aspects of his or her imaginary beliefs. With the hidden conflict exposed to consciousness, including the forbidden impulse and the method of defense, the failed compromise that is expressed in an emotional symptom becomes superfluous. Similar insight is afforded to the patient regarding his or her unconscious perceptions of others and their internal influence; though when these derive from detrimental behaviors of the therapist, this type of effort must also be accompanied by a rectification or correction of the therapist's hurtful attitudes or interventions.

Freud presented us with two models of unconscious thinking and fantasizing. In the first there is a forbidden (instinctual drive or id) wish or thought and a defense that has been erected against its expression or fulfillment. Both the wish and the defense exist outside of the patient's direct awareness, expressing themselves through displacement and disguise. The entire conflict is often communicated through an emotional symptom that represents both the hidden wish and the failed defense.

In light of this model, the therapist, as noted, presses the patient to remove his or her defenses and to become directly aware of the forbidden impulse. If the defenses are strong and the patient resists the emergence into consciousness of the unconscious fantasy, the therapist has simply to identify the defense in order to remove it and allow the underlying images access to awareness. In these instances, the cure comes about when the patient recognizes the unconscious basis of his or her symptom, resolves the inner or intrapsychic conflict, and no longer needs to express it through an emotional disorder.

Anna O.'s refusal to drink liquids after observing the dog who drank water from the lady-companion's glass may be used as an illustration of this model. It may be speculated that the unconscious id wish is to have a man perform cunnilingus on her. This wish creates anxiety and is repugnant to the patient. Her defense is to become entirely unaware of the impulse—the use of repression. She also repudiates the wish and expresses this attitude by refusing to drink liquids. This latter is a failed compromise that represents both the impulse (to be sucked from) and the defense (not to allow this to happen). The expression is symbolic and displaced from the raw fantasy-wish onto the drinking issue. The symptom is an encoded communication that reflects the patient's unresolved conflicts.

The insight-oriented therapist's goal in this model (considerably over-simplified in this illustration) would be to help the patient to become aware of the totality of her unconscious conflict—a conflict represented in disguised form in the symptom. If the wish is known and understood, and if inappropriate, renounced, the conflict is resolved and the symptom is no longer necessary. If the patient resists conveying an encoded expression of the intrapsychic problem, the therapist's job would be to help her to understand the basis for her avoidance to the point where she would modify this second level of defense and permit a disguised expression of the conflict to emerge.

This basic model of the structure of a symptom is rather complex. Freud tended to simplify the structure, believing that the unconscious wish was directly available for observation once a defense had been cleared away. At times, however, he used a second model in which encoded or disguised representations of the underlying conflict were given their full due. Most of these ideas were laid down in the *Studies on Hysteria* and developed with greater clarity some four years later in *The Interpretation of Dreams* (Freud 1900).

In this more elaborate conception, unconscious daydreams (and perceptions) as they relate to neurosis are understood to always be expressed in some *encoded* form. The manifest associations from the patient that contain these encoded messages are called *derivatives*. The manifest content contains within it the latent content, which the patient has disguised. The hidden fantasy can be identified because of the patient's ability to communicate on two levels simultaneously. The first meaning is direct and conscious, while the second is indirect and encoded. The latent message is contained within the manifest message, even though the individual conveying it is entirely unaware of its disguised presence. The encoding is carried out automatically and unconsciously by the human mind through a variety of measures. No amount of direct probing will make these encoded messages accessible. Instead the therapist requires a decoding device that will reveal the hidden messages already communicated in the expressions from the patient.

In this model, a symptom itself is an encoded message—a form of maladaptive communication. Further, much of what the therapist expresses to the patient contains similarly encoded messages. By decoding these messages, the therapist helps the patient to understand the unconscious sources of anxiety and conflict that

have led the patient to express himself or herself outside of awareness. Simply being aware of the underlying message is not enough.
Understanding the anxieties and other factors that led to encoding
and defensiveness, as well as symptom formation, are essential in
the treatment process.

Freud, in the 1880s, appears to have sensed on some level the
demoniacal world that he would have to enter if he wished to
pursue the underlying basis of emotional disturbances. Despite an
abundant knowledge of hypnosis, and even though he already well
knew Breuer's remarkable discoveries with Anna O., Freud, as
noted, did not make use of hypnotic techniques of any kind in his
own work with patients until the late 1880s. It seems that he only
made use of hypnotic suggestion at first. However, he soon turned
to the exploratory and cathartic approach described to him by
Breuer. He combined these efforts with prescriptions of baths for
his patients and administered body massages to them as well.

To this point, Freud appears to have been distinctly of two
minds. On the one hand, he was intrigued with the discoveries of
Breuer and sensed their enormous potential; on the other hand, he
seems to have been fearful and to have withdrawn from the pursuit
of these insights. His own ambivalence may well have contributed
to his failure to convince Breuer to publish the case of Anna O.

The struggle with Breuer, and what was undoubtedly a powerful
inner struggle for Freud personally, continued on for some eight
years. While it is difficult to imagine, one must realize that during
this period Freud had no cogent explanation for the powerful
feelings and impulses that were stirred up in patients, and undoubtedly to some extent in therapists as well, when hypnotic
techniques were applied. These responses occurred even when the
therapist made use only of hypnotic suggestion. Freud seems to
have clearly sensed that efforts by the therapist to probe into the
sources and meanings of a patient's symptoms under hypnosis
would unleash even more powerful and unmanageable forces. Without a scientific explanation of the basis for these highly disturbing
experiences, he would be at the mercy of their effects. Breuer had
already fled their sphere of influence. Freud struggled against
entering their domain, used hypnotic techniques gingerly at first,
and eventually discovered a means of staying in the arena despite
the dangers—the discovery or invention of transference.

Transference is first mentioned in *Studies on Hysteria*. As Chertok (1968) has pointed out after careful investigation, Freud did not mark the date of this momentous insight—a brilliant moment, and as shall soon be seen, one filled with conspiratorial influence. There is evidence Freud was considerably concerned about making use of Breuer's exploratory hypnotic method lest he himself would experience an untoward reaction from a patient not unlike the culmination of Breuer's treatment with Anna O. In many passages, Freud wrote in highly glowing and positive terms of his first hysterical patients. There is evidence that he found them both fascinating and attractive, and there are also signs that he experienced considerable threat in his relationships with women patients (Freud 1905, 1920). In later years, Freud offered two excerpts from analytic work with adolescent girls. There were distinct signs of difficulty on his part. With both, he dismissed them summarily as unmotivated and untreatable.

Many therapists who have attempted to utilize psychoanalytic technique have experienced powerful emotions—dramatic and stark conscious fantasies and wishes—emanating from their patients toward themselves. With any measure of sensitivity, such interludes can be enormously disturbing for patient and analyst alike. Their sources are another matter. For the moment, it is well to realize that Freud was struggling with one of the most powerful forms of emotional encounter known to humankind.

Apparently, Freud eventually mobilized himself first to make use of hypnosis, and then 18 months later, to begin to use the more probing technique. The focus remained on the patient and his or her symptoms, and once again little attention was afforded to the interaction between physician and patient. It is evident, however, that Freud soon began to realize that the relationship needed to remain on good terms and that a disturbance in this regard could lead to an aggravation of the patient's symptoms. These observations seem to have been relatively peripheral, however, and not subjected to careful investigation.

Freud himself eventually wrote of something seductive and powerful that he experienced while using hypnosis. He had virtually nothing to say, however, of the possibility of erotic responses in his patients until his experience with the woman patient who threw her arms around him while emerging from the hypnotic state. This event, which appears to have occurred sometime in 1891, must have shaken Freud to his core. He now experienced directly a form of the unmistakably erotic involvement that he had pondered in regard to Breuer. How is it that he too did not immediately take flight? How was he able to cope where Breuer had failed to do so?

As we know, the answer lies in Freud's statement that the patient's evident attraction had nothing whatsoever to do with himself. With this pronouncement, he immediately interposed a third party, some other figure toward whom the impulse was actually directed. While the patient experienced her feelings toward her therapist as real enough, they were actually unfounded and unreal. They had nothing whatsoever to do with the realities of the relationship between herself and her hypnotist-therapist; they belonged to an entirely different relationship. The therapist was a mere pawn of the patient.

Since Freud could believe he was not really involved, he could stay on as a passive partner, an observer. He could interpret the patient's behavior as a mistake, implicitly maintaining his innocence and lack of contribution. A therapy could be designed to trace out the source in other relationships, present and past, for these inappropriate behaviors and fantasies of patients—transferences as they were called. This treatment became known as psychoanalysis, and it exists today, nearly one hundred years later, in basically the same form as developed by Freud in the mid-1890s when he eventually abandoned hypnosis and simply made use of free association.

The fundamental belief in the nature of transference has remained essentially the same. While 'transference' has been considerably elaborated, virtually all psychoanalysts still maintain that it reflects the patient's fantasy life and virtually nothing of themselves. The very hypothesis of an experience in one individual in the presence of, and in interaction with, a second individual that has nothing whatsoever to do with the second party inherently smacks of falsification. When the patient accepts this proposition—and countless patients have done so—there are the makings of a major therapeutic conspiracy. On the face of it, it seems unthinkable with any measure of reflection that the psychoanalyst does nothing whatsoever to stimulate the fantasies and behaviors of his or her patients.

Transference has to do with the relationship between patient and therapist. An emotionally ill individual turns to a supposedly healthy therapeutic practitioner in the hope of obtaining relief from his or her symptoms. Clearly, such a relationship must take on very powerful meanings—all the more so because the basis for the emotional illness in the patient is primitive, terrifying, highly conflictual, and involved with forbidden and threatening realizations. The situation is enormously charged. It is not surprising to discover that Freud, and virtually every therapist who has followed him through the years, has needed some form of inappropriate protection against the powerful forces unleashed in such a treatment experience. The inevitability of conspiracy is once more upon us.

Not unexpectedly in light of our present understanding, Freud never reported the case of the woman who threw her arms around him. In *Studies on Hysteria*, however, he did present his work with four woman patients of his own. Most revealing for our topic is the first of these patients, Frau Emmy von N. This patient is described by Freud as the first person whom he treated with the cathartic method, though he still employed supplementary measures such as direct suggestion, hypnosis, and body massages. The treatment took place sometime in 1888 or 1889. The case report concentrates on Freud's efforts to trace out the origins of a series of disturbing symptoms experienced by this woman. The treatment was carried out, at Freud's recommendation, in a sanitorium.

Of special interest for this discussion is a footnote that Freud made regarding his session with Frau Emmy von N. on the morning of May 15 (1888 or 1889). Freud had made it a practice to record a summary of each session with this woman during the first three weeks of her treatment. The footnotes were appended upon the presentation of this material in the volume coauthored by Breuer.

To understand the footnote, one must turn to the final section in *Studies in Hysteria* (Breuer and Freud 1893–95). The book was structured so that it contained the five case histories in the first part, a six-part theoretical discussion by Breuer on the nature of hysterical symptoms, and a section by Freud on the psychotherapy of hysteria. In this latter discussion, Freud stressed the role of sexual factors in the etiology of hysterical symptoms and offered a dynamic or conflict theory as a basis for understanding this form of emotional illness.

The basic model proposes that these symptoms arise from a distressing, shameful idea against which the patient erects some type of defense so that the idea does not reach, or is forced out of, consciousness and memory. When a therapist then attempts to pursue these defended against or repressed ideas, he is met with some type of resistance or opposition from the patient. These resistances correspond to the patient's initial defenses erected against the awareness of the threatening idea.

In Freud's hands, the cathartic technique began to center upon the creation of pressures on the patient designed to remove these resistances. Freud detailed rather carefully the unconscious issues in resistance and the techniques with which they could be overcome by the therapist. This led to an extended discussion of unconscious motives and ideas and of the unconscious factors in hysteria. This brought Freud finally to a last topic, which he stated, "plays an undesirably large part in the carrying out of cathartic analyses such as these" (Breuer and Freud 1893–95, p. 301). It concerned a third possible reason for a failure of the pressure technique. Earlier Freud had suggested that such an outcome could occur because there was actually nothing more to be found or because of a resistance that could be overcome only later on. The final possibility was that the patient's relation to the physician had been disturbed. In this regard, Freud proposes three principal cases: (1) if there is a personal estrangement between the therapist and patient, such as the patient feeling that he or she has been neglected or hearing an unfavorable comment about the physician or method of treatment (Freud indicates that this obstacle can be overcome through discussion and explanation); (2) a dread within the patient of becoming too accustomed to the physician personally and of losing his or her independence in relation to the physician (the fear may even include that of becoming sexually dependent on the physician); and (3) in Freud's words, "If the patient is frightened at finding that she is transferring on to the figure of the physician the distressing ideas which arise from the content of the analysis. This is a frequent, and indeed in some analyses a regular, occurrence. Transference on to the physician takes place through *a false connection*" (Breuer and Freud 1893–95, p. 302).

To illustrate this last possibility, Freud described an hysterical woman patient whose symptom derived from a repressed wish that a man to whom she had once spoken might boldly take the initiative and give her a kiss. At the end of a particular session, a similar wish came up in her about Freud. The patient was horrified, spent a sleepless night, and was useless for work in the following session.

Once Freud had discovered the obstacle and removed it, the work proceeded further. Following his effort, which Freud did not describe in detail, the frightening wish made its appearance as the next of her pathogenic recollections.

In analyzing this incident, Freud stated that the wish appeared in the patient's consciousness initially without any memory of the surrounding circumstances that would have assigned it to a past time. It existed within the patient and was linked to Freud's person because of a compulsion to associate that was dominant in her consciousness. The result of this *mésalliance*, which Freud described as a false connection, was that the same affect was provoked which had initially forced the patient to repudiate her forbidden wish.

With this discovery, Freud stated that it became possible for him, whenever he found himself similarly involved personally, to presume that a transference of this kind based on a false connection had once more taken place. He added that, oddly enough, the patient was deceived afresh every time this was repeated. Freud then concluded by describing how these transferences were involved in highly important obstacles to therapeutic work, adding that their analysis proved quite salutary for the treatment: "The patients, too, gradually learnt to realize that in these transferences on to the figure of the physician it was a question of a compulsion and an illusion which melted away with the conclusion of the analysis" (Breuer and Freud 1893–95, p. 304) Thus both patient and analyst were convinced that the patient's feelings and wishes toward the therapist were instances of self-deception for the patient. An illusion was involved that had no basis in the therapeutic relationship. A feeling emerged toward the analyst because of an inner compulsion to make such a connection, without any contribution on the analyst's part.

Transference wishes are highly disturbing conscious impulses and fantasies in and of themselves. The suggestion by Freud that they are baseless in the actual relationship with the therapist provided a sense of immediate relief to both participants to treatment. For the patient, the frightening or shameful impulses were not to be taken seriously; they were quite unreal and illusory, despite their vivid and immediate qualities. They were not really meant for the therapist, and at bottom had virtually nothing to do with him. The tension was greatly lessened through the realization that the fantasy and feelings belonged to an earlier time and involved another person entirely. Sometimes the impulse even made considerable sense when understood in light of the earlier relationship. With that, the seemingly irrational and even crazy impulses toward the analyst appeared far more sensible and far less threatening.

For the therapist, there was considerable safety in the belief that he had done nothing to stimulate the patient's fantasies and impulses. There was a great diminution of anxiety and threat in the proposition that impulses vividly experienced toward the therapist belonged elsewhere. Instead of being confronted with intensely real seductive wishes and impulses that might be difficult to manage, he was reassured by the proposition that the entire experience was actually quite unreal and illusory and unrelated to his personal relationship with the patient. Additional protection was afforded to him in the belief that he had in no way contributed to or aroused the patient's experience. The image of the innocent observer-interpreter of the patient's experience also afforded the therapist considerable protection.

There is a strong possibility of collusion in Freud's statement, true to this day, that patients soon accept their analysts' interpretations that their feelings and fantasies toward the analyst come from an inner compulsion and involve an illusion. Suppose it turns out that the analyst has behaved in some seductive fashion? He or she may have done so quite overtly or quite unconsciously and indirectly. If this were the case, then the analyst's uninvolvement—his or her total innocence—would be a myth. The experience would not be based solely on the patient's fantasies and memories. The patient's conscious or unconscious valid perceptions would be present. The entire proposition of transference would be false. An interactional experience in which a therapist had in some fashion stimulated his or her patient's erotic or hostile feelings and fantasies, and in which the patient's communications contained in part accurate but encoded unconscious perceptions of the true nature of the therapist's interventions, would have been falsely labeled as figments of the patient's imagination.

Basic to the thesis of transference, then, is a rather blatant denial by the analyst of his contributions to the patient's experience. Such denial enables the analyst to remain safely ensconced in the therapeutic relationship; though it would lead the analyst to many false formulations and interpretations as well.

In his later analysis of the transactions between Breuer and Anna O., Freud suggested that his colleague was unable to manage the erotic transference of his patient. Both he and his biographer, Ernest Jones, also indicated their belief that Breuer himself had experienced major countertransference reactions to his patient, that he had responded in ways that reflected his own emotional difficulties. Thus, unrecognized and unanalyzed transferences, and unmastered countertransferences, were used to account for the precipitous termination of Anna O.'s treatment and for the later symptoms with which she suffered.

In terming Anna O.'s hysterical fantasy of pregnancy and delivery a manifestation of transference, the implications were several: that the image of impregnation, gestation, and delivery was entirely the product of her own imagination; that even though she stated that the baby was Breuer's, he had in no way helped to stimulate this fantasy; that instead, the belief that the fantasy child was Breuer's was an unrealistic illusion; and lastly, that the ultimate source of this particular fantasy resided in unresolved aspects of the patient's relationship with her father, much of it in the form of repressed and repugnant sexual wishes, including the wish to have his baby.

Wishes of this kind may well have existed in Anna O. long before she met Breuer. There is considerable evidence that such fantasies were indeed present. They are rather typical in the growing child, and they may contribute to the development of emotional symptoms. Less well recognized, however, is the existence of seductive behaviors and indirectly seductive communications from parents, which lead children to perceive, most often quite unconsciously, expressions of the hidden sexual fantasies and wishes within the adults who surround them. Unconscious fantasies in a father toward his daughter are universal, and include sexual and impregnation wishes. Emotional disturbance comes as much from this type of unconscious communication and perception when it is excessive, as it does from the imagination of the child. There is an extensive interplay between these two sources: outer and inner.

The same applies to the psychotherapeutic and psychoanalytic situations. Whether or not a therapist chooses to be cognitive of the unconscious interaction with a patient, such an interaction does indeed take place. Every expression from the therapist is filled with conscious and unconscious implications, and the same is true of the expressions from the patient. The patient's experiences are a product of the direct and indirect inputs from the therapist as much as they arise from his or her own inner tendencies and imagination.

On this basis, it may be readily recognized that situations may well exist in which transference as Freud defined it actually plays a major role. Under these circumstances, the therapist behaves well, manages his relationship with the patient in keeping with the patient's therapeutic needs, and does little that is inappropriate to stimulate the patient's wishes and imagination. As will eventually be shown, however, in present-day practice such conditions are rarely met. Thus true transference reactions in patients are extremely uncommon.

Instead, therapists do a great deal to stimulate and arouse fantasies and other kinds of images and disturbed responses in their patients. Once the sources of these reactions are understood, and their disguised realizations in the patient's communications are decoded, the reader will learn that a great deal of what the patient experiences under such conditions is based on highly accurate unconscious perceptions of the therapist and his or her wishes. Still, this does not preclude a contribution from the patient, which is always present. Instead, it offers a more accurate and balanced picture of what is happening between the patient and therapist, and within the patient himself or herself. It enables us to take more fully into account the actual contributions of the therapist to the experiences of the patient. In simple language, it also affords a far less crazy or sick view of the patient than that proposed by most therapists, including Breuer and Freud. When we know something of what has aroused a response in a patient, it often appears far more sensible than when viewed in isolation. As already noted, this applies to the pseudocyesis of Anna O., which while symptomatic, appears far less peculiar in light of the evidence of Breuer's unconscious seductiveness than it seemed when taken as an isolated symptom.

Valid unconscious functioning often helps to account for many apparent disturbances in patients, the vast majority of which have been stimulated by disturbances in their therapists. There is often a combination of both transference and nontransference, a mixture of valid perception and inappropriate fantasy.

It is most important to realize that an interpretation to Anna O. that her pseudocyesis was based on an unconscious or unrecognized wish to be impregnated by her father would take a grain of truth and use it as a way of falsifying or covering over far more important and immediate truths as they pertained to the interaction between Breuer and his patient. Such a formulation and interpretation would clearly be a way of denying the therapist's own unconscious wishes and their expression in his interaction with the patient. They would be an inappropriate disavowal of his contribution to the fantasy and to the experience itself—a conjuring up of the past as a means of denying the present. They would also dump all of the inappropriate and pathological elements in the situation into the patient, ridding the therapist of any burden in this regard. For the patient to accept such an interpretation—and many have done so—a particular form of unconscious collusion would clearly have to be in operation.

In sum, then, a distorting influence based on past relationships—transference—can indeed exist under proper conditions in a psychotherapeutic or psychoanalytic relationship. However, quite often a patient's reactions to a therapist, direct and encoded, are in keeping with sound unconscious perceptions of the implications of the therapist's interventions. It is a defensive error for a therapist to apply the term transference to such occurrences, which are best considered as forms of nontransference or valid reactions. The differentiation depends largely upon an in-depth evaluation of the implications of the therapist's own interventions.

Josef Breuer paid no attention to these problems, while Sigmund Freud introduced the concept of transference almost as an addendum to *Studies on Hysteria*. The term does not appear in any of the footnotes he prepared for this work, nor is it included in the discussions of the individual cases. It emerges instead as a kind of afterthought, which suggests uncertainties and problems. The defensive and collusive qualities involved have already been documented. A further study of Freud's specific work with his early patients will help to extend our understanding of Freud's use of the concept of transference and the additional origins of psychotherapeutic conspiracy.

CHAPTER 11
FREUD'S EARLY THERAPEUTIC WORK

Freud's report of the case of Frau Emmy von N. in *Studies on Hysteria* shows extensive evidence of collusion. As noted, Freud did not make use of the concept of transference to explain away his contribution to this patient's experiences. That attitude first appears in concrete form in a later case, the analysis of a patient Freud called Dora, which took place in 1900 and was published in 1905. With Frau Emmy von N., the collusion and defensiveness took the more common form for its time, of denying any personal involvement between patient and therapist and of focusing entirely on the patient and her symptoms without regard for the therapeutic relationship and interaction.

The case report is of special interest, however, in that it contains the first recorded reference by Freud to the presence of false connections, the basis for transference. This appears in a footnote, and evidently was not used in intervening with the patient. Oddly enough, while Freud mentions the false connection theme, he does not propose the concept of transference at that juncture. Nonetheless, the particular reference is fraught with implied meaning.

Freud saw Frau Emmy von N. in the sanitorium in the morning and again in the evening on virtually every day of her initial stay. The morning session of May 15 is the one that most concerns us here. In the morning session of May 14, the patient seemed well and spoke, among other matters, of an earlier attack of abdominal inflammation. The morning before, Freud had removed her gastric pains by stroking her across the upper gastrium. Under hypnosis, the patient responded to a query by indicating that she still felt unprepared to take part in social life. She reported a memory of men coming out from behind bushes, one of them a harmless lunatic. She spoke of her country house being broken into. In the evening, she was quite frightened and hated herself. She had had a visit from Dr. Breuer, which had caused a state of alarm and had led him to assure her that it was "only this once." Sometime earlier, Breuer had been this woman's physician; it was he who had referred her to Freud.

Previously, during the evening session with Freud on May 9, Frau Emmy von N. had made fun of her treatment with Freud's colleague. She had described how a chance remark made by Dr. Breuer enabled her to find a way of giving up the therapy. Freud had reacted with surprise to this comment, and the patient had become frightened and self-accusatory. Her ensuing images under hypnosis had involved an insane cousin and a period of time when her own mother had been in an asylum. When the disturbance over the remark Freud had made regarding Breuer carried over to the morning of May 10, Freud pacified his patient with what he termed a "white lie" and told her that he had known about the incident all along. Freud then noted that while he was massaging her, which he did with some regularity, the patient became quieter, clearer in the head; his influence had begun to take effect.

Returning to the evening session of May 14, Freud picked up the patient's self-reproaches and evidently offered some ineffective forms of reassurance. Under hypnosis, the patient recalled horrifying images of bloody heads on every wave of the sea at a time when she had been in Abbazia. Freud made the patient repeat the lessons he had given her while she was awake.

On the morning of May 15, the patient showed a return of her symptoms, including a tick, clacking, and speech-inhibition. She was frightened to death once again. In reply to a query, the patient connected her fear with a lift used by her children, which she did not trust. The pension (landlord) had himself said that the lift was dangerous. A countess had been killed in Rome in an accident involving a lift.

Freud tried to dissuade the patient from her fear. He discounted the patient's comment about the pension as a paramnesia brought about by anxiety—a false recollection. She agreed her fears were improbable. On that basis, Freud decided to put the question of the source of her anxiety to Frau Emmy von N.'s hypnotic consciousness. Before doing so, there were exchanges during the massage, which Freud had resumed after a few days' interval. The patient spoke of a toad that was found in a cellar and of an eccentric mother who looked after her idiot child in a strange fashion. The woman had been shut up in an asylum because of melancholia. (In symbolic form, is the patient talking here of the search for unconscious factors, and could she be expressing her surprising and encoded views of Freud's treatment methods?)

When the question of the patient's restlessness was posed to her under hypnosis, the response was quite different. She then stated that she was actually afraid that her period was going to start again and that it would interfere once more with the massages. It is to this comment that Freud appended a very lengthy footnote regarding false connections.

In essence, Freud proposed that the patient was anxious and her consciousness did not present her with the real cause of the anxiety. That cause emerged only under hypnosis. Patients have a need to explain their sense of disturbance, and when the true causation evades conscious perception, they attempt to make another connection, which they then believe although it is false. He accounts for this phenomenon through two factors: a split in the contents of consciousness and the need to give meaning to experience.

In clarifying, Freud turned to Frau Emmy's belief that the cool hip-baths he prescribed had caused her to be depressed. The patient profoundly mistrusted Freud's therapeutic recommendations, though she would not fully oppose them directly. Freud then pretended to give up his proposal, while in her next hypnosis he suggested that she herself should put forward the idea of cool baths. When awake the patient did so, unwittingly using the arguments that Freud had previously presented to her. Freud agreed without much enthusiasm, but then found the patient in a deep depression after the cool bath. With exploration, it was discovered that the cool bath reaction had nothing to do with the patient's depression, but that instead, she was concerned about a revolution in San Domingo where her brother was now living.

Freud then stated that many neuropaths react in this manner to the therapeutic procedures recommended by their physicians. The patient who develops a symptom on a particular day is inclined to attribute it to his doctor's latest advice. The underlying factor is set to the side. Two conditions seem to be necessary for bringing about a false condition of this kind: mistrust and a splitting of consciousness. In addition, patients tend to avoid the true causes of their disorders because they tend to be unwilling to be reminded of that share of the cause for which they themselves are to blame.

In this way, Freud introduced the concept of unconscious factors in the symptoms of emotionally disturbed patients. He attempted as well to develop an understanding of the basis for resistances. The sequence suggests that Freud connected these unconscious factors and symptom formation to the mistrustful reactions in patients to their physicians, though he did this only through a sequential affinity and in a manner that seems to be both accusatory and hostile.

The false connection theme is taken up again in Freud's discussion of the nature of hysteria, and is based on an earlier discussion of the neurophsychoses of defense (Freud 1894). In the main, Freud proposed that an affect or feeling is often separated from the idea to which it is related. In order to avoid and cover over the underlying motive for the disturbing affect, the patient establishes some type of surface, but false, connection between the affect and an event that is different from the experience that actually provoked it and thus accounts for the sense of disturbance.

Then, as already noted, in the final pages of *Studies on Hysteria*, Freud first used the definitive term *transference*, specifically stating that, "The patient is frightened at finding that she is transferring on to the figure of the physician the distressing ideas which arise from the content of the analysis" (p. 302). This occurs through a false connection in which the patient's sense of disturbance is actually based on an experience with someone else, present or past. The distressing ideas connected with that other experience arise in the patient's associations. Because of a need to defend against the recollection of the disturbing experience which would actually account for the distressing affects or other disturbance, the patient connects these distressing ideas to the physician. This is, according to this reasoning, a mistaken connection which tends also to interfere with the progress of the treatment. The goal then becomes that of discovering the unconscious motive and memory which actually accounts for the distressing idea in order to show to the patient that it does not belong at all to the relationship with the physician, but instead belongs to the earlier experience. Thus the concept of transference was born.

Frau Emmy von N. herself seems to have had an unconscious commentary on her interaction with Freud in this historical session. When the patient expressed anxiety that her massages might be interrupted, Freud quickly changed the subject to her leg pains, ignoring the allusion to himself. The patient responded by describing a series of incidents that each time had aggravated her symptoms. She also described neck cramps. Freud's efforts to show his patient that this complex of symptoms represented some type of recollection failed entirely. There was some connection to an experience that the patient had had while nursing her brother during his delirium but nothing meaningful could be identified. The patient stated that she did not know from where the attack had come.

The footnote under discussion draws its importance as a first allusion to false connection and as an attempt to deal with the subject of resistance. Freud also offerred one of his first comments on the subject of dreams. However, the material also points to the kinds of therapeutic conspiracies in which Freud engaged with his patients. It was necessary for him to totally avoid the subject of the massages he gave to this patient, and Freud learned little when his efforts to change the topic back to the patient's symptoms led to a blind alley. It may well be that this was one of the first instances in which Freud was confronted with disturbing communications about himself from a patient, expressions fraught with manifest and latent meaning. Under similar circumstances, and in particular when faced with the pseudocyesis, Breuer had simply made a countersuggestion and taken flight. Freud, now daring to probe into the unconscious meanings of symptoms, adopted a different tactic. He stayed physically with the situation, though psychologically he moved the patient away from the dangerous material. In his discussion, he readily blamed his patient for her resistances and saw no accounting for them (even in part) in the nature of his own defensive and critical interventions. By implication, Freud also invoked here a potential allusion to transference as a means of avoiding contributions that his body massages were making to this patient's associations and disturbance. All of these conspiratorial defenses are in use by therapists and analysts to this very day.

Both repression and denial are basic to the psychotherapeutic conspiracies that have existed and still exist between patients and therapists. Repression is an intrapsychic defense through which a threatening fantasy (or perception) is removed from conscious awareness, either entirely or in a manner that permits only a disguised representation to appear in consciousness. Denial is a means of dealing with readily perceived conscious thoughts or external realities by negating their existence. Often, no representation whatsoever is permitted of the blocked perception. Complementing these defenses is the basic use of displacement, the means by which disguised versions of threatening fantasies and perceptions are worked over in a second sphere.

Psychological defenses of this kind are one of the means by which we survive as emotional human beings. Not only do we deny our responsibility for the sometimes inappropriate sexual stimulation and even the suffering of others, but we must also in some healthy fashion deny the inevitability of our demise and helplessness lest we be overwhelmed with unbearable anxiety. Psychological defenses of this kind can be quite adaptive. They shade into the use of the same defenses in ways that are inappropriate and pathological and which, instead of freeing us for growth and creative functioning, bind us down to our suffering and narrow our options. The line between a healthy and pathological defense is often difficult to discern. Sometimes, a defense that is blatantly misapplied enables a person to function in a situation that he or she could not otherwise handle. Considerable creativity and inventiveness can follow, but the initial false connection—to use Freud's term in a different sense—the initial defense, the initial self-deception, must be maintained at all costs. Should the original denial fail, the entire superstructure for which it is the foundation would collapse and crumble.

Prior to the cathartic method, physicians were content to leave the communications of their patients unexplored. Since the symptoms were distressing, however, they allowed themselves to attempt to alter the patient's state of equilibrium—mainly through nonpsychological modes of cure, an approach that is to this day still highly attractive. Some therapists attempted direct psychological suggestion, specific efforts to chase away the patient's suffering, but even they did not tamper with what lay beneath the surface.

Breuer, of course, at the behest of his patient Anna O., began to tamper with the hidden basis for his patient's emotional disorder. With an unconscious sensitivity that is rather typical of patients,

Anna O. altered her defenses only a small measure. She revealed to Breuer only that which he could tolerate hearing and confronting. Her messages regarding the unconscious factors in her illness were all highly encoded and quite symbolic.

Anna O. said nothing directly of her conscious and unconscious perceptions of Breuer's erotic involvement with her. She said nothing of the fantasies that these perceptions stimulated. She maintained a level of defense that protected both herself and her physician even while under hypnosis. Because defenses are usually viewed exclusively as protectors of the individuals who use them (i.e., patients), it is well to underscore the way in which these protective measures also spared Breuer more than he could handle (i.e., the way in which the patients' defenses serve their therapists).

When the sexual perceptions and fantasies intensified, Anna O. made use of highly disguised, symbolic communication. She spoke of snakes and saw herself with snakes for fingers. She spoke of a dog lapping water from a glass of a woman companion. She called her therapeutic procedure with Breuer chimney sweeping. Each of these involved rather evident symbolic expressions with highly sexual implications. To the ear and mind that wished not to behold anything sexual, these would be seen as concrete hallucinations and memories and as a playful way of naming a treatment method. To listen symbolically requires strength and courage.

It is of interest, of course, that psychoanalysis began as chimney sweeping, a symbol of the man (therapist) inside of the woman (patient). While most analysts would to this day see this representation as the hysterical fantasy of a sick woman, there is every reason to believe that this representation contains within it a perceptive reading of an unconscious meaning that the cathartic method had for its founder—and for many later-day analysts as well. In all cases of perception outside of awareness, perceptions registered and expressed through encoded and disguised means, there is a typical mixture of valid perceptiveness with extension into fantasy in the mind of the beholder. Freud entirely denied the perceptive side, and Breuer either did not sense it at all or sensed it all too well. It is this aspect that has been so neglected by analysts and therapists during the first 100 years of probing psychotherapy.

Anna O. maintained her defenses as long as Breuer continued as her therapist. Once he terminated (abandoned?) her, she threw aside these mental barriers and exposed her physician to the secrets for which they had allowed but highly disguised expression. "Here comes Breuer's baby" is a blatantly sexual statement and a rather undisguised commentary on the therapeutic transactions. It speaks for their bilateral sexuality in clear terms. In light of the death of Breuer's mother in childbirth, it speaks too of murderous consequences. Such were the rewards for Breuer and Anna O. for their bold venture.

In a way, Breuer was more insightful and honest than Freud. He seems to have known that his patient was right—something sexual had indeed taken place. He had no choice but to undo what had happened and to take his leave. He was unable to state, as Freud might have: "This pregnancy had nothing whatsoever to do with me, such a thought is based on a false connection. It arises from her father, or from someone else. I am blameless." In his way, Breuer knew the truth was otherwise. His problem was that he had no way of mastering the truth and turning it toward therapeutic benefit for his patient—or even for himself.

This too was prophetic. Those therapists who have discovered the truth of the therapeutic interaction, and of their own unconscious inputs into the treatment situation, have found their discovery overwhelming. They have seldom allowed these truths to reach even their own direct awareness. Most often, they have simply abandoned the pursuit of insight and adopted some other mode of treatment that would prevent its emergence. All the while, however, by shifting to a deviant approach, they continue to unconsciously stimulate their patients in ways they wish not to know. Paradoxically, even then, the patient sometimes finds relief. Some of it arises from the unconsciously observed contradictions in the therapist's approach; some of it from other sources that will be identified in later chapters.

Throughout his career, Freud implicitly and explicitly showed a deep commitment to the discovery of the truths that form the unconscious basis of neuroses. He wrote of truth very sparingly, however. Still, as a scientist and physician, he stated quite directly his commitment to search out the truth of emotional illness wherever it lay. His monumental writings are a reflection of a man dedicated to this type of unrelenting search.

Thus it is all the more strange to find in Freud's report of the case of Frau Emmy von N. a reference to a deliberate "white lie," which he had told the patient in connection with his apparently defensive reaction to her criticism of her work with Breuer. When his response upset the patient, Freud pacified her with the lie by claiming he had known about the situation all along. His patient's agitation eased at that very moment. This is perhaps the first documentation of the manner in which direct falsifications to patients can provide them with symptomatic relief. It is indeed a strange mode of treatment in which conscious lies can prove curative. That too was a prophetic moment.

Freud also engaged in a type of lie in pretending to give up his recommendations of cool baths to his patient and in then suggesting under hypnosis that she herself should put forward this very idea. Here are signs of cure through deliberate deception. Falseness is in evidence—and this in a passage that soon follows Freud's own comments on the false connections made by his patients!

Breuer, knowing or sensing the truth, found it unbearable and took flight. Freud, undoubtedly sensing but not consciously knowing the truth, remained. How was he able to do so? Freud seems to have built up, perhaps through early efforts at self-analysis or through his own natural and evolved propensities, a capacity to tolerate from his patients relatively open expressions of sexuality. It may well be that in reality he experienced little conscious attraction to the women with whom he worked. There is much in his biography to support such a contention. It seems certain that he did not get involved with any of his patients in the way in which Breuer became entangled with Anna O.

Still, there is evidence that Freud was attracted to hysterical women. There are also signs that he tended to deny this attraction with defenses that did not always hold. For example, he rather abruptly sent away the two young women whose treatment is described in part in his writings, Dora and an unnamed woman who was struggling with homosexual problems (Freud 1905, 1920). By then, Freud was in the position of dismissing patients who threatened his defenses, rather than leaving the field himself.

In his work with Frau Emmy von N., there is an overabundance of symbolic sexual material. The patient had fallen ill when her industrialist husband, much older than she, died shortly after they were married. Her associations, even in her early sessions, as they are summarized by Freud, touched only occasionally and peripherally on sexual matters. However, issues of this kind emerged quite openly soon after the session of May 14.

Freud's great sense of distance from his women patients seems to have served him well in his initial efforts to probe more deeply into their inner mental worlds. In contrast, it is likely that some of Breuer's feelings toward Anna O. were conscious and even evident to others, including his patient. At best it can be surmised that Freud did not experience this level of blatant erotic feeling and fantasy toward his patients. Of course, Freud was not devoid of such feelings and fantasies unconsciously; he simply managed better to defend himself against their expression. He probably avoided anything more than an occasional direct thought of this kind. While the facts may never be known, Freud's entire approach to the therapeutic relationship is in keeping with these speculations.

It seems likely, then, that Freud did not have Breuer's problems in dealing with his own openly conscious erotic feelings and reactions. As Freud said, for that, one has to be a Breuer—and there remain among us, inevitably, many such Breuer-therapists. To be a Freud, one's erotic and sexual feelings and fantasies toward patients must be subjected to rigid or truly adaptive and effective defenses and remain mostly outside of consciousness. To be a Freud, a therapist may well experience some kind of general attraction or vague positive feelings toward a patient, though he or she would not become preoccupied with the patient or caught up in extensive daydreams. Being human, he or she might have an occasional dream of the patient, but would quickly discount its meanings and influence.

It is the nature of the human mind to entertain feelings and fantasies of this kind. The difference between a Breuer and Freud is one of manifest expression. The difference between health and pathology is one of control, management, understanding, and the use of healthy defenses so that the underlying fantasies do not interfere with the therapist's functioning or with his daily life.

Given the intimacy of the therapeutic relationship, such stirrings are absolutely inevitable. A therapist has no choice but to deal with them. As a consequence of these efforts at coping, some therapists remain insight-oriented and others shift to quite a different approach. The manner in which a therapist deals with his or her own erotic and hostile feelings and fantasies aroused in the context of a treatment relationship is a major determinant of the therapeutic measures of use both in the field at large and in regard to the personal choice of each individual therapist. It is also a key factor in the nature of the psychotherapeutic conspiracy that a therapist offers to a patient.

For a variety of reasons, then, Freud interacted with his patient, Frau Emmy von N., in a manner that indicated to her a moderately good tolerance for disguised and even thinly disguised erotic allusions. This set the stage for the fateful moment of the session of May 15. During the actual experience, Freud apparently sensed a hidden motive for his patient's anxiety. There is no indication whatsoever that he consciously realized it had anything to do with her relationship with him. Even when his patient stated that it involved the anticipation of her period, which would interfere with Freud's giving her body massages, Freud simply moved on to inquire into the history of her leg pains. He too took to flight, but it was in words rather than in action. He stayed with the patient and simply changed the subject. He maintained a focus on the contents of the patient's thoughts and feelings, and totally ignored his relationship with her.

It must be remembered that Freud wrote the footnotes for *Studies on Hysteria* sometime in 1893 or early 1894. By then, he had experienced the incident in which one of his own women patients had thrown her arms around his neck while coming out of hypnosis. As mentioned earlier, it was actually in response to that moment that Freud had discovered—invented is the far more accurate term—transference. Freud invoked the concept of false connection as a means of denying his own influence on the patient's sexual behavior. In denying that his own personal charm could in any way account for her action, Freud was simultaneously denying any contribution whatsoever to her behavior. "She had put her arms around the wrong man" was Freud's statement of false connection and transference. The material of the analysis had aroused her; instead of recognizing the actual source of this arousal, the patient had mistakenly taken Freud as the object of her erotic feelings. The patient was lying to herself, deceiving herself regarding Freud. The work of the analysis would be to show her the sources of her misconception.

There is a strange quality to the realization that the invention of transference involved a lie or self-deception on the part of Freud. There is evidence that this came about partially because Freud was beginning to experience the influence of his patient's unconscious perceptions of the erotic qualities of his treatment efforts. While it is quite unclear and unstated, Freud specifically wrote regarding Frau Emmy that he had stopped giving her massages for a few days. The patient's own material suggests that she may have had her period at that time. However, it seems likely that there would have been a comment regarding the resumption of her menses if it had taken place just a few days after the prior period of menstruation.

While entirely speculative, it may well be that Freud in some way sensed that his patient was becoming too aroused by the procedure. Therapists do indeed detect unconsciously, entirely outside of their own direct awareness, erotic and hostile messages from their patients. Freud had not as yet written *The Interpretation of Dreams* (1900), nor studied in definitive fashion the nature of unconscious or encoded communication. He was probing where virtually no one had dared to probe. He was dealing with messages and communications that no one had as yet clearly defined. There are many indications, however, that Freud's unconscious sensitivity in these areas was enormous.

In any case, it is in response to the reference to the massage that Freud, in the 1890s, grown wiser and perhaps more defensive through experience, wrote the footnote regarding the false connection. The patient's source of anxiety was not her concern for her children being killed through an accident in a lift, but her fear that her period was going to start and interfere with the massages.

The image of the lift involves an enclosure, a vehicle out of control, and a connection to a countess who had died in such an accident. It could well contain an unconscious perception of Freud's anxieties and concerns in first making use of the cathartic method, as well as the patient's own responsive fantasies and fears. It could well be an encoded message filled with meaning for the therapeutic interaction.

Under hypnosis, when the deeper source of the patient's anxiety was revealed, Freud used the material to demonstrate how a conscious thought could be falsely connected to an affect. The unconscious thought, which could more meaningfully account for the affect, could be discovered with analysis. Thus the affect was falsely connected to the surface idea and correctly connected with an unconscious idea.

It is a reflection of Freud's unconscious genius that his first comments on false connections were offered in light of specific clinical material that involved an allusion to himself. Struggling with this area, Freud later wrote the footnote on ways in which patients bring about false connections between their physicians and some other incident and person. Freud himself saw mistrust of the therapist as an element in this type of unconscious error by the patient. The insights presented here suggest a reasonable basis for this mistrust, but also reveal that the false connection is often not so false after all.

Freud seems to have known something was amiss in his relationship with his patient. In her own way, Frau Emmy appeared to have been attempting to tell Freud that she was becoming disturbed by the inner feelings, fantasies, and perceptions of her physician being stirred up by the body massages. Freud simply treated this situation as if the patient were talking about some other topic. While he did extend his footnote comments into false connections that involved the therapist, he did not try to illuminate the incident of the May 15 session. This type of confusion, uncertainty, and ultimate avoidance is typical of how therapists and analysts react to the details, conscious and unconscious, of their interaction with their patients.

In the discussion section of *Studies on Hysteria*, Freud's introducing transference as a false connection implies that Frau Emmy's reactions to the body massages would eventually have been interpreted as deriving their sources in the patient's relationship with her children, and ultimately in that with her brother—since it was he who was mentioned in the hour. But already, signs of additional difficulty emerge. In his discussion of transference, Freud was suggesting that the conscious feelings and fantasies directed toward the therapist did not apply to him. Yet in the example with Frau Emmy von N., which becomes the basis for the first clinical discussion of false connections, it is the patient's manifest thoughts about her children that serve to conceal thoughts about Freud. Had Freud more clearly seen this relationship, he might have then more thoroughly analyzed his patient's reactions to himself. Instead, Freud did not subject this particular incident to careful analysis, nor did he return to it in his discussion of transference.

For some time in subsequent works, Freud made only passing allusions to the concept of transference, most of them in *The Interpretation of Dreams* (1900), where he used transference in a more general or universal sense to refer to a basic form of displacement (transfer). Freud then dropped the specific issue of transference until he wrote of his analytic work with Dora in 1905. As Brian Bird (1972), a psychoanalyst, has pointed out, Freud tended to discover and then repress and then rediscover his realizations regarding transference. He showed signs throughout his psychoanalytic career of enormous difficulties with the concept.

All of this is for good reason. A patient's feelings and fantasies toward his or her analyst, as expressed directly and manifestly as well as through symbolic representations, pose an enormous problem and burden for the analyst. Clues have already been presented that indicate that these communications contain highly sensitive unconscious perceptions of the therapist, including aspects of his or her own personality and work of which he or she is mercifully (though unfortunately) unaware. Many of these encoded perceptions touch upon his or her greatest areas of vulnerability. In addition, transference fantasies involve rather terrifying and primitive images and memories. It is therefore much to Freud's credit that he dared probe deeper, though he was then exposed to revelations to which he was unable to respond adaptively. One must therefore understand his defensiveness, an issue with which, for the moment, he alone was attempting to cope.

By stating that the patient's conscious feelings and fantasies toward himself as analyst were falsifications and unrelated to himself, Freud was able to create a fictional system that enabled him to remain a psychoanalyst. Had he sorted out his own unconscious contributions to his patients' experiences, with the same painful analytic dissection he applied to his patients, he might well have been every bit as frightened and appalled as Breuer. What Breuer knew to some extent on the surface, Freud could have discovered through genuine self-analysis. Freud appears to have avoided this level of self-discovery, a heritage that has been passed on to psychoanalysts for several generations. For them, too, the myth of transference serves as a protective barrier between themselves and their own inner stirrings. The myth protects them while creating a fictional mode of therapy that supports their defensiveness without truly understanding the patient. In this context, it is not surprising that patients willingly accept this treatment form. Psychoanalysis is but one of many forms of therapeutic conspiracy between patients and their healers.

This is *not* to propose that there is no such phenomenon as transference. Patients do indeed distort their images of their therapists and respond to them inappropriately based on the influence of earlier interpersonal relationships. However, this type of reaction and communication tends to appear mainly when the therapist has intervened properly and in the absence of disruptive inputs. All reactions to the therapist are a mixture of transference (the influence of distortion) and nontransference (much of it based on valid unconscious perceptions of the implications of the therapist's interventions).

When the therapist has directly or even unconsciously traumatized or otherwise disturbed the patient, the latter responds mainly in terms of a sensitive unconscious reading of the implications of the therapist's hurtful effort. Here the paradigm is rather different from that which pertains to transference. Instead of the past having a distorting influence on the patient's view of the present, the present is in actuality a repetition of the past—i.e., the therapist is in some real (however unconscious) manner repeating a behavior with the patient that is very much like the behaviors of earlier figures; behaviors that involved transactions that helped to create and sustain the patient's emotional illness. In transference, the present with the therapist is by definition different from the past, even though the patient reacts as if this were not so. In nontransference, the present is the same as the past, and the patient's usually unconscious belief that this is the case is essentially correct.

It is clear in retrospect that the experiences that Freud studied, and that formed the basis for his invocation of the concept of transference, were mainly those in which his own inputs were highly charged. Because of this, the larger portion of his patient's responses actually were quite in keeping with the unconscious implications of his interventions. To this, some small or large measure of distortion (true transference) was undoubtedly added. Still, the essential point remains that Freud invoked the concept of transference when the more valid discovery would have been that of nontransference or of a mixture of both. The very realization of an interplay between the past and present, between earlier experiences and those currently with the therapist or analyst, was in itself a major insight. Nonetheless, the concept of transference clearly implies that the therapist has not in any way behaved in a fashion in keeping with the behaviors of the earlier figure, a point made quite clearly many years ago by the British psychoanalyst Margaret Little (1951).

Freud invoked the concept of transference quite specifically to deny his personal charm and, more broadly, his causative role in the patient's responses. A far more accurate conceptualization would have acknowledged the unconscious inputs from Freud and then more carefully studied the extent to which the patient's reactions were in keeping with those unconscious implications, and the degree to which they extended clearly beyond them. In addition, it would be necessary to account for distinct differences in how patients react to their unconscious perceptions of the therapist. Clearly, some patients might recoil from a therapist's unconscious seductiveness, while others would indeed respond, as had Freud's patient, by blatantly attempting to bring the underlying unconscious erotic interplay out into the open.

On balance, Freud's invention of transference contained a small measure of truth and a large measure of falsification. The false connection that he attributed to his patients was mainly his own. The connection that the patient was making between Freud and the past figure was largely valid, and in only some extreme way—given the nature of Freud's interventions—was it falsified. The pursuit of truth has been greatly impaired by the lie-foundation that proved necessary for the creation of the psychoanalytic method.

CHAPTER 12

PERCEPTIONS OF FREUD BY HIS PATIENTS

The vicissitudes of Freud's conception of the role of sexuality in the etiology of neuroses provide additional insights into the nature of the therapeutic conspiracy developed between Freud and his patients. Considerable conflict existed within Freud regarding this area. Early on, a notable source of his hesitation in using hypnosis to treat hysteric patients appears to have been his observation of Breuer's flight from Anna O. and Freud's sense of its underlying sexual sources. This anxiety over sexuality in hysterics was counterbalanced to some extent by Freud's observations of Charcot in 1885.

The French hypnotist, Charcot, studied hysteria quite scientifically, with a strong sense of equanimity and without any evident fear of its erotic manifestations. Some of the patients hypnotized by Charcot showed sexual responses that sometimes reached orgasm. These scenes must have disturbed Freud. After all, while in Paris he was engaged and committed to his future wife Martha. There are many indications that Freud maintained a state of sexual continence while in the midst of considerable sexual openness. The aroused conflicts may well have had a great deal to do with Freud's thoughts of leaving Paris prematurely, a decision that he did not explicate. Some writers (e.g., Chertok and de Saussure 1973) believed that Charcot and his pupils were able to adopt a relatively impersonal and mechanical approach to sexual manifestations in hysterical patients by reducing them to strictly physiological and impersonal processes. This approach may well have offered a defensive protection that enabled Freud to maintain his interest in both hysteria and hypnotic techniques.

In the 1880s, Freud himself played down the role of sexual factors in the etiology of hysteria. It was only in the mid 1890s that he clearly shifted his position. During the earlier period, Freud actually seemed to have repressed a number of comments made by such important persons in his life as Charcot and Breuer regarding the genital sources of this emotional disorder. It was apparently a tribute to his own capacity to modify his defensiveness that Freud began to openly recognize the role of sexual trauma, events, and ultimately, fantasies, in hysterical illness.

The material collected by Chertok and de Saussure appears to support the hypothesis stated earlier that Freud was able to maintain himself as a psychotherapist because of relatively strong defenses directed against conscious sexual thoughts and expressions. Biographical data indicate that Freud had little contact with women before meeting Martha Bernays. His intense commitment to his fiancé during the four-and-a-half years of their engagement appears to have been accompanied by sexual abstinence. It seems likely that this commitment helped Freud to establish rather powerful defenses against outside sources of sexual stimulation, the temptations of other women, and the possibility of experiencing his women patients in any type of erotic fashion.

There is evidence too that Freud's defenses were overly intense in this regard. Thus Freud seems to have had little conscious awareness of the seductive qualities of hypnosis and the hypnotic relationship. Further, there is no indication whatsoever in his writings of an awareness of the potentially sexually stimulating aspects of the full body massages with which he personally provided his patients. Here too Freud's defenses border on the maladaptive use of denial. It appears that when these particular defenses failed in the face of the amorous reaction of at least one hypnotic patient, Freud required a new line of protection. Genius that he was, he invented the concept of transference for this purpose.

Freud's detailed notes on Frau Emmy von N. offer a number of examples in which the patient appears to have unconsciously perceived aspects of Freud's technique and personality that she dared not indicate to him directly, though she found some encoded means of letting him know what she had perceived. At the time, Freud paid little attention to his patient's indirect comments about himself and showed no appreciation of this type of encoded communication. This attitude is typical of present-day analysts as well.

In regard to conscious thoughts and feelings about Freud, his reactions to such communications from his patients are best illustrated through a more careful review of the sequence of sessions that began on May 9. During Frau Emmy's morning session with Freud, Breuer came in suddenly with the house-physician. The patient became frightened and began to make her clacking noise, and the two quickly departed. She commented on the visit, but it seems that Freud, in what was then rather typical fashion, placed her under hypnosis and shifted the focus to her gastric pains. He then helped her to get rid of them by stroking her.

That evening the patient was cheerful and made fun of her treatment by Freud's medical predecessor, Breuer. Through displacement, she could well have been ridiculing some of Freud's own techniques. She went on to describe how she was able to rid herself of Breuer by virtue of a chance remark he happened to make. When Freud was surprised at what he heard, she grew frightened and blamed herself for being indiscreet—this too could well have been un unconscious perception of Freud's inappropriate reaction. Freud then reassured her.

When Freud shifted to hypnosis, he immediately changed the subject and asked about other experiences that had given her a lasting fright. Her response involved a cousin and her mother who had both been in an insane asylum. When the patient returned to the giving away of Doctor Breuer, Freud pacified her with his white lie. Freud stated in his records that, at this point, he was already beginning to influence his patient and to quiet her down. When he asked the patient under hypnosis what had made her upset, she again alluded to her indiscreet talk and to pains caused by being so uncomfortable in her bath. Freud shifted to an inquiry regarding her phrase, "keep still," and the patient connected this to animal shapes and to an illness of her brother's.

In keeping with Freud's lack of attention to the therapeutic relationship, Freud responded with negation when, in the evening session of May 10, Frau Emmy asked him directly if he was annoyed with something she had said during the massage in the morning. Typically, Freud shifted immediately to an effort to regulate his patient's periods through hypnotic suggestions. Freud saw Frau Emmy von N.'s allusion to the words "don't touch me" as completely unconnected to the twice-daily body massages he administered to her. This reaction is comparable to Freud's response when his patient alluded to these massages in the session of May 15, and he reacted by immediately asking her about the history of the pains in her leg.

There are two striking examples from Frau Emmy von. N. of possible unconscious perceptions of the collusive implications of Freud's interventions with her. The first occurs in the evening session of May 16. The patient stated that she had been frightened by an enormous mouse, which had whisked across her hand in the garden. She seemed confused, and Freud asked her under hypnosis what it was that really had frightened her. She repeated the story of the mouse, and Freud told her that these were hallucinations and that she need not be afraid of mice—only drunkards saw them (the patient disliked drunkards intensely). Freud then told the patient the story of Bishop Hatto who, according to legend, was eaten by rats. Frau Emmy listened to him with extreme horror. Freud then asked her why she had thought about the circus. The patient responded that she had heard horses stamping in the nearby stables; they were being tied to their halters, which might injure them. Freud denied that there were stables nearby and also saw as a misperception the patient's belief that she heard someone in the next room groan. The patient was disoriented and thought she was elsewhere. She recalled memories from Rugen —where she had recently believed herself to be—in which she had frightful pains in her legs and arms, had lost her way several times in a fog, and twice, while on a walk, had been pursued by a bull.

These last images in particular could well represent in encoded form Frau Emmy von N.'s experience of Freud as someone who seemed to be lost or dislocated in his efforts to help his patient, and as someone who had an unconscious need to injure or pursue his patient by such measures as telling her the terrible tale of the Bishop who was eaten by rats. Freud's intervention was well-meaning, though he failed to recognize the highly threatening unconscious qualities that it contained. In the illustrations of present-day psychotherapies, a number of such well-meaning, yet intrusive, interventions were offered by therapists from rather different persuasions. All of them owe their heritage to Freud, whose early techniques appear indeed to have been relatively sadistic. They seem to have often been readily accepted by his patients, who might well have been gratifying their responsive masochistic (self-punitive) wishes and needs.

Returning to the case, the next morning Frau Emmy said she now felt well. Earlier, she had given out screams in her bran bath because she took the bran for worms; the treatment had frightened her. Her cheerfulness seemed exaggerated, and she reported a dream of walking on a lot of leeches. She then remembered some horrible dreams from the previous night in which she had to lay out a number of dead people and put them in coffins, but would not put on the lids. Freud suggested that this recollection obviously involved her husband, though he made no connection to the story of the Bishop and his own interventions.

However, if Freud's tale is taken as the stimulus for this material, a number of encoded perceptions of Freud can be identified in this sequence. The story was intended as a well-motivated intervention to the patient, a form of treatment like the bran baths. The supposedly helpful substance turns into frightening worms, suggesting that the story, despite its therapeutic intention, had also frightened her. She was being forced to make contact with creatures that she found quite fearful, such as leeches. Further, in her dream she laid out a number of dead people, much as Freud exposed her to the story of the dead Bishop. Her refusal to put the lids on the coffins may well contain the unconscious perception of the way in which Freud was unnecessarily exposing his patient to threatening material, rather than helping her to develop useful defenses against the underlying disturbance.

In the session, Frau Emmy then described a bat that had become caught in her wardrobe so that she had rushed out of her room without putting on any clothes. To cure her of this fear, her brother had given her a lovely brooch in the form of a bat, but she had never been able to wear it. This last image seemed to exquisitely represent through disguise Freud's attempt through deconditioning to cure his patient's fear of mice by telling her the tale of how a Bishop was eaten by a similar creature. The encoded communications from the patient indicate that such measures are not especially curative and are bound to fail.

The second incident occurred during a second period of treatment Freud provided his patient. Much of the manifest work involved disagreeable impresssions that the patient had developed regarding her daughter's treatment by a gynecologist whom Freud had recommended, and the patient's own treatment during a stay in a sanatorium. In the latter situation, there was much suppressed anger toward the physician involved, who compelled her to spell the word "toad" while under hypnosis in an effort to desensitize the patient from one of her great fears. (Note the evident connection to the above interlude with Freud).

During this treatment, which Freud carried out in the patient's home, Freud observed Frau Emmy discarding food. On inquiry, it turned out that the patient ate very little and found that drinking water or minerals ruined her digestion. When Freud took a specimen of her urine and found it highly concentrated with urates, he recommended that she drink more and increase her intake of food. The patient did so under pressure, but then became depressed and ungracious. She complained of violent gastric pains and recriminated Freud that she had told him this would happen. She complained bitterly, and Freud responded with direct reassurance.

At this point, the patient for the first time could not be hypnotized. Freud felt she was in open rebellion and gave up on the effort. Instead, he gave her 24 hours to think things over and accept his view that her gastric pains came only from her fear. At the end of the time, Freud would ask her if she still believed her digestion could be ruined for a week by drinking a glass of mineral water and eating a modest meal. If she said yes, he would ask her to leave.

Twenty-four hours later, Frau Emmy von N. was docile and submissive. When asked the inevitable question, she answered that she thought her gastric pains came from her anxiety, but only because Freud said so. Freud put her under hypnosis and asked again why she couldn't eat more. The answer involved a series of recollections. When she was a child, she often refused to eat her meal at dinner out of sheer naughtiness. Her mother was severe about it, and under the threat of punishment, she was obliged two hours later to eat the meat that had been left standing on the plate. The meat was cold and the fat set hard, and the patient reacted with disgust.

Frau Emmy went over the memory in detail and then went on to another recollection of her brother, who had had a horrible disease. It was contagious and the patient was afraid of making a mistake and picking up his knife and fork. Despite that, she ate her meals with him so that no one would know he was ill. Soon after, she nursed another brother when he had consumption. She sat by his bed, and his spittoon stood on the table. He had a habit of spitting across the plate into the spittoon, which made Frau Emmy sick; but she could not show her feelings for fear of hurting her brother.

Freud cleared away these stories under hypnosis and inquired into her inability to drink water. She connected this to a time when she had contracted gastric catarrah owing to bad drinking water. The other members of her family who developed these symptoms were quickly relieved by medical attention, though she was not. Nor did she improve when mineral water was recommended. When the doctor had prescribed it, she had thought at once that it would not be of any use.

Despite the many valid unconscious perceptions of the hurtful qualities of Freud's ultimatum that abound encoded in this material, the patient had a rather positive symptomatic response to these recollections. Nonetheless, in disguised fashion, she recalled her mother's punitive attitude in response to her early refusals to eat. Her images then shifted to illness in others and a fear of showing any awareness of these disturbances lest she hurt someone else's feelings. To this very day, when therapists respond to their patients with noninterpretive interventions such as ultimatums, patients unconsciously view them as ill, and often as punitive and manipulative. It is under these conditions that therapists are repeating the patient's pathogenic past, the conditions under which the patient fell ill, rather than distinguishing themselves from these past figures. Such therapeutic procedures, in the words of this patient, are not of any use.

Why then do they sometimes, as suggested here, lead to symptom alleviation? Unfortunately, Freud does not provide the further associations that would be necessary to understand the patient's response. Perhaps the closest one can come to hazarding a guess is that the patient's guilt over the illnesses of her brothers was assauaged to some extent by Freud's punitive attitude. Further, since Freud was seen as having problems not unlike her mother's, the patient could then excuse her mother for her destructiveness. Then too, aroused fears of the mother and of further punishment, and of the loss of her relationship with her physician, could also have contributed. (In later chapters, the means by which patients paradoxically respond to hostile therapeutic measures with symptom relief will be studied.)

There is evidence, then, that despite important valid unconscious perceptions of problems within Freud and his techniques, Frau Emmy von N. accepted these therapeutic measures to a large extent. Her overt rebellion against Freud's direct interventions may well have been based on a deeper and unconscious appreciation for the problems rampant in his method. This may be one of the first instances in which a patient proved capable of directly criticizing a therapist's technique, though typically, then as now, such attitudes are treated as resistance and as signs of illness in the patient. These direct efforts appear to have been supplemented by unconscious communications, which had some quality of wishing to be therapeutic toward Freud, as well as involving attempts to let him know the unnoticed implications of his efforts.

The reader must again be reminded here that while transference was invented or discovered in *Studies on Hysteria*, countertransference was totally ignored. The emotional problems of the analyst, and the broader subject of the conscious and unconscious nature of his or her contributions to the patient's therapeutic experience, was afforded virtually no consideration at all. Even at a time when there was considerable uncertainty regarding therapeutic techniques, and when Freud was utilizing a new and somewhat experimental technical measure, there was little or no sense of the possibility of error, of ineffectual therapeutic efforts, or of justified mistrust of therapeutic procedures on the part of the patient.

The interventions described by Freud in the case of Emmy von N. range far and wide. They include a variety of personal opinions, direct efforts at reassurance, personal discussions, and even telling her such tales as the story of Bishop Hatto. It is easy today, through hindsight, to recognize the powerful traumatic effects that interventions of this kind would have on a patient. Freud ignored such a possibility. Many therapists to this day intervene in this fashion without the least bit of awareness of the evident underlying implications of these techniques.

The next step, the realization that interventions from the therapist could be a reflection of his or her own emotional problems—i.e., could be expressions of countertransference in the narrow (pathological) sense of the term—is even further removed from Freud's thinking in the 1890s. As is well known, Freud (1910) did indeed have the genius to coin the term countertransference and to identify it as a limiting factor in analytic work. However, he never wrote a major paper on the subject and afforded it only minimal attention in his later writings. His attitude, already stated in the *Studies on Hysteria*, was to the effect that erroneous interventions tend to be harmless and have little influence on the patient, much as water rolls off the back of a duck (Freud 1937). In the realm of countertransference, Freud's use of denial was more extensive and powerful than in the realm of transference. Thus his blind spots regarding himself were even greater than those in respect to his patients. Here too Freud proved unfortunately to be a strong model for future therapists.

In general, it can be suggested that symptom relief that takes place under conditions where a therapist totally avoids the ongoing communicative therapeutic interaction must derive in large part from a sharing of the therapist's use of avoidance and defense. It can arise too from unconscious responses to the unconscious realization that the therapist is indeed in difficulty and under pressures similar to those experienced by the patient. At times the defenses and lie-barrier systems generated in this fashion prove serviceable to the patient, while at the other moments they do not do so.

As the case of Anna O. clearly demonstrates, patients sometimes violently object to the lie-barrier systems that they have shared with their therapists. They undo these defenses and confront the therapist suddenly with a blatantly clear message loaded with meaning. Virtually always, the therapist who requires denial and defensiveness in both himself and his patient is totally unprepared for such an experience. He or she will react violently and defensively to these circumstances, and often do considerable psychological harm to the patient who dares to violate the defensive misalliance that they have created together.

Still other therapists, and most psychoanalysts are among them, acknowledge the importance of the patient's reactions to his or her therapist. However, they define the therapeutic interaction almost entirely in terms of transference. They account for the patient's experiences of the therapist almost entirely in terms of past relationships. Their own inputs into these experiences, especially on an unconscious level, are almost totally ignored. They accept in full the heritage offered to them by Freud to engage in a treatment experience with patients in which the patient is held entirely accountable for his or her own sickness and for any disturbance in the therapeutic experience. Transference is the guiding concept. Nontransference is given little thought.

Later it will be shown that this particular conspiratorial arrangement offers something to both patient and therapist. It also appears to have been a necessary defense for many therapists, enabling them to use treatment techniques of an uncovering nature. Without the concept of transference—the personal denial of their own inputs—it appears that therapists would have been, and still would be, so overwhelmed by the therapeutic situation and patient as to have no other recourse but to flee. Transference is the false concept that enables them to endure.

Under these conditions, the patient gets virtually all of the blame for any disturbance in the therapeutic interaction. The emphasis is on the sickness of the patient and the implied health of the therapist. In this way, patients who are guilt-ridden receive a strong measure of accusation and punishment, which may provide them with some type of relief from their emotional suffering. Other strange and unusual advantages also accrue to the patient in these conditions, and they are considered later in this book. In part, they involve the satisfaction of functioning unconsciously as therapist to the therapist.

For therapists or analysts, the advantages are more evident. They are able to deny their own pathology or countertransferences, and to maintain an image of the patient as the sick member of the therapeutic dyad. They are also able unconsciously to place their own pathology into their transactions with their patients and to work over their own sickness on an unconscious level, all in the guise of consciously working with the pathology of the patient. Further, they are able to observe psychopathological phenomena secure with the false reassurance that it has nothing whatsoever to do with themselves.

Protected by the armor of the defensive use of the concept of transference, Freud became the world's first psychoanalyst. He was able to make monumental discoveries regarding the nature of human emotional functioning and of unconscious mental processes. True, once the error in his thinking is recognized, some revisions in the psychoanalytic theory of emotional disorders are required. Nonetheless, most of that theory remains valid, despite the basic flaws in the psychoanalytic method and in the conception of the therapeutic experience. Psychoanalysis is an art and science that has discovered many truths about human functioning and emotional disturbance while using a basically erroneous therapeutic technique. The truths that were supposedly discovered in respect to the patient are actually more applicable to the therapist. Nonetheless, since they involve valid statements regarding the nature of human psychological functioning, they are essentially correct on a general level. In addition, the therapist has the advantage of being able to use these truths for his own self-protection.

It seems unlikely that Freud could have developed psychoanalysis without the psychoanalytic conspiracy that he created between himself and his patients, and between himself and his colleagues. Because of the enormity of the threat involved, it may well be that there would have never been a psychoanalytic movement were it not for the defensive use of the concept of transference. There is every indication that the underlying truths of a patient's emotional disturbance, as constituted by both threatening perceptions and threatening fantasies, are more disturbing than most minds can bear. Patients can experience these truths only if they are relatively disguised; indeed, direct experience of such truths is often part of a psychosis, or may well lead to one. Therapists require some way of muting these truths lest they too go mad.

It seems to have taken a full 100 years to mobilize the intellectual and emotional resources to attempt to deal with emotional illness in terms of their truths, rather than through one or another form of falsification and avoidance. Yet, it may well be that the dangers in doing sound and truthful psychotherapy have been exaggerated. If this is the case, a truth therapy paradigm is not only feasible but desirable.

PART III
EMOTIONAL ILLNESS AND UNCONSCIOUS COMMUNICATION

CHAPTER 13

THE SOURCES OF EMOTIONAL PROBLEMS

Throughout the histories of medicine, psychiatry, and psychotherapy, physicians and therapists have attempted to understand the basis of their patients' afflictions. It should not be surprising that understanding of emotional dysfunction has tended to lag behind those understandings developed in spheres of medicine that rely heavily upon anatomical, cytological, physiological, and biochemical researches and findings. Some of the difficulties in the psychological-emotional sphere arise from the multiple sources of ultimate disturbance, as well as from the finding that no one source is consistently the most important factor in the etiology of the disturbance.

There appears to be a strong correlation between a particular theory of emotional disturbance and the nature of the therapeutic measures utilized for its alleviation. There is a spiraling interplay between theory and technique. At times, the technique is arrived at empirically and the theory derived from clinical observations based on the particular procedure at hand. Further elaborations of the theory tend to be developed mainly as a means of giving sense to and justifying the technical procedures in use. Depending on the focus of the procedure, the theory itself tends to be concentrated at the same level of observation and thinking.

For example, as long as hysteria and other emotional disorders were thought to be derived from states of general tension or to have some type of organic basis, treatment measures involved massages, baths, methods of relaxation, and procedures designed to extirpate possible organic foci. Freud himself recommended the surgical removal of nasal infections and obstructions at a time when he believed that certain types of hysterical symptoms, such as gastric pains, derived from nasal pathology. He recommended this type of surgery for a particular patient whose code name in *The Interpretation of Dreams* (Freud 1900) is Irma—now known to have been a friend of Freud's wife and family, Emma. This particular surgery had disastrous results when the surgeon, Wilhelm Fliess, Freud's closest friend and associate at the time, left a segment of iodoform gauze in the patient's sinunasal cavity. Freud himself had made use of similar surgery for some of his own emotional symptoms during this period—the mid-1890s.

In the years before Breuer and Freud, when there was little understanding of the etiology of emotional disorders, symptoms were treated as inanimate entities without meaning. The physical procedures utilized were expected to mechanically promote the elimination of the disturbance. Some physicians also made use of hypnosis in order to create a state of consciousness in which suggestibility was at its height. Under these conditions they tried through a variety of often forceful means to suggest away the patient's emotional suffering.

Even today, each and every form of psychotherapy has its own theory of emotional disturbance. To some, the answer lies in the absence of meaning, and the treatment efforts aim at direct removal of the illness using methods not unlike those adopted in the 19th century. For others, the theory is more elaborate, though focused on a particular level of etiology. The treatment method is then shaped in keeping with these concepts.

Before tracing out the origins of psychoanalysis and psychotherapy, and the theory of neurosis to which they were attached, the possible levels of experience that may contribute to an individual's emotional disturbance must be explored. From what is known today, the following factors are involved: (1) congenital—innate and emotional givens; (2) physical–structural—measurable physiological and physical factors that contribute to the individual's emotional and coping capacities; (3) internal psychological factors

—intrapsychic determinants; (4) interpersonal factors—family and other immediate relationships; (5) cultural—the broader influence of society.

The treatment of emotional disturbances is confounded by the finding that, in a particular person, a given emotional problem may arise overwhelmingly from any one of these major factors or, at the other extreme, from an even mixture of all five. In regard to cure, matters are made even more difficult by the finding, to be discussed later on, that sound treatment procedures sometimes evoke paradoxical negative therapeutic reactions, while hurtful and downright destructive therapies may lead to symptom alleviation.

It was Breuer, following the lead of his patient, Anna O., who began to realize that hysterical symptoms were derived from hidden ideas and feelings, many of them related to recent memories. His observations of his patient suggested that an altered or clouded state of consciousness—a hypnoid state—at the time of the trauma was an important contributing factor. Under these conditions, the affective or feeling response to a hurtful experience was strangulated rather than discharged. It remained within the individual as a pent-up disturbance that expressed itself through a variety of symptoms. Some of the psychic difficulties were converted into physical problems, such as anesthesias and paralyses. The mechanism of *conversion* was postulated as a means by which pent-up affects and ideas were transformed into physical symptoms that symbolized the underlying ideas and memories.

In circular fashion, it was Breuer's observation of symptom alleviation, which followed the release of the covered-over (repressed) memories and affects, that led him to his theoretical formulations. On the whole, the theory of emotional disturbance generated by Breuer and Freud was based on their clinical observations derived from the use of the cathartic method. Through his troubled but ingenious decision to listen to his patient, Anna O., Breuer had opened up an area of clinical observation never before investigated. As already noted, he apparently did so out of his commitment as a scientist and because of some infatuation with his patient. He also did so at the risk of tampering with previously maintained defenses and, in consequence, of being exposed to less disguised and more disturbing communications from his patient. In the end, he was of course overwhelmed by the Pandora's box that he was the first brave soul to unlock. Many therapies today are designed to avoid this very type of catastrophic reaction, not so much in patients but in their therapists.

Breuer's thinking concentrated on isolated symptoms and their inner sources—the internal psychological realm. Freud extended this intrapsychic focus and subjected it to extensive study in the more than 40 years that followed. In Freud's formulations, initiated in his own contributions to *Studies on Hysteria*, unconscious inner mental struggles (conflicts) were the central factor in emotional disturbance. External reality and relationships with others were acknowledged only peripherally, mainly as sources of gratification or trauma. While Freud eventually did provide a basis for a study of the role of what are called object relationships in emotional disturbances, it remained for modern-day psychoanalysts to begin to take this sphere—the interpersonal sphere—into account. To this very day, this factor is afforded only limited consideration, though there are trends toward a more elaborate accounting of its role in the development and maintenance of neuroses.

Freud postulated an almost conscious struggle in his patients as the source of their symptoms. While he initially accepted the possible role of an altered state of consciousness—the so-called hypnoid state—in the onset of an emotional disturbance, his own thinking concentrated on the role of impulse and defense, ideas incompatible with the main body of thinking within an individual (the ego) and the ego's use of defensive operations. In this way, the role of intrapsychic conflict, and of unconscious fantasies—memories and imaginary ideas that exist within the individual outside of his or her awareness, expressed in some encoded and symbolic form—were seen as factors in the creation of symptoms.

Freud quickly recognized the role of shame, self-reproach, and concern for physical harm as hidden or unconscious motives for the repression of pathogenic ideas aroused by an earlier trauma. By the time he developed his contribution to *Studies on Hysteria*, he was able to stress the importance of sexual traumas in particular in the etiology of hysteria and other forms of emotional disturbance. For a while, he believed that these traumas involved actual and blatant sexual seductions by family figures during the childhood of the patient. After his own self-analysis, he gave up the seduction theory and attributed the sexual etiology of neuroses to conscious and unconscious fantasy formations—to the imagination of the patient. Nonetheless, Freud never resolved the question of whether these early sexual traumas were entirely imaginary or quite real. As late as 1918, and again in 1926, Freud postulated the presence of real seductions in many of his patients. And yet, he continued to maintain on a theoretical level that such events were by and large the product of unconscious fantasy rather than quite real.

This question of real trauma, sexual and otherwise, as a factor in neurosis, as compared to the role of intrapsychic unconscious fantasies, remains a matter of dispute to the present day. While some analysts believe that children are born with preformed unconscious fantasy systems, most would agree that these develop through an interplay between the child's innate emotional and imaginative capacities and the stimuli emanating from his or her important interpersonal relationships, particularly from that with the mother. As a result, the child's unconscious fantasy systems are derived in part from actual conscious and unconscious inputs from the parental figure and in part through elaborations based on his or her own inner proclivities. At times the interpersonal inputs can be the major determinant of an early emotional disturbance, while at other times, psychophysiologically founded dysfunctions in thinking and imagination may play the major role.

Freud sensed a dynamic inner struggle within his patients. At first there was a trauma that had invoked an impulse, wish, or fantasy, which had in turn prompted a reaction of shame or self-reproach. Often, there was no discharge of the sexual wish involved, and as a result, there was an internal strangulation of affect and a damning of libido (sexual energy). Freud's early thinking was that anxiety was a physical (transformed) consequence of this dammed up libido. Many years later, mainly in 1926, he revised his thinking and saw anxiety as a response to trauma and psychic danger. In that particular theory, anxiety leads to defense, which leads to sexual repression, rather than the other way around.

The earlier theory arose largely because Freud's thinking was quite phenomenological. Even though he postulated the presence of unconscious motives and unconscious fantasies, much of his work involved conscious struggles within the patient. To these he applied direct pressures on the patient to overcome the patient's defenses and to gain direct access to the painful memories that were being almost consciously suppressed, rather than unconsciously repressed.

Still, the important definitions of the role of psychic trauma in emotional disturbance and of intrapsychic conflict were spelled out quite clearly in this first extended volume. Hysterical symptoms were defined as mnemic (memory) residues and symbols of traumatic events. They were the consequence of the compromise between impulse and defense. Further, when the therapist attempted to undo the defense, the patient *resisted* the therapist's efforts. As a result, it became necessary for the therapist to remove these resistances, and in time, Freud viewed the analysis of the unconscious basis for such resistances as a critical part of therapeutic work.

In *Studies on Hysteria*, Freud made only a few brief remarks on the connection between disturbances in the relationship with the therapist (which he defined as transference) and resistances. Eventually, he postulated that transference resistances (obstacles directed against the recovery of painful memories related to fantasies about the therapist, and later on, more broadly, directed against therapeutic work of any kind that arose in the context of the relationship with the therapist) were the most significant obstacles to therapy. At the same time, analysis of these very difficulties revealed an enormous amount about the patient's emotional disturbance.

Freud's theory of neurosis went through a number of elaborations and transformations, though its basic elements were clearly stated in *Studies on Hysteria*. Some dissatisfaction with the therapeutic results obtained through the cathartic method in part led Freud to give up the use of hypnosis. His own dread of the seemingly unbridled sexual feelings and impulses that were released in the course of hypnotic work also seems to have played a role. Then too, some growing realization of the erotic qualities of the hypnotic relationship for both himself as therapist and his patients may have been a factor. And Freud repeatedly indicated that his inability to hypnotize many patients also played a role. Finally, once he invoked the concept of transference as a way of denying any contribution on his part to the patient's erotic reactions, it may well have been necessary for Freud to give up hypnosis as a means of attempting to preclude in reality any such contribution on his part.

Whatever the totality of reasons, Freud did indeed soon give up hypnosis and adopt a technique through which he pressed on his patients' foreheads and encouraged—forced—them to free associate and to give up their defenses. In little time, he ceased all physical contact with his patients, and placed them on a couch where they could not see him; while he sat back and allowed them to free associate. However, virtually every description of his actual analytic work indicates a fairly high level of activity on his part, even with this last, free association paradigm.

As Freud became less actively involved with his patients, the theory of neurosis became more exclusively intrapsychic. There was a strong correlation between the theory that transference is entirely a product of the imagination of the patient and the belief that emotional disturbance develops in comparable fashion—from within. Thus there is the additional correlation between the technique of therapy, the theory of neurosis, and the therapist's thinking on the nature of his or her own as well as the patient's contributions to the treatment process.

In the final section of this book, these correlations are studied for a number of treatment forms. In general, the therapist who uses deconditioning, or unlearning, maintains a theory of neurosis that views emotional disturbance as internally determined through poor learning patterns. The relationship between the patient and therapist is relatively inconsequential to the treatment process. The focus is on the symptom and its removal, a later-day version of Breuer's original technique, though with a different emphasis—a shift from strangulated affect to poor learning patterns.

Primal scream therapists are perhaps closest to Breuer among present-day thinkers in respect to their theory of neurosis and their technique, though they are perhaps more closely tied to Freud's abreactive efforts without hypnosis than to those with hypnotherapy. Their theory in essence involves the role of repressed memories and strangulated affects in mental illness, factors that require release and discharge. Their techniques are designed to create this very effect, and their patients' sense of relief is taken as confirmation of the theory.

Family therapists, of course, have developed a theory of therapy and of neurosis in which familial interpersonal reactions and interplay are seen as most crucial. Their techniques are designed to modify disturbed family patterns and, in general, do not touch upon intrapsychic contributions from within the family members.

Since virtually anything can provide a patient with symptom relief, almost everything has been tried in the name of psychotherapy. The choice of treatment modality and the development of new treatment paradigms seem to be based in the therapist on a mixture of therapeutic desire and personal need. With so many levels of determinants, a rationale for a treatment modality is relatively easy to develop.

Virtually no one has examined the transactions within any of these treatment modalities in depth. While it is certainly clear that a therapist can help a patient to obtain symptom relief through such diverse means as revealing the nature of an unconscious fantasy and by placing him or her into an entirely new culture, the level at which a treatment experience is offered need not preclude a careful and in-depth analysis of the basis for symptom alleviation.

For example, a rash may be treated by a surface ointment, a pill taken by mouth, or an injection. A full understanding of the basis on which the rash disappears would, however, require careful cellular and physiological–biochemical studies. Similarly, whether a patient is treated through cultural change, deconditioning, or psychoanalysis, an understanding of the basis for change in the patient would require that the therapist take into account the influence of all five factors defined for the development of an emotional disturbance. In the absence of such careful and detailed exploration, anything goes.

CHAPTER 14

THE FEAR
OF THE INNER
MENTAL WORLD

Physically, everything ultimately comes down to physiological and biochemical cellular and organ changes. Similarly, psychologically, everything funnels into conscious and unconscious intrapsychic and interpersonal transactions. It is at this level that the individual equation has its greatest meaning.

Freud and many who have followed him have been able to show that an unconscious intrapsychic factor that leads the individual to a maladaptive reaction to current stimuli is basic to the nature of an emotional disturbance. Neurosis or emotional disturbance is, by definition, a form of maladaptation or sickness. It is an emotional reaction that is disturbing and costly to the individual and often to those around him or her. It is a response that cannot be accounted for in terms of the actualities at hand. Thus a frightened response or hurtful reaction to an actual trauma that is in keeping with the nature of the trauma is not a sign of neurosis; instead, it is an indication of an adaptive effort to a hurtful experience. It is only when these efforts at coping begin to fail and become disproportionate to the nature of the trauma that a true emotional disturbance is present.

Many therapists have failed to make this distinction.

Their treatment efforts involve nonneurotic reactions and are successful because they simply lessen the traumatic qualities of the patient's surroundings. They need not concern themselves with unconscious factors since they are not especially relevant.

Other treatment modalities accept the definition of neurotic behaviors as inappropriate to reality stimuli, and as therefore based on internal and unconscious factors within the individual, but they choose nonetheless to avoid probing these factors. Instead, their procedures are designed to create changes in some other sphere, which could then, in ways that do not interest these therapists, have a positive effect on the patient's inner mental world and symptoms.

In general, only psychoanalysis and psychoanalytic psychotherapy are designed to help the patient become aware of the unconscious factors in his or her neurotic reaction. It is their theory that such conscious awareness helps to diminish anxiety, to reduce inevitable unconscious distortions, and to provide a means by which a patient may consciously and directly resolve a conflict that had previously been entirely unconscious. Through these and other means, symptom alleviation based on insight into unconscious factors in neurosis-formation is obtained.

Clearly, there are a great number of psychotherapeutic modalities that make no effort whatsoever to gain access to the hidden or unconscious basis for a patient's inappropriate reactions to reality stimuli. There seem to be two major ways to account for this pattern: (1) the belief that insight of this kind is of little or no value in resolving an emotional disturbance, or (2) the possibility that the actual nature of the intrapsychic disturbance that forms the basis for neurosis is so terrifying and potentially overwhelming for patients and/or therapists that few dare to approach the truths behind neuroses and most prefer avoidance and flight.

In a way, it becomes a question whether a therapist hopes to be a Breuer or a Freud, though even Freud, it would seem, did not allow himself to get in touch with the totality of the unconscious basis of his patient's emotional symptoms. He permitted himself to deal only with unconscious fantasies and ignored unconscious perceptions—the influence of actual interpersonal inputs.

This basic choice could be the source of an extended and great debate. However, insight into the true unconscious basis of a patient's emotional disturbance may actually provide the patient with what is probably the best means available of resolving a neurosis and of having the resources to cope with future emotional traumas. Evidence on this point will be cited in the final section of this book, and it seems to follow that therapists and patients have avoided this type of treatment approach mainly because of a deep and abiding dread of the inner basis of a patient's emotional symptoms. In the present chapter, some of the reasons for this overwhelming fear, which has so significantly contributed to the search for alternate treatment modalities, will be defined. Such anxiety cannot exist on such a massive scale without due cause. Understanding its sources will provide a valuable perspective on the popularity of noninsightful treatment methods.

The patients with whom Breuer and Freud worked, described in *Studies on Hysteria*, suffered in the main from a form of grand hysteria seldom seen in present-day practice. Their level of anxiety, the pervasiveness of their hallucinations and delusions, and other symptomatic disturbances and problems in reality-testing, have led subsequent writers to suggest that patients like Anna O. and Emmy von N. were actually psychotic, schizophrenic. Still, the symptoms reported by these women were terrifying in themselves. Anna O. showed disturbances in speech and vision, paralyses and contractions, somnabulism, and a variety of terrifying hallucinations that included black snakes and changes in her own body. Frau Emmy von N. stammered and made a clacking sound from her mouth, showed tic-like movements of her face and neck, and would cry out in fear, "Keep still!—Don't say anything!—Don't touch me!" while having what appeared to be terrifying hallucinations. She experienced a wide variety of horrible animal scenes and images of corpses. Her memories, too, were nightmarish and overwhelming.

Emotional symptoms both reveal and defend against underlying disturbances. With Anna O., these were traced to her internal conflicts regarding her relationship with her dying father. With Frau Emmy von N. they involved the death of her husband and periods of fright in her childhood, some of which related to the deaths of several of her siblings. They also involved frightening experiences with men who jumped at her from behind bushes and with a particular man who hid in her room while she attended a resort.

By and large, the sexual factor in these traumas and anxieties was moderately disguised. With the three other patients whom

Freud described in *Studies on Hysteria*, Miss Lucy R., Katharina, and Fraulein Elisabeth von R., sexual traumas and longings were far more in evidence. For example, Katharina, whom Freud worked with but once while on a vacation, ultimately remembered being seduced by her "uncle," who, Freud later revealed, was actually her father.

This brief survey points to some of the reasons why patients and therapists prefer to avoid the truths that underlie patients' emotional disturbances. These truths involve highly traumatic memories and their subsequent elaboration in fantasy. They involve traumas with those whom the patient at one time or another deeply loved and who nonetheless proved to be hurtful. They entail losses that are painful to acknowledge and are often best treated through avoidance and quiet denial. They also touch upon inner impulses that are the source of considerable anxiety, guilt, depression, shame, and revulsion. Gaining direct access to these recollection-fantasy complexes is therefore enormously disturbing.

In dredging up symptom-related memories of traumas that have evoked this kind of inner conflict and mental pain, the turmoil that the patient experiences has two sources. There is, as has been repeatedly emphasized, the realization of his or her own depressing and threatening fantasies. But in addition, an important role is played by disturbing perceptions of the other persons involved in the illness-producing experiences.

Until quite recently, the role played by actual and valid unconscious perceptions of highly disruptive inputs from other individuals has been quite neglected in the etiology of emotional disturbances. This difficulty has arisen in part because these perceptions are registered outside the awareness of the perceiver and expressed in therapy in disguised and symbolic form. Then too, many of these perceptions immediately involve the therapist, which has led to a defensive neglect of this particular level of experience. There is, then, a strong relationship between the formulation of the basis for emotional symptoms and the therapist's thoughts regarding the nature of the therapeutic interaction and experience.

The inner mental basis of an emotional disturbance involves all that is forbidden, repugnant, repulsive, primitive, and terrifying. The early nascent mental functioning of the child remains within the adult, covered over though not entirely sealed off. On that level, experience is fragmented, uncertain, and highly instinctualized with both aggressive and sexual qualities. Incest is rampant, as is murder and dismemberment. The primitive conscience operates largely by the law of Talion: an eye for an eye, a tooth for a tooth. A murderous mutilating fantasy contains within it the threat of mutilating punishment. A murderous mutilating unconscious perception of the mother leads to helplessness, fear of annihilation, and fantasies of mutilating revenge.

In another sense, it is the helplessness, the horrible contradictions in our images of ourselves and others, the tumultuous realizations that we can no longer fuse with mother and, instead, must indeed ultimately die, which are the unconscious basis of the perceptions and conflicts that drive us crazy. Interpersonally, there are the inevitable maternal and paternal contradictions and failures. Then too there are the infuriating arrivals of siblings who will compete for affection and interfere with our own personal needs. There are also the inevitable realizations that we are by no means omnipotent, and the unavoidable disappointments and frustrations that further account for neurosis.

To these factors, add the influence of specific conflicts, failings, disturbed self-image, and emotional problems in the parental figures, which are communicated consciously and unconsciously to the child. The perception and experience of these failings and hidden but expressed fantasies, the terror of an unconscious realization of a parent's wish to destroy his or her child, create some of the overwhelming affects that prompt the defenses we need in order to preserve our sanity and some semblance of emotional equilibrium. No one is immune. Small wonder we are all neurotic and even psychotic in some lesser or greater way. Reality and other persons will inevitably fail us, and coping efforts can never be entirely successful. The very mechanisms by which we protect ourselves— repression, denial, displacement, disguise, and other defenses—are the same means by which we become neurotic and react inappropriately to situations in our daily life.

Conflict, defense, and compromise abound. There is the struggle between the impulse and restraint, between what we validly and painfully perceive and the need to deny, between the pressure to express our innermost fantasies and the need to cover them over, and more broadly between expression and concealment. Toward those who traumatize us, we react with mistrust and fear. While we must express our reaction to the horrors they create within ourselves, we must also insure our safety in the face of the dangers they present; we therefore seek out compromise and defense. Unconsciously, we attempt to find clever ways to react, to find revenge, to defend ourselves, while all the while maintaining innocence and affection. Intrapsychically and interpersonally, neuroses arise from turmoil, chaos, and pain, and out of the necessity for simultaneous expression and defense.

Neuroses arise from the ever-present contradictions in others and in ourselves. When our defenses and other efforts at coping succeed, we get along reasonably well. When they fail, we develop symptoms that enable us to cope, though at considerable cost.

Two other elements of the emotional nightmares that lead to symptom formation must be stressed. The first involves the relationship with the therapist. At the very moment a patient decides to contact a therapist, the therapist becomes an important figure in the patient's emotional life. Based on the hope for cure and on the special meaning that the therapist has for the patient, the therapeutic relationship quickly becomes the major organizing force in the maintenance of the patient's emotional disturbance and in its resolution.

Because of this remarkably intense investment in the relationship with the therapist, patients become exquisitely perceptive of every nuance reflected in the therapist's behavior and interventions. These nuances are filled with unconscious meanings and functions, and patients are highly sensitive to these hidden levels of interchange. Whenever a therapist departs from a basically sound holding and therapeutic manner of relating to the patient, and from the interpretations needed to explain the unconscious basis of a patient's neurosis, the therapist is experienced by the patient as fulfilling his or her own pathological needs, and as in some way failing and traumatizing the patient. If sound therapeutic work is to succeed at such crossroads, it must then be concentrated on an understanding of the patient's communications in light of these hurtful inputs from the therapist. In actuality, no neurosis can be insightfully and fundamentally resolved without taking fully into account the spiraling conscious and especially unconscious communicative interaction between patients and their healers.

Before Freud, the relationship between the patient and therapist, hypnotist or other, was almost entirely ignored. From time to time, a sensitive observer would recognize the special bond between the hypnotist and hypnotized, and would even sense its child-parent and erotic qualities. For the most part, however, the relationship was taken for granted. The focus was on the patient's symptoms and, sometime later, on the patient's symptoms in light of earlier life experiences. The therapist was free to explore the illness, probe its meanings, and comment upon it. The patient's reactions were understood entirely on an emotional–intellectual plane as a response to the direct and manifest qualities of the therapist's comments.

With Freud and the discovery-invention of transference, it was recognized that the therapist was a bit more involved with the patient. The therapist became a player whom the patient could direct and employ for fantasy purposes—an instrument of the patient's intrapsychic fantasy life. The therapist's presence was acknowledged, though total innocence was maintained. There was no sense of interaction or interplay.

For a hundred years, then, psychoanalytic therapists have probed the unconscious bases of the emotional disturbances within their patients. Their focus has been almost exclusively on the patient alone, with an occasional nod to factors within the therapist or analyst. Those analysts who began to study the interaction between patient and therapist tended to do so quite superficially. They made little effort to account for unconscious perceptions within either participant to treatment, and especially for the patient's special sensitivities in this regard. They were prepared to probe the patient's neurosis as an entity of imagination within the patient, and as derived from his or her own early life experiences. The therapists were not prepared to admit that they were now an inherent part of this neurosis and that their every move could have an influence on the patient's emotional disturbance. They were especially unprepared to acknowledge those situations in which their interventions were such that they enhanced the patient's emotional illness rather than insightfully diminishing it. Because of this, it was difficult for these therapists to acknowledge the role of the perceptions of others in the development of emotional ills. Here too there was a significant correlation between a therapist's view of his or her own role in the therapeutic experience and his or her ideas regarding the nature of emotional illness.

Freud provided psychoanalysts with a heritage that enabled them to enter the field under false premises. The denial of sickness

within the therapist or analyst, and especially of his or her contribution to the patient's ongoing illness, made it tolerable for
someone to be a therapist. It helped in part to depersonalize the
therapeutic relationship. It created a sense of distance and nonpar-
ticipation that was protective. Many valid aspects of the underlying
basis of emotional illness in patients could be mapped out through
this means. Still, critical blind spots were inevitable. Ironically, then,
psychoanalysis, with its fierce claim to the pursuit of the underlying
truths of the patient's emotional illness, required built-in falsifications and blind spots in order to maintain its otherwise relentless
probing of the unconscious mind.

While some analysts are now engaged in attempts to correct
these basic errors and to face the unconscious basis of a patient's
neurosis full force, regardless of its sources (including their own
inputs), there is as yet no major and acknowledged mode of treatment in use that consistently takes this key factor into account.
There is, however, a new descendant of psychoanalysis that is
beginning to stake its claim in this respect. It is called the *bipersonal*
or *communicative* (interactional) *approach* to psychotherapy, and it
will be discussed in more detail in Part IV of this volume. For the
moment, this long-standing void is a sad and yet telling testimony to
the difficulties experienced by both patients and therapists in attempting to identify the true basis for an emotional illness.

The second qualifying point involves the nature of emotional
symptoms. Today, emotional disturbance may take the form of a
particularly idiosyncratic way of living, an odd but necessary mode
of relatedness, or a tendency to behave in a particular fashion. There
may be more distinct symptoms such as anxiety, obsessions and
compulsions, and phobic fears such as those of heights and air-
planes. There may be various kinds of suspiciousness, sometimes to
the point of blatant delusions. There may be the need to always be
with others or the opposite, the need to be entirely alone. Many
patients cannot rationally justify the symptoms with which they are
suffering. They have little awareness of the circumstances of their
origins and little to say of their underlying basis. They feel suspicious
or fearful of heights, but they really do not know why. They may
attempt to rationalize their fear, but their reasoning is unsound.

If a therapist undertakes an analysis of the patient's associations
to a particular symptom, he or she soon discovers certain unconscious meanings and motives. The high place may symbolize the

parental bed or the process of birth, a strongly feminine type of fantasy. It may symbolically represent experiences of parental intercourse and images of parents as terrifying giants.

For example, Anna O.'s hallucination of the snake that was about to attack her father might have symbolically represented an unconscious perception of seductiveness on his part. At some point, he might have exposed his penis to his daughter and aroused in her highly disturbing perceptions and fantasies. In her envy of her brother, Anna O. might well have experienced a conflicted wish that she were a man. The hallucination of the phallic snake might have been in some symbolic fashion a way of gratifying that wish. Or perhaps she had an image of her father's penis as attacking and poisonous, and in the hallucination imagined a Talion punishment upon him. Perhaps she too wished she were a man so that she could seduce her father, or even her mother, and the terrifying hallucination both gratified these fantasies and punished her for them.

These hypothetical formulations could be confirmed only through a study of the free associations of this patient. For the moment, they are cited here as a way of demonstrating how we adopt a special language when faced with inner emotional disturbance, perception, or fantasy. It is a language filled with *displacements* from primary issues and relationships to secondary ones, and it involves the use of disguise and symbol. It embodies a mode of thinking that is rather different from the one we use in our everyday lives when solving problems and relating directly to others. It lacks logic and often shows little or no concern for reality. It combines several images into one, rather than treating each in discrete fashion.

In order to understand the nature of neuroses, and the manner in which they constitute forms of communication and expression, it is essential to understand this special form of thinking. Remarkably, and as an expression of his great genius, Freud offered such an understanding early in his writings. In *Studies on Hysteria*, he defined the dynamic nature of emotional illness and attempted to formulate its inner basis. Four years later, in *The Interpretation of Dreams* (Freud 1900), he provided a series of brilliant insights into the nature of neurotic and unconscious communication.

Oddly enough, psychoanalysts have tended subsequently to concentrate their interest on defining the dynamics of emotional illness. They have paid far less attention to the nature of unconscious communication. Here too defensive needs have played an exceedingly notable role. Inevitably, such an investigation would lead them to their own use of unconscious expressions. Until now, they have resisted such an effort. While stating openly their wish to know as well as humanly possible all there is to understand about themselves and their patients, they have been quite self-protective when it comes to self-realizations.

CHAPTER 15
THE FATEFUL DREAM OF PSYCHOANALYSIS

In *Studies on Hysteria*, Freud offered only two passing comments on the subject of dreams. In the first, he alluded to the symbolic connection between a precipitating trauma and a pathological emotional response. He stated that the connection is comparable to the type of thinking seen in healthy people within their dreams. Here of course Freud was suggesting that some type of encoding process is a factor in both symptoms and dream formation. The second comment is broader, but along similar lines. There, Freud stated that hysterical patients are insane when they are in an altered state of consciousness, a hypnoid state, adding, "Insane, as we all are in dreams" (Breuer and Freud 1893-95, p. 13).

In addition, in the footnote to the case of Frau Emmy von N., which has already been discussed in some detail, Freud began with his comments on false connections (the precursor of the concept of transference), moved to a discussion of the mistrust in patients of the therapeutic procedures recommended by their physicians (one in which he stressed the patient's defensiveness and, again, the role of false connections), and then touched upon the role of false connections in the development of dreams. There, Freud wrote of a compulsion to associate on the part of an unconscious complex that must find some connection to ideas present in consciousness. This surface idea then serves to represent and yet falsify the underlying unconscious conflicts.

Freud remarked too that he was already in the process of writing down and attempting to solve his dreams. He found two factors consistently present: (1) the necessity to work out in dreams ideas that were dwelt upon only cursorily during the day, and (2) the compulsion to link together ideas present in the same state of consciousness. The latter was used to account for the senseless and contradictory character of dreams.

From the beginning of his work as a therapist, Freud showed some measure of interest in the dreams that his patients reported to him. However, he wrote little on the subject until the publication of his monumental volume, *The Interpretation of Dreams*, in late 1899. By then, he stated that he had analyzed thousands of dreams from his patients, and indicated that he had subjected many of his own dreams to systematic self-analysis. In fact, the analysis of dreams played a role in Freud's heroic undertaking, carried out in the middle and late 1890s, of a detailed effort at self-analysis. It was through this particular and unique endeavor that Freud discovered the importance of infantile sexuality and clarified the basic secrets of neurosis.

While Freud apparently made sporadic efforts at dream analysis, it was in July of 1895, just two months after the publication of *Studies on Hysteria*, that Freud subjected a dream of his own to a thorough and systematic analysis. The dream is the well-known specimen dream reported in Chapter 2 of *The Interpretation of Dreams*, the Irma dream. On the basis of his analysis of this dream, Freud crystalized some of the most crucial factors in dream production and dream formation. In this way, he cleared a path for the study of conscious and unconscious mental functioning, and normal and neurotic states, which is still being explored to this day.

The Interpretation of Dreams, and the circumstances of the Irma dream in particular, are critical in three ways. First, the dream itself and its analysis is a major component of the origins of psychotherapy. An understanding of the circumstances under which the dream was dreamt and some of its meanings will provide critical insights into the hazards of exploratory psychotherapy. Second, there is Freud's discovery that human communication can at times be multi-leveled or layered with meaning, and that it can take place in encoded rather than direct form. Ingeniously, Freud thereby generated insights into the special form of communication that accounts for emotional disorders. An understanding of this particular type of communicative expression is critical to the comprehension of the unconscious meanings of the varieties of therapeutic interaction that are the main subject of this book. Manifest contents, or self-evident meanings, are quite insufficient in this regard. However, as shall soon be seen, the simplistic forms of decoding which Freud first developed often produce erroneous readings. Only by adopting a particular form of decoding effort, one that Freud himself also presented, but that has been relatively neglected, can one arrive at a decoding process that does true justice to the patient's intended though disguised communications.

Third and finally, the very first sentence of the preamble to the Irma dream introduces the final factor necessary for a comprehensive understanding of the psychotherapies—the basic conditions and ground rules of the therapeutic situation and relationship (i.e., the rules of procedure, interaction, and all else that provides a basic structure to the treatment interaction).

Freud's first words in the Preamble are surprising:

During the summer of 1895 I had been giving psycho-analytic treatment to a young lady who was on very friendly terms with me and my family. It will be readily understood that a mixed relationship such as this may be a source of many disturbed feelings in a physician and particularly in a psychotherapist. While the physician's personal interest is greater, his authority is less; any failure would bring a threat to the old-established friendship with the patient's family (Freud 1900, p. 106).

The manner in which Freud's unconscious genius could unknowingly connect seemingly separate topics that had important hidden and unrecognized links has already been shown. It is proposed here that among the many determinants of the Irma dream was Freud's great concern regarding the contaminating ground-rule factor that his patient, Irma (whose real name was Emma), was the personal friend of Freud and his family.

At the time of the dream, Freud was in a summer house at Bellevue, a suburb of Vienna. On the day prior to the dream, Freud's wife, who was pregnant, had told him she expected that a number of friends, including Irma, would be coming to visit them on her birthday, two or three days hence. The dream was dreamt in anticipation of that particular occurrence.

The situation was compounded by the fact that Freud had only been partially successful in treating Irma's symptoms. She had been relieved of her hysterical anxiety, but continued to suffer from somatic symptoms. Thus another stimulus for this dream of discovery was the failings of Freud's psychoanalytic techniques. This particular stimulus for the dream may well have been linked to the recent publication of *Studies on Hysteria*. The volume included the descriptions of patients whose responses to the treatment procedures developed by Breuer and then by Freud were distinctly mixed. At the time, Freud appears to have been aware of some of the omissions made by his colleague regarding the treatment of Anna O. There are suggestions too that the mixed results of his own first cathartic-analytic effort with Emmy von N. (note here the similarity between the code name Emmy and the real name Emma) may also have continued to concern him. The Irma dream contains a number of themes that are readily linked to Freud's case report on this patient.

There are many aspects to this landmark dream that will not be considered here (see Elms 1980). At the time, Freud appears to have been on relatively good terms with Breuer, though there had been a recent period of estrangement, and some measure of tension was undoubtedly present. Freud had become involved in a complex relationship with Wilhelm Fleiss, an ear, nose, and throat specialist who was involved in developing a series of complex ideas regarding nasal functions and sexuality. Fleiss soon became Freud's confidant and correspondent and, until the break-up of their relationship in the early 1900s, one of the most significant figures in Freud's life. The Irma dream dealt with Freud's intense ambivalence toward Fleiss, Freud's dawning doubts about his colleague, and his continued need to idiolize the one individual who seemed to best understand his labors and struggles.

As with almost everything connected with the origins of psychoanalysis, one can readily experience the conflicting concerns and forces with which Freud was dealing at the time of this dream. It is another tribute to his great genius that he dealt with these highly troublesome personal and professional problems by dreaming a dream whose analysis enabled him to descend once again into the realms of the Mothers, and to return with a new series of brilliant insights.

In a number of ways, the Irma dream is another critical point of origin for psychoanalysis and all insightful psychotherapies. Its richness defies full comprehension. Freud himself provided only a limited number of associations to the dream, and much is left for speculation. The dream was as follows:

A large hall—numerous guests, whom we were receiving.—Among them was Irma. I had once took her on one side, as though to answer her letter and to reproach her for not having accepted my "solution" yet. I said to her: "If you still get pains, it's really only your fault." She replied: "If you only knew what pains I've got now in my throat and stomach and abdomen—it's choking me"—I was alarmed and looked at her. She looked pale and puffy. I thought to myself that after all I must be missing some organic trouble. I took her to the window and looked down her throat, and she showed signs of recalcitrance, like women with artificial dentures. I thought to myself that there was really no need for her to do that.—She then opened her mouth properly and on the right I found a big white patch; at another place I saw extensive whitish grey scabs upon some remarkable curly structures which were evidently modelled on the turbinal bones of the nose.—I had once called in Dr. M., and he repeated the examination and confirmed it. . . . Dr. M. looked quite different from usual; he was very pale, he walked with a limp and his chin was clean-shaven. . . . My friend Otto was now standing beside her as well, and my friend Leopold was percussing her through her bodice and saying: "She has a dull area low down on the left." He also indicated that a portion of the skin on the left shoulder was infiltrated. (I noticed this, just as he did, in spite of her dress.) . . . M. said: "There's no doubt it's an infection, but no matter; dysentery will supervene and the toxin will be eliminated." . . . We were directly aware, too, of the origin of the infection. Not only before, when she was feeling unwell, my friend Otto had given her an injection of a preparation of propyl, propyls . . . proprionic acid . . . trimethylamin (and I saw before me the formula for this printed in heavy type). . . . Injections of that sort ought not to be made so thoughtlessly . . . And probably the syringe had not been clean (Freud 1900, p. 107).

Through his analysis of this dream, Freud discovered the four basic mechanisms through which a threatening raw fantasy, a latent dream thought, is subjected to an encoding process that produces the manifest dream. It is the operation of these mechanisms—condensation, displacement, symbolization, and concerns for surface representability—that constitutes the unique form of mentation or thinking that takes place outside of awareness and in sleep. It is these mechanisms that account for the peculiar qualities of a dream. They stand in contrast to our waking way of thinking, which is single-minded rather than a condensation of multiple images, direct rather than displaced, concrete and realistic rather than symbolic, and single-leveled rather than multi-leveled. In addition, Freud discovered that dreams were the fulfillment of unconscious and infantile wishes.

Before studying in detail these unconscious modes of expression, the Irma dream can be reviewed as a reflection of Freud's unconscious concern with his involvement with his patients in various forms of psychotherapeutic conspiracies. The first of these worries touch upon the conditions of treatment, the ground rules of psychotherapy. As already noted, this theme is prominent in the initial part of Freud's preface to the dream. Similarly, the dream itself begins in a large hall and at a social situation. Rather quickly, its setting is somewhat modified and the situation soon becomes quite professional. The dream itself centers around Irma's failure to get well and its causes, and Freud's evident struggle with his strong sense of guilt for not having produced a cure. This area will be examined in greater detail later on; it can be stated at this point that Freud apparently had an unconscious appreciation that the contaminants in his relationship with Irma were a factor in the unsuccessful outcome of her psychotherapy. In this regard, it appears that Freud not only had a social relationship with his patient but also spoke of her with several of his colleagues, including Josef Breuer, as well as with his wife. The dream itself represents several third parties to the treatment situation. This is an alteration in the basic one-to-one relationship that prevails in the ideal therapeutic situation.

The theme of therapeutic conspiracy is revealed in this landmark dream. By implication, the suggestion has already been made that one (newly identified) type of conspiracy involves the acceptance of a treatment relationship by patients and therapists alike under conditions of basic framework compromise. There quickly appears a more familiar type of collusion when Freud reproaches Irma for not having accepted the solution to her illness. The reproach is not unlike the one Freud directed at Frau Emmy von N. when he gave her the ultimatum to accept his view of her gastric pains as coming only from her fears rather than from the water or minerals that Freud had advised her to drink.

To this day, many therapists lack a dynamic conception of resistances within patients to their curative efforts. Even more unfortunate is the failure among virtually all therapists to recognize their own contributions to such resistances. They tend to treat such opposition as inappropriate, pathological, and as arising from the inner (intrapsychic) conflicts of their patients. The notion that such resistances may be quite appropriate and realistic in light of the therapist's treatment efforts has gained little credence as yet. This exists despite the impression that, much as in the situation in 1895 with Freud, the most superficial examination of the therapeutic techniques involved reveals clear indications of difficulties within the therapist.

More broadly, and of considerable general significance, is the realization that the Irma dream appears to reflect a monumental struggle within Freud regarding his functioning as a therapist and the nature of his treatment techniques. Freud's sense of guilt in this regard is more than evident, and it emerges with even greater intensity in his many associations to the dream. Among these, there is his need to vindicate his work as a physician under other circumstances and to reassure himself that his therapeutic ministrations are beyond reproach. These themes are also reflected in the manifest dream itself, which on the surface exculpates Freud from all blame for his patient's continued symptoms.

Freud's efforts at exoneration are not entirely successful. It is well established that every figure in a dream and every dream element are reflections of some aspect of the dreamer. On this level, then, the discovery that Irma's illness is iatrogenic (physician caused) is an encoded but final note of self-condemnation, one that hints symbolically at unconscious sexual factors (the syringe and injections). It may well be that, plagued with guilt and unable to resolve his doubts about his current psychoanalytic procedures, Freud found relief and resolution by turning his self-accusatory dream into a moment of brilliant discovery. Not unlike the ways in which patients benefit from traumatic and hurtful moments in psychotherapy, Freud reacted to the problems in his therapeutic work with remarkable inventiveness.

The seriousness and depth of Freud's concerns about the nature of his psychotherapeutic techniques (which he named "psychoanalytic" the year after the dream), emerges dramatically in Freud's further associations to the dream. In associating to the words "at once," Freud recalled an occasion when he produced a severe toxic state in a woman patient by prescribing what was then considered a harmless remedy, sulphonal. The patient eventually succumbed to the poison. Clearly, an accepted and well-meaning therapeutic technique had proven to be fatal.

The same theme is even more painfully developed in Freud's association to the white patch and turbinal bones with scabs on them, which he saw in Irma's throat. This led Freud to recall his own near-disastrous involvement with cocaine and the discovery of its anesthetic property (a drug, by the way, that Freud actively took for his nasal difficulties at the time of the dream). Freud's efforts to utilize the drug as a substitute for morphine in the belief that it was not addicting failed when it was discovered that the substance did indeed have addictive powers. Freud was seriously reproached, as he mentioned in his associations, and was accused of having created the third scourge of humanity, the other two being alcohol and morphine.

On a more personal note, Freud had prescribed the drug for his close friend and colleague, Fleischl von Marxow, who had been suffering from intractable pain caused by neuromas that had developed after an amputation. Here too, despite the hope that the cocaine would prove to be a nonaddictive substitute for morphine, the effort failed when von Marxow became addicted to the substance and made use of large dosage injections of the new drug. The addiction contributed to his death, and while there was room for rationalization and justification, Freud's sense of guilt was considerable.

Moreover, the contradiction within Freud's view of psychotherapy is striking. On a conscious level, and for good reason, he was in the process of developing what would soon be the technique of psychoanalysis. On the surface, he felt concern and yet confident and optimistic, seemingly convinced that the emerging therapeutic procedure would prove uniquely curative for neuroses. And yet, on another level, much of it quite unconscious—though revealed in this dream and Freud's associations to it—Freud deeply feared that in some way the psychoanalytic procedure was toxic and would prove fatal to its clients—and by Talion punishment, or through direct involvement, to its therapist as well.

This dread of destroying and being destroyed is a powerful motive for the psychotherapeutic conspiracy. An abiding fear of the unconscious mind of both patient and therapist alike is present. Here the problem arises partly because the therapeutic relationship is not defined with sufficient clarity, though the grave consequences of this particular contamination are not at all recognized consciously. Again, to this day, therapists engage in alterations of the ideal conditions for therapy of the kind reflected in the Irma dream and its associations, consciously believing there are no detrimental consequences. And yet, in their dreams and encoded fantasies, there is little doubt that present-day therapists also entertain doubts, regrets, and guilt not unlike those with which Freud struggled in July of 1895. One can only hope that some of these therapists will find solutions every bit as creative as the one to which Freud turned on that occasion.

In light of this analysis, the Irma dream is in certain ways remarkably similar to the two dreams of the paradigmatic psychoanalyst described in Chapter 3. There too a fierce investment in a manifest technique and a latent (unconscious and encoded) realization and dread of its destructive powers were evident. The resolution through psychotherapeutic conspiracy can be understood in better perspective when it is recognized that the issues involved are indeed experienced as matters of life and death.

Freud stands here on what seems to be experienced as a precipice, though in actuality it was a gradual entry into the world of psychoanalysis. In this light, the Irma dream reveals the deep and abiding concerns within therapists regarding the consequences to those who dare to probe and master the unconscious mind, patients and therapists alike. Faced with anxieties as grave as these, an enormous number of psychotherapists back off and invent self-protective alternatives.

The impression that the Irma dream concerns itself with the origins of psychoanalysis is strongly supported by its occurrence within two months of the publication of *Studies on Hysteria*. Freud had indeed invited numerous guests into the chamber of insight psychotherapy. Clearly, he dreaded what they would discover; he feared that his invention was laced with psychopathology (cf. the patches and scabs discovered upon investigating Irma's oral cavity, as well as the dull area low down on the left and the infiltration of the left shoulder). The Doctor M. in the dream is known to have been Josef Breuer, coauthor of *Studies on Hysteria*, and on the night of the dream, Freud had written notes on the Irma case for Breuer to review. Otto is known to have been Oscar Rie, a pediatrician with whom Freud coauthored a volume on paralyses in children. All of this stands in strong support of the thesis that the Irma dream is not only a dream through which Freud discovered the secrets of unconscious communication, but also an intense effort to work out deep and abiding conflicts regarding the psychoanalytic procedure.

In this connection, Irma's recalcitrance as if she were a woman with artificial dentures proves to be an interesting detail of the dream. Freud associated this element with an examination of a governness who appeared youthful and beautiful and yet had taken measures to conceal her dental plates. This led to recollections of other medical examinations and of the secrets that they revealed. In this connection, Freud's thought in the dream that there was no need for her to do that reminded him of a friend of Irma of whom Freud had a very high opinion. She suffered from hysterical choking, as did Irma, and Freud had often fantasied that she might come to him to ask him to relieve her of her symptoms. Freud knew this was unlikely since the woman was quite reserved and recalcitrant; nor was there a need for her to do so since she appeared to be strong enough to master her condition without outside help.

This particular element, then, touches upon the theme of exposing secrets through medical examinations, a theme that runs like a thread through much of the dream. For example, Freud's physician friend Leopold percusses Irma through her bodice; psychoanalysis is indeed a probing and exploration carried out with the patient fully dressed. Here too the idea is to the effect that digging for secrets can be dangerous, and perhaps they are best left alone. Freud's own conflict in this regard, his questions and doubts about using the psychoanalytic procedure, are reflected not only in his thoughts of a patient who would not enter treatment with him, but also in other associations to a young man with hysterical bowel symptoms for whom Freud recommended a trip rather than psychoanalysis. On the voyage, the patient's symptoms were aggravated, and Freud felt a new sense of guilt. Perhaps the message here is that the dangerous images connected with the psychoanalytic procedure need to be analyzed and understood, rather than forming the basis for flight and avoidance. Turning away from the pursuit of insight only makes matters worse after all.

Freud himself did not associate to the evident themes of artificiality, falseness, and secrets. It may well be that he was dealing here with issues of lies and deception. It appears likely, as already noted, that Freud was aware of the omissions made by his colleague Breuer in his report of Anna O. in *Studies on Hysteria*. One may sincerely wonder whether Freud himself was involved in similar kinds of omissions and distortions in his eagerness to advocate the cathartic method. In Freud's report of the case of Emmy von N., he recorded the use of a white lie to his patient in an effort to allay her anxieties regarding her revelations to him about his colleague Breuer. It is to Freud's credit that he repudiated the actual use of concealment, and dreamt of its use as unnecessary.

On a broader level, one may wonder whether Freud was not also concerned, quite unconsciously, with that aspect of the psychoanalytic conspiracy that involves the analyst's use of protective deceptions. In this connection, while Freud did not associate to the theme of transference, it is possible to show a strong connection between Freud's use of transference as a means of personal defense and his repudiation of responsibility for Irma's illness. The rejoinder in and of itself reveals his contribution to the patient's sickness: thus, while on one level Freud denied having caused Irma's illness, and claimed that he could not be held accountable for his failure to cure her, on another level the illness was traced to an erroneous toxic medical procedure. In like vein, as already seen, Freud used the concept of transference to hold the patient accountable for his or her sickness and as a way of repudiating responsibility for therapeutic failure through the concept of transference resistance (obstacles within the patient that arise in connection with his or her relationship with the physician, but that are based on earlier relationships).

Remarkably, then, the Irma dream suggests that, despite Freud's firm and persistent use of the concept of transference, he himself entertained grave doubts on some unconscious level regarding the extent to which the patient alone was responsible for the continua-

tion of his or her illness in the course of an analysis. This suggests
again that psychotherapists are deeply divided regarding their participation in psychotherapeutic forms of collusion, often doing so
manifestly while filled with latent doubts. It will be possible later
on to show that patients are typically similarly divided, a state of
affairs that is more easy to demonstrate since it is possible to have
the full associations of the patient available for analysis.

The Irma dream is replete with mechanisms used to this day by
therapists to exonerate themselves from responsibility for their
patients' failures to get well. There is the common reproach of
patients who fail on the surface to accept their therapist's interventions or solutions. There is often the direct and angry blaming
of the patient for not improving. Irma's response in the dream, in
which she implored Freud that her suffering was beyond his understanding, is a common *unconscious* (encoded) though rarely direct
reaction in patients and even in therapists as well. It implies that
the problem lies not so much for the moment in the patient's
stubbornness and psychopathology, but in the therapist's lack of
knowledge (not knowing). It is this type of unconscious communicative message, however, that present-day therapists do not allow
to register consciously. It is striking to see that within this dream,
and on some unconscious level, Freud himself appears to have
been deeply concerned with the consequences of areas in which he
lacked understanding. While he was not able to state this failing
directly, it is readily detectable in the latent dream.

Another cop-out used by patients and therapists alike is to
attribute essentially emotional disorders to some organic trouble.
Much as Freud in the dream, therapists who are incapable of
understanding unconscious factors in emotional disorders often
press for the discovery of an organic basis for their patient's
difficulties, and regardless of the findings, will make extensive use
of medication and other physical therapeutic methods. It appears
that in this dream, quite unconsciously, Freud was comparing the
psychoanalytic method (which he himself feared greatly, partly
because of his own misunderstandings and pathological fantasies)
with alternative methods of uninsightful cure. Strikingly, these
other approaches exist today as they did then. It is a tribute to
Freud's courage and wisdom that he himself did not succumb to
their deceptive attraction.

Freud's use of the assistance of other physicians is not unlike certain forms of group and family therapy that make use of multiple therapists. The dream suggests that this practice derives in part from the failings of a single therapist to understand and manage the patient's complaints. Further, the colleagues are called in to support the primary therapist's disavowal of blame for the continuation of the patient's illness and to strenghthen the defenses of the original therapist. In light of the sexual implications of the treatment procedure that emerge toward the end of the dream, the presence of others in the treatment space may well serve also as a protection against a loss of control by the participants to a one-to-one therapy. Such again are the motives of therapeutic conspiracy.

As already noted, psychotherapy began with an almost total denial of an interaction between the patient and therapist. With the invocation of transference, Freud acknowledged the unilateral involvement of the patient. The physician or therapist was merely the observer and the interpreter. In keeping with usual medical thinking, there was no concern about the mental health of the healer. His or her job was to advise and understand, a seemingly simple enough effort.

These are, of course, familiar attitudes. Little effort is made even today to diagnose and screen out therapists whose emotional difficulties might seriously interfere with their therapeutic work. The subject itself is quite complicated, since quite often, with some effort at personal therapy, emotionally disturbed but gifted therapists can contribute more to their patients and to the field than those who are far less ill.

At issue for the moment is Freud's initial failure to recognize that the psychotherapeutic relationship is a deeply emotional interaction that is inevitably influenced by the emotional condition of the therapist. And while it is known today that disturbed reactions in therapists (countertransferences) can be used to understand the patient, the potentially serious consequences and limitations that this type of disorder might have on the course of therapy for a patient was not as yet recognized at the time of the Irma dream. It was as late as 1910 that Freud coined the term countertransference and indicated his belief that no analysis could go further than the limitations imposed by its presence in a psychoanalyst. Freud himself never wrote a major paper on this subject, and it was not until 1950 that other psychoanalysts began to investigate the topic in earnest. The discovery of countertransference some 20 years after the discovery of transference is an indication of a trend that persists until the present: the therapist concentrates on the pathology of the patient partly as an effort to deny his or her own emotional problems.

The Irma dream can be understood to reflect an *unconscious* struggle within Freud regarding his countertransferences in his relationship with this patient. Here again one can develop a formulation that encourages one to make use of the unconscious sensitivities of psychotherapists when confronted with their overt failings. It may well be that consistent self-analysis and analysis of therapists will prove to be the only effective means of resolving major aspects of the psychotherapeutic conspiracy.

The most important clue to Freud's concern about his own psychopathology (countertransferences) appears in his association to that part of the dream where Leopold indicated that a portion of the skin of the left shoulder was infiltrated. Freud was able to notice this in spite of the patient's dress, implying that he already had some special knowledge of this lesion. In his association to this element, he stated that he had immediately realized that the infiltration was the rheumatism in his own shoulder, which he invariably noticed if he sat up late into the night. Freud also clarified that his comment about noticing this infiltration was meant to indicate that he had noticed it on his own body in the dream.

Clearly, then, Freud was indicating through these dream images that both he and Irma, therapist and patient alike, shared some type of pathological problem. In the presence of active countertransference, the patient and therapist are indeed quite similar: both are emotionally ill and suffering, and the important distinction and gradient, which exists when the therapist is healthier than the patient, is lost. Through countertransference, patient and therapist share an emotional disturbance rather than resolving it. In conspiracy this type of sharing can often be quite reassuring for patients. They will usually detect these shared difficulties unconsciously and respond in turn with encoded messages of their own.

It may well be, then, that in his search to understand the sources of Irma's failure to get well, Freud touched upon a number of factors that had indeed contributed to the therapeutic failure. Each involved a type of conspiracy between patient and therapist, and each seems to have been recognized only unconsciously by Freud, who expressed these realizations through his encoded dream. In his own analysis of the dream, Freud simply stressed his wish to exonerate himself for the therapeutic failure with Irma, either by blaming an organic illness or the failings of a colleague. By blaming both Dr. M. (Breuer) and Otto (Oscar Rie), Freud also took revenge on two of his critics. (Otto in particular had helped to trigger this dream by critically reporting to Freud that he had seen Irma and that she was not doing very well.)

The deeper and unconscious (encoded) wisdom contained in this dream reflects that Freud was in the process of creating psychoanalysis and was fully cognizant of its highly dangerous qualities for both patient and therapist alike. The therapeutic procedure was by no means fully developed and was replete with flaws. Freud began his preamble of the dream itself with the first of these, the contaminations that arose because of his mixed relationship with Irma, both personal and professional.

In the reproach to Irma for not having accepted his solution, Freud touched upon another flaw, which took the form of his noninterpretive interventions and his efforts to pressure his patients to get well. This commonly practiced pressure technique often fails to produce sound therapeutic results.

Next, there is the theme of "If you only knew," which touches upon the lacunae in Freud's understanding of his patient's neuroses and of the therapeutic interaction itself. This theme is reinforced in Freud's allusion to missing some organic trouble; indeed, a great deal was being missed, though much of it was in the unconscious communicative interaction between himself and his patient.

The artificial dentures may be taken to allude to the defensive and lie-barrier qualities of the psychoanalytic technique, including the false use of the concept of transference to blame the patient for her own pathology, and for whatever was awry in the psychoanalytic treatment situation. This theme was announced earlier in the dream when Freud blamed his patient for continuing to be ill.

The discovery of lesions on various parts of Irma's body may be taken at this level as Freud's unconscious efforts to identify his own countertransferences and their influence. In this connection, the allusion to Irma's nose conjures up another situation in which a well-meaning medical procedure nearly proved fatal. As stated earlier, Freud had referred Irma to his close friend and colleague

from Berlin, Wilhelm Fleiss. Fleiss had performed surgery on Irma
and inadvertently left behind a piece of iodoform gauze. Subsequently, another consultant discovered and removed this gauze in
the presence of Freud, who nearly fainted at the sight of the purulent
and bloody exudent, which was made even more terrible by the
horrible odor that was also present. Here too the theme of iatrogenic
pathology in the patient, a sickness caused by a well-meaning
physician and therapy, found vivid expression. How deeply Freud
worried about the psychoanalytic procedure is more than evident.
These are, as noted, the very fears that unfortunately move many
similarly frightened therapists away from the insight approach.

The theme of the therapist-caused illness received its final representation in the discovery that Irma's sickness was caused by a
thoughtless injection and an unclean syringe. It is here that some of
the unconscious central meanings of psychoanalytic investigation
and penetration for both patient and therapist (for the moment, the
latter in particular) find expression. It is unconscious meanings of
this kind, misunderstood and not mastered, that also cause guilt
and anxiety in many therapists who shy away from (and even use)
the psychoanalytic method. At this point in the dream, through an
encoded perception, Freud indicated that Irma's continued sickness was indeed the product of his own countertransferences. It is
extremely difficult for a therapist who unwittingly makes use of a
well-meaning but hurtful technique to acknowledge and bear the
responsibility for the error of his or her ways. Instead, through
conspiracy, most therapists deny their role in the continuation of
the patient's illness and create techniques and theories that will
support this denial.

Finally, there is the striking mode of ultimate cure represented in
the dream. "Dysentery will supervene and the toxin will be eliminated." Freud appears to have been quite discouraged regarding
the use of interpretations as a means of resolving neurosis. As a
result, he took recourse first to the use of an injection and thereby
to cure through medication. In addition, there would be a cure
through evacuation. The patient herself, having been made ill by
the physician, would find a means of ridding herself of the toxin.

Here, of course, is the model for many present-day psychotherapeutic techniques that involve cure through not only encouraging
patients to abreact and to get rid of the sick stuff inside of themselves, dumping it into whomever may be around; but also, a cure

in which the therapist himself or herself dumps his or her own inner toxic psychological stuff into the patient. This type of almost bizarre curative procedure aptly characterizes many forms of present-day psychotherapy. The suggestion here is that it is accepted by patients because it affords them an opportunity to become a channel through which the toxic sickness of both their therapists and themselves can be eliminated.

The Irma dream contains several messages regarding the nature of psychopathology. The problems lie in hidden lesions, concealed secrets that patients are loathe to reveal. They involve highly charged sexual wishes, which are experienced as poisonous and must be eliminated. Then too emotional illness stems from the well-meaning ministrations of others, the psychotherapist in particular, who inadvertently harm and disturb the patient whose own illness is thereby reinforced and extended. It derives too from relationships that lack clear definition and boundaries, contaminated in ways that disturb rather than heal.

The Irma dream of Freud is perhaps the most important dream ever dreamt by a psychoanalyst or psychotherapist. It occurred at a momentous point in Freud's career, when he was on the verge of enormous understanding and of developing an important and new psychotherapeutic technique. It was a time of great personal conflict and concern (Martha was pregnant with their sixth child, Anna). It lent itself to several formulations by Freud, and was the avenue to major analytic and personal insights. Later writers have developed at least ten major interpretations of this incredible dream. Its use here in order to illuminate the theme of therapeutic conspiracy adds but one more dimension to this multi-faceted gem.

As for the origins of psychoanalysis, the Irma dream sheds considerable light on the deep struggles within Sigmund Freud as he developed his technical procedures. The sources of many psychotherapeutic conspiracies, then and now, are thereby illuminated. The dream reveals a strong sense of the split in many psychotherapists: plunging onward with one or another therapeutic technique while filled unconsciously with not only doubts and guilt, but also with the untapped wisdom to revise their ways.

The Irma dream ends on a most moving and telling note: "Injections of that sort ought not to be made so thoughtlessly . . . " This is Freud's unconscious commentary on countertransference-dominated psychotherapies and on all psychotherapeutic conspiracies: they are the product of the carelessness of the physician or therapist and ought not be used. Unable to draw upon his own unconscious wisdom in certain important areas, Freud failed to apply this message to his own countertransferences and to his false use of the concept of transference.

How many therapists since Freud have communicated similar messages to themselves and yet failed to see the wisdom of their own unconscious insights? One of the reasons for the chaos in the field of psychotherapy today, and for much emotional suffering, is the inability of patients and therapists alike to make conscious and direct use of their own unconscious wisdom. It requires an inordinate amount of tolerance and understanding to make this critical transition. The pain involved is great, but then so are the rewards.

CHAPTER 16

UNCONSCIOUS THINKING

It has been established that psychoanalysis and psychotherapy were born out of conflict and were the cause of considerable inner struggle in those who shaped their destinies. *Studies on Hysteria* initiated a century of efforts to define the nature of emotional disorders. *The Interpretation of Dreams* stands as the origin of serious efforts to comprehend the language of emotional illness, and the nature of neurotic communication.

Without exception, every form of uninsightful therapy now in existence is based on therapeutic efforts that entirely ignore the distinction between neurotic and nonneurotic communication. Even psychoanalysis itself stands confused on this issue. Almost all therapeutic work in existence is founded on an understanding of a patient's manifest (surface) communications, what are termed manifest contents. Quite rarely, and only in selected psychoanalytic and psychotherapeutic instances, will a therapist make an effort to arrive at the nature of encoded messages hidden and contained within these manifest elements. Then too, with few exceptions, these hidden messages are formulated as the imaginary products (fantasies) of the patient, with no attention to the influence of the ongoing therapeutic interaction and unconscious perceptions.

Through *The Interpretation of Dreams* and later writings, Freud offered a distinctly mixed heritage to psychoanalysts and psychotherapists. With true brilliance, he was able to detect and clearly demonstrate the presence of hidden meanings in his own dreams as well as in those of his patients. He was able to integrate these impressions with a study of his patients' productions in treatment, their free associations. There too, he was able to show the existence of hidden messages and their bearing on the understanding of neuroses.

The discovery of hidden meanings in dreams and other messages is, of course, hardly original. In the Bible, Joseph is able to decipher the Pharoah's dream and is richly rewarded. Symbolic and other forms of rote decoding had long been in existence before Freud. Freud himself was quite interested in this type of dream decoding, and actually made use of it with his own dreams and the dreams of others.

The Interpretation of Dreams includes many important insights. Most relevant for this discussion is Freud's realization that the highly specific and personal, but concealed implications contained within manifest dreams could be revealed by the dreamer's associations to the dream elements. The use of free association as a means of arriving at the hidden (latent) contents of dreams was ingenious.

On the basis of his self-analysis of the Irma dream, supplemented by a study of many other dream-associational networks, Freud was also able to define the fundamental psychic mechanisms through which a dream is constructed. His findings hold well to this very day. Freud was quick to sense that the kind of mentation or thinking reflected in a dream was distinctly different from our usual, waking mode of thought. He also realized that this very same kind of thinking, which he termed *primary process thinking*, took place in many waking psychotic individuals and in the unconcious thinking of normal persons (i.e., their thinking outside of direct awareness). It is this same mode of thinking that also accounts for emotional disturbances.

The discovery that we are capable of two distinct ways of thinking, according to primary and secondary processes (the latter is realistic, discrete, and logical), emerged from Freud's analysis of the Irma dream. Faced with many strange messages, Freud permitted himself to free associate. He made use of the totality of his own communications (the dream and his associations to it) in order to identify a series of underlying dream thoughts or raw messages.

It was these threatening images that had been subjected to the encoding process in order to produce the manifest dream. It was the use of these encoding or primary process mechanisms that accounted for the unusual qualities of the dream experience.

With a brilliant leap of insight, Freud recognized that it was this same type of thinking that not only accounted for an emotional symptom, but also constituted the means by which patients communicated to their therapists about the underlying nature of their illnesses. Unable to state the cause of their symptoms directly (since these factors were outside of awareness—i.e., unconscious), patients quite automatically found a means of doing so through encoded messages. It was only through decoding messages of this kind that one could understand the basis of an emotional disturbance.

For example, suppose a patient has a fear of walking in the street. She has never had an accident or any untoward incident while doing so. If this latter were the case, her fear would be logical and understandable. Lacking such cause, her fear is evidently irrational and must derive from some inner source within her own thinking.

If asked to free associate about the fear (to considerably oversimplify), suppose the patient thinks of a woman friend who has too much freedom. Once, the friend was roaming in a field and was accosted by a man who raped her. In light of this association, one could suppose that the street unconsciously stands for the field—i.e., through displacement, one situation has been substituted for another. The danger in the field is one of rape, so one could then suggest that the patient either fears being raped in the street or wishes that such an event would happen. To protect herself from her fears and/or wishes, she avoids going out.

There is no logical reason to fear being raped in the street. Nor is it logical to expect that such a wish, even if present, would be gratified simply by going outside. There would be a small measure of (secondary process) logic if the patient feared going into a field by herself. Because of her friend's experience, this fear would have some measure of sensibility and could be readily fathomed. Then one would not immediately consider the patient's sense of caution a symptom of an emotional disorder.

Because of the use of displacement, and because the street has now symbolically become a place of rape, however, the patient's fear of going outside has an inner meaning that defies conscious logic. In conscious thinking, a fear of a field remains a fear of a field; it does not become a fear of walking in the street. In unconscious thinking, such displacements readily occur. As a result, the patient's fear appears to be logically unfounded, though its unconscious meaning can be identified. Because of the lack of surface logic, however, the fear of walking in the street is, by definition, an emotional symptom.

To take the matter a bit further, it is indeed possible to alleviate (remove) the symptom by showing the patient the unconscious meaning that the street has acquired for her. A therapist would hope also to analyze the genetic and dynamic sources of the patient's fears and wishes to be raped in order to provide the patient with a full sense of insight. Once the displacement and the unconscious wishes can be understood, the patient can resolve the problem intrapsychically and come to terms with her fantasies and impulses. At that juncture, the symptom would disappear, since the symbolic meaning of the street would be given up, and the defensive avoidance would no longer be necessary.

But notice too that the patient's symptoms could also be "cured" if she became a nun and she was required to remain within the nunnery. It could be cured too through deconditioning, by having her make repeated visits onto the street until she would be desensitized to the point where her anxiety would disappear. If the symptom was an isolated one, there would be little concern that its underlying meanings had not been understood and resolved. Through another approach a therapist might help her to acknowledge the irrationality of her fear and simply give it up. With sufficient pressure, this might actually occur. Still another therapist might goad or try to force the patient into surrendering her illness.

With the exception of the psychotherapist who would seek to understand the unconscious basis of the patient's symptom, and who would include a conceptualization of its mobilization and continuation in light of the ongoing therapeutic interaction, each of these therapists could offer this patient the hope of cure without full and true insight. They would do so by fracturing her defenses or by offering her fictions and lie-barrier systems designed to seal off and better defend against the underlying fantasies and anxieties. In each instance, then, there would be a psychotherapeutic conspiracy designed to avoid the truth of the patient's emotional illness, especially once it came into play with the therapist's own inputs into the situation.

To briefly illustrate this last point, suppose the therapist adopted an extremely forceful, attacking, and challenging technique with the patient. The patient's fear of the street might then intensify, and she would require a companion not only on the street but in the waiting room of the therapist's office. She would soon become fearful of coming to her sessions. The therapist would see nothing logical in these fears and angrily try to persuade the patient to give them up. With some material, he would manage to interpret the patient's wish to be raped and attempt to hold this fantasy accountable for the patient's illness.

It can be readily seen that the therapist on some unconscious level would actually be engaged in a mental rape of this patient. As long as he does not recognize this quality of his technique and continues its practice, the patient will have an unconscious reason to intensify her symptoms. They have now found an important source in the actualities of the therapeutic interaction. Once this occurs, true cure could only take place if the therapist corrected his ways and properly interpreted the basis of the patient's present anxieties.

Throughout this type of therapy, the patient would find encoded ways of communicating to her therapist her raw perceptions and fantasies of these interventions and their unconscious implications. She might, for example, dream of a man with a moustache (like the one sported by the therapist) who was drilling a hole through the wall of a house. If the patient had been using secondary-process logical thinking, she would have simply said to the therapist that she felt that his interventions were an attempt to penetrate her. However, because she was making use of primary process mechanisms, the patient symbolizes her own self through dreaming of a house and the therapist's attacking interventions through the drilling procedure. When an image stands not so much for itself but for something else, it embodies the kind of thinking on which dreams are founded and which account for symptoms.

To emphasize this point, then, the concept of neurosis or emotional disturbance is invoked only when a particular behavior or experience is not in keeping with logic and reality. Similarly, when one feels anxious at a party or in a crowd, one's anxiety has no logical and rational basis. Yet there is some hidden or unconscious reason for this anxiety. It was Freud who discovered that such symptoms are based on unconscious forms of thinking and unconscious images. For Freud, these images were in the form of fantasies and memories, while today some therapists rightly propose that, in addition, frightening perceptions of others may also be experienced quite unconsciously and expressed in encoded fashion.

Anxiety, conflict, a sense of danger, and other disturbing affects prompt individuals to cover over or repress their (raw) conscious fantasies and perceptions. Repression brings relief and may at times be quite successful. When it fails to handle the inner problems and the relationship conflicts with which a person is struggling, a compromise may be effected. With the use of unconscious communicative mechanisms, a symptom will appear that expresses the forbidden impulse or perception, as well as the patient's defenses against its realization. In this light, an emotional symptom is seen as a form of communication based on primary process mechanisms, rather than on logical reality-oriented thought (secondary processes).

Freud also recognized that virtually everything of any importance that is related to a neurosis is experienced or expressed in a form greatly influenced by primary process mechanisms. This mode of thinking and experiencing, which takes place outside of awareness, follows rather different laws or rules than does logical conscious thinking. This particular mode of expression accounts not only for the nature of a patient's emotional disturbance, but also serves as the only basis through which one can understand the unconscious aspects of the interaction between a patient and therapist. A great deal that is emotionally meaningful takes place on an unconscious level. Of course, there may be surface sources of disturbance, but once an individual reacts in a neurotic manner, the *explanation* for his or her behavior must be couched in primary process terms.

We are so accustomed to secondary process thinking that we hardly pay any attention to it. It is so much a part of ourselves that we are also generally unaware that there is another way in which our minds work. Secondary process thinking is (hopefully) reflected in the sentences and paragraphs of this book. The author states directly what he means, and his words convey just that and little else. In our daily lives, as we work and learn, relate socially, solve problems, and do so much more, we make use of logical reasoning and thinking. If we want to build a shelf in a closet, the shelf is indeed a place on which to rest objects and the closet is a place within which to contain them. If we shift to the other mode of thinking, the shelf might become a penis and the closet a vagina. Still, in our waking thinking, out of utter adaptive necessity, we are usually quite straightforward and direct. As Freud is said to have put it, there are times when a cigar is nothing more than a good smoke.

Logical thinking of this kind does not, as already emphasized, account for emotional disorders. If we are accosted by someone with a gun, we react with fear and out of an entirely sensible dread. There are many realistic causes for anxiety and emotional disturbance. As long as our responses are in keeping with these stimuli, we are not dealing with an emotional disorder. It is only when our responses are not in keeping with reality (though they are, of course, in keeping with some inner mental reality—fantasy or perception) that we think of emotional disorder. Even when an emotional disturbance derives from our relationships with others, it does so through unconscious perceptions rather than those that are conscious. Consciously perceived hostility can be dealt with in straightforward fashion. Unconsciously communicated and unconsciously perceived hostility deprives us of this option, and often becomes the soil for inappropriate reactions and neurosis.

Thus a patient may perceive unconscious hostility in his mother, dare not register it consciously, and become inappropriately fearful of a teacher who is on the surface quite kind. Through displacement, his conflict with his mother is displaced onto his relationship with the teacher. While self-protective, it is this kind of displacement that is critical to both primary process thinking and to the development of an emotional disorder. As long as we are aware of a problem, react to it directly, and understand its impact upon us, it is unlikely that we will become emotionally ill. It is only when issues and conflicts unfold outside of our awareness and are subjected to the primary process mechanisms, that emotional disturbance unfolds.

Through his analysis of the Irma dream, Freud discovered the characteristics of this peculiar form of primary process thinking. He noticed that there was a distinct disregard for reality, a tolerance for contradictions, and an ease through which one image stood for and represented another. Freud identified four basic

mechanisms involved in this type of thinking. Through their application, a threatening *raw perception or fantasy* is encoded into a
conscious day dream or night dream. A decoding process would, of
course, require the undoing of the changes and disguises produced
by these mechanisms.

The primary process mechanisms are those of (1) *condensation*,
the bringing together of two or more images in a single thought or
image so that a particular dream or fantasy element actually
stands for several other underlying elements; (2) *displacement*,
through which there is a shift from one scene to another or from
one person to another; (3) *symbolization*, through which one image
stands for and represents in some meaningful fashion another
image; and (4) *secondary revision* and *concern for matters of
representability*, through which the human mind produces a surface or manifest message that is essentially logical and meaningful
in its own right, while it simultaneously contains in encoded form
an essentially illogical or unconscious message of notable importance.

The Irma dream illustrates each of these mechanisms. Were
Irma's entrance into the large hall an actuality, one would be dealing with a single image with a clearly defined meaning: Irma was
entering a room as the guest of Freud and his wife at Martha's
birthday celebration. Freud and Martha would react to Irma almost
entirely in these terms and not as a symbol or stand-in for someone
else. If, on the other hand, Freud suddenly became angry with Irma
because of an unconscious sense of anger he felt toward his own
mother, his response would be inappropriate to the realities of the
situation and therefore neurotic. Irma would have then been treated
in waking life as a figure *displaced* from Freud's mother and as a
symbolic stand-in for this woman. When an individual reacts in
terms of primary process mechanisms in his or her daily life, he or
she is considered neurotic because the responses are strange and
discordant with consensually validated reality.

It is therefore safe, innovative, and adaptive to use such mechanisms while asleep, though the individual has little choice but to do
so. It appears that the human mind shifts to primary process
functioning at such times, much as it will under intense emotional
stress and, at times, when a patient is in a psychotherapeutic
situation. With primary process mechanisms at work in Freud's

dream, the arrival of Irma actually represented and condensed the appearance of several different women. Freud *condensed* physical-emotional images of each of them into the single image of Irma. One is able to recognize this process of condensation because, in Freud's associations to the dream, he conjures up a number of figures: the close woman friend of Irma, the woman patient of Freud who died of drug toxicity, Freud's daughter Mathilde who had the same name as this woman patient, and Freud's own wife. Thus a single individual, who stands for herself alone in waking thought and experience, is used in a dream to represent a number of different persons, including Freud himself (the principle that each figure in a dream at the very least represents that person and the dreamer himself or herself is well established).

The operation of condensation may be detected through Freud's free associations, which touch upon each of these other figures. Further, each of these individuals conjures up a diverse set of memories and meanings. Thus, by means of condensation, not only are a number of figures portrayed through one image, but also a panorama of intricate meanings is compacted into a single dream element. This means, of course, that while secondary process thinking is realistic, it is quite constricted in its potential; in contrast, primary process mentation is a form of thinking in which an enormous amount of information (memories, fantasies, perceptions, adaptive responses, etcetera) can be tightly packed into a single brief image.

It is the magnificent gift of the human mind to be capable of functioning with primary or secondary processes according to the nature of the situation and the conditions of the mind itself. Remarkably, when realistic responses are absolutely vital for adaptation and even survival, the mind usually functions in keeping with secondary process mechanisms in a very direct and responsive fashion. When the problem is one of an emotional trauma, and multiple meanings are aroused and must be dealt with, the mind shifts to primary process functioning.

The human mind, then, is capable of both single-minded and multiple-meaning messages, and is able to shift from one mode of communication to another depending on a variety of conditions. Here it is essential to understand both modes of thinking, and especially the primary-process mode, because this is the particular form and mode of communication through which patients express themselves in regard to what is really happening in a psychotherapeutic experience.

Until now, most efforts at understanding the patient's perceptions of the therapeutic interaction have been restricted to secondary process thinking and to his or her linear (direct and manifest) statements. This level of expression proves highly inaccurate and uninformative in regard to the nature of the therapeutic experience, while encoded communication (a synonym for primary process expression) proves to be rich in both meaning and perceptiveness. One's concept of the nature of the treatment process changes dramatically when attention is paid to these encoded messages, and as a result, one's conception of the best mode of treatment for a patient is also influenced by this kind of understanding.

The use of the mechanism of *displacement* is also in evidence. To the extent that Freud was working over perceptions, feelings, and fantasies related to these other figures, displacement was used in representing them through Irma. For example, Freud's concerns about his wife's pregnancy were displaced onto Irma. The clue to the presence of this displacement is the image of Irma as looking pale and puffy, an association undoubtedly related to Martha's state of pregnancy—a point supported by Freud's own association. Thus, rather than dreaming directly about his conflicts regarding his wife's pregnancy, Freud through displacement dreamed about Irma. He thereby shifted his concerns regarding one relationship onto a relationship with someone else. The same principle can be applied to all of the other figures Freud had in his mind regarding whom he displaced his thoughts onto Irma.

Almost inherently, the human mind, when under stress and the influence of anxiety, is hard put to work over a troublesome problem quite directly. By displacing the issue onto a different relationship or situation, the individual is freed from a sense of immediate threat and danger and develops a space for the safer displaced and encoded working over of the anxieties and conflicts involved. Displacement proves to be a highly effective and universal defense, though its overuse can, as has already been seen, actually lead to neurosis. Once again, the very mental mechanisms that protect sanity can also lead to mental problems.

Symbolic representation, or *symbolism*, is the third primary process mechanism. Not only are persons and situations displaced from one to another, but they are also used to represent or portray qualities that exist in others. In addition, events and objects with particular shapes and implications are utilized to represent meaningful hidden (repressed) events and objects that are too threatening to experience or allude to directly. In symbolism, one thing meaningfully represents another.

For example, in the Irma dream, the unclean injection given to Irma represented (i.e., stood for or symbolized) Freud's use of a seemingly harmless drug, sulphonal, in a manner that produced a severe toxic state in a woman patient. The allusion to trimethylamin stood for, or symbolized, the chemistry of sexual processes. The syringe may well have had a phallic meaning, just as Irma's mouth and throat suggested the vaginal orifice. In each instance, a relatively innocuous object or anatomical part was used to represent and symbolize a more threatening anatomical part, incident, person, subject, or whatever. Here too the defensive protection and adaptive value is self-evident.

Through condensation, displacement, and symbolism, an individual is able to work over and adapt to extremely charged and threatening perceptions and fantasies that would otherwise overwhelm him or her if experienced directly. Thus these mechanisms involve not only a special and encoded form of communication within onself and with others, but also a form of rather primitive but highly adaptive means of thinking that permits the constructive working over and resolution of highly charged emotional problems.

Freud also showed that unconscious thinking is shaped by *concerns of representability*. Dream thinking occurs through a sequence of images that involve, as a rule, a particular narrative. It is therefore necessary for the three mechanisms involved in transforming a raw dream thought into a dream image to do so in a manner that proves to be mindful of the story of the manifest dream. Similarly, free associations involve ideas and images that touch upon such matters as current events, early memories, and the like. To the extent that free associations are formed through the use of primary process mechanisms, the mind of the individual must unconsciously select surface associations that readily represent the underlying messages which are under the influence of the primary process mechanisms. This is a truly remarkable accomplishment, though virtually every one is capable of achieving it under the proper conditions.

For example, Freud was dealing with a number of raw thoughts and fantasies about sexuality and its role in neuroses. He required a dream image that could be part of the narrative of the dream and yet represent these underlying thoughts and concerns. He accomplished this by alluding to the injection that Irma had received and through the image of trimethylamin, whose formula appeared visually before his eyes. This particular chemical formula condensed Freud's unconscious concerns regarding the latent sexual qualities of the psychoanalytic process with other worries about doing harm to his patients, concerns that Freud was working over regarding Irma's psychotherapy that were displaced onto worries about injections and chemicals. A sexual symbol was employed to represent an underlying sexual fantasy. The entire effort took place unconsciously and automatically in the course of the dream. It is indeed a staggering accomplishment of the human mind, though Freud's ability to (consciously) detect the operation of these critical mechanisms was an even greater achievement.

Freud's discovery that the dreamer or communicator has a need to appear and experience himself or herself as rational relates to concerns of representability. This leads to what Freud called a *secondary revision* of these loose and seemingly illogical images and representations. Through this revision, the patient's dream or conscious thoughts (free associations) take on a seemingly logical cast that helps to cover over their underlying irrationality. Even in dreams, one unconsciously attempts to tell a fairly sensible story. Certainly, this effort may break down, though it does not do so very often. More so, in free associating, the patient attempts on the surface to report a logical sequence of events and recollections. However, encoded and contained within these direct reports are the hidden, primary process dominated messages through which both neurosis and the unconscious dimension of the therapeutic interaction can and must be understood.

Freud made several other major discoveries regarding dreams. The most monumental for him was the realization that dreams express the hidden or unconscious wishes of the dreamer and, further, that these wishes involve instincts and drives that took shape in early childhood. Every dream can be traced to its sources in such infantile wishes and fantasies. Today one would add to these wishes the presence of infantile unconscious perceptions as well.

On the other side of the time continuum, Freud also discovered that every dream is prompted by the events of the day or two prior to the dream experience. He called these events *day residues*, the immediate *triggers* of dreams. He found that these day residues often involve unfinished problems and tasks. Sometimes, the day stimuli involve experiences of considerable emotional significance. At other times, they seem quite innocuous and take on their meaning largely because of some special link to an infantile wish stirring within the dreamer.

With these insights, it is possible to recognize three different ways in which dreams and all encoded mental productions can be *decoded*. These processes, which depend on a comprehensive understanding of the nature of unconscious thinking, enhance appreciation of the nature of psychotherapies and their conspiracies. Preliminary insight is gained through consideration of how a dream is formed. In therapy or in daily experience, one is usually faced first with the dream and must then trace out its origins and sources. Reversing this process and identifying just how the dream took shape helps to clarify these seemingly mysterious primary process mechanisms that Freud discovered.

One day residue or stimulus for the Irma dream was the conversation between Freud and his physician friend, Otto, who implied that Irma, Freud's patient, whom he had recently seen, was better but not quite well. There was a tone of reproof and a feeling that Otto was siding against Freud. Freud responded consciously by writing out Irma's case history with the idea of giving it to Breuer in order to justify himself. This is a logical and sensible, adaptive response. Freud also responded with the Irma dream.

In the Irma dream, Freud's friend Otto stood beside Irma, as did Dr. M. It was Otto who, sometime earlier, when Irma was feeling unwell, had given her the chemical injection that Freud then reproved and criticized because the syringe had not been clean. Clearly, the waking stimulus of Otto's criticism of Freud was been turned into Freud's criticism of Otto. This particular theme is rather prominent in Freud's own associations. One of his most immediate wishes in response to Otto's doubts was to be able to prove that he himself was not responsible for the persistence of

Irma's symptoms. Another wish was for revenge on Otto, who had by implication accused Freud of an incomplete cure. This revenge was accomplished by dreaming that Otto had made Irma ill.

What, then, transpired mentally within Freud to create a dream from this particular day residue? To answer, one must understand some of the latent or hidden implications of the stimulus itself. While attractive and simplistic, it is insufficient to simply suggest that Freud merely transformed Otto's implied criticism of himself into a direct criticism of Otto. While apparently true, such an analysis lacks the subtlety required in order to understand unconscious expression.

A closer examination of the situation suggests first that Freud did indeed make use of two of the dream mechanisms he subsequently identified: displacement and symbolization. The displacement is from himself onto Otto, shifting the blame away from Freud. If it were postulated in addition that Otto's remark had mobilized in Freud a sense of concern and guilt regarding his own treatment procedures, the displacement onto Otto would appear to be a crucial protective (defensive) mechanism. In this instance, the raw unconscious perception would be, "I (Freud) feel guilty over failing to cure Irma." Such a feeling would likely have evoked highly disturbing affects within Freud and a need for defensive protection. Freud might well have been motivated to repress his sense of failure and guilt, and to defend himself against their realization. One can readily sense in the Irma dream both a disguised expression of Freud's worries and guilt, as well as his defense against these disturbing affects.

A similar compromise can be seen in the way Freud dreamed of the origin of Irma's symptoms. She had become ill because of a treatment procedure, but the procedure had nothing to do with psychoanalysis or Freud. Emotionally laden communications, including dream elements, tend to consistently reveal and express such compromises between expression and obliteration, disturbance and defense.

Through displacement, Freud shifted the cause of Irma's illness away from himself and away from his psychoanalytic techniques. Instead, the illness had been caused by a contaminated injection given by Otto. In addition to displacement, it is clear that symbolization was also used. A treatment procedure that involved talking with the patient had been portrayed as a medical procedure in the form of an injection. Freud had taken his disturbing raw perceptions of psychoanalysis and encoded and disguised his worried view of them by shifting them to concerns about more commonly accepted medical treatment procedures. In doing this, Freud had also been able, quite unconsciously, to reassure himself that there are detrimental side effects to other types of medical procedures. If patients in psychoanalysis fail to get well, the blow is lessened if one remembers that patients treated through other medical means also sometimes fare badly.

If one accepts the assumption proposed earlier that Freud was simultaneously working over his concerns about the treatment of Frau Emmy von N., one may further postulate the existence of condensation. Thus Freud's reproach to Irma for not having accepted his solution combined a reprimand to both patients. At the same time, Freud displaced the blame for the treatment failure from himself onto still another group of individuals—here, his patients. It is typical of dreams to include multiple representations of a particular disturbing raw unconscious perception or fantasy, and to then treat each representation with a fresh form of defensiveness. In the Irma dream, Freud attempted to deal with the issue of failed treatment procedures several times over. Each message has a distinctive form and involves a specific compromise—a disguised representation of the disturbing raw message and an attempt at defense.

Concerns for representability are more than evident in the Irma dream, which adopts a visual form typical of dreaming. The use of secondary revision in order to develop a sensible sequential narrative is also apparent. Thus it was possible to separate out each segment of the dream for separate associations that took on considerable meaning. Nonetheless, the dream also has meaning as a totality. The separate dream elements are woven together in an unconscious effort to tell a seemingly logical and sensible story.

In decoding dreams, as well as any other form of expression that contains latent messages, it is necessary to undo the effects of the dream mechanisms—the primary process mode of thought in which condensation, displacement, and symbolization reign supreme.

CHAPTER 17
DECODING DREAMS

When we are alert in school, at business, or engaged in a relatively unemotional social conversation, we make use of logical, reality-oriented secondary process thinking. In the absence of a deliberate attempt at lying, we say what we mean and mean what we say. We develop a conscious message, impart it to the listener, and await his or her response.

There are, of course, a number of implicit or unconscious qualities to what we have expressed. There is our tone, our accompanying body posture, the sentence structure and syntax, the sequence of presentation, the possible use of words and sentences with double meanings, and a variety of nuances of that kind. These are, however, the inevitable added implications of our daily cognitive (rational) efforts at communication. While some small portion will contain specific encoded messages, they are in general of minor import. Most of these are found in a particular choice of words and sentences and in the sequence of the presentation. Most can be inferred through direct listening and require no specific decoding key.

Under special conditions, secondary process gives way to primary process. This occurs, as noted, when we sleep and dream, when we are experiencing intense emotional stress, and under particular conditions such as the use of psychedelic and other special classes of drugs, in exposure to extreme sensory isolation and deprivation, and in the hypnotic state. This type of expression also tends to take over when a relationship is designed to alleviate the emotional suffering of one of the persons involved—i.e., when the relationship is designed primarily as psychotherapeutic. The type of primary process thinking that takes place under these various conditions will be rather comparable, regardless of the reason for the shift in mode of thought. The thinking will, in addition, be somewhat distinctive, depending on the exact nature of this causative factor and personal propensities within each individual so exposed.

With primary process thinking, threatening raw messages are treated in a special fashion. Instead of being subjected to logical considerations and realistic elaborations, they are handled through displacement, condensation, symbolization, and the rest. When there is a shift to primary process thinking in the waking state, an individual uses the same words as those in use in daily functioning. Instead of a dream, there is a story—a narrative or some other kind of verbal communication. The message appears on the surface to be secondary process dominated: it is usually logical, realistic, and clearly stated. As a rule, it is only when primary process thinking emerges in the context of an altered state of consciousness that one may observe unusual forms of presentation such as images and hallucinations.

Every human being has the remarkable capacity under certain stressful conditions to communicate simultaneously on at least two distinctive levels. For example, the patient in psychotherapy may be telling a narrative tale of an upsetting incident that took place on the day prior to his treatment session. Simultaneously, and entirely unconsciously, the same narrative may contain a series of encoded messages regarding the interaction with the therapist. It is this unique capability that enables the patient to express highly threatening messages while simultaneously defending himself or herself against the dangers involved.

Therapists have tended to ignore the encoded messages contained in their patients' associations. They have shaped their therapeutic techniques based on manifest communications, with virtually no regard for hidden expressions. A brief clinical excerpt demonstrates this kind of two-tiered communication and the different ways in which therapists have attempted to decode their patients' hidden messages—when they have tried to do so at all.

A CLINICAL VIGNETTE

Mrs. Able was in psychotherapy with Dr. Baker, who saw her once a week, face-to-face. She began one session as follows:

"I had a dream. It was frightening. A man with a moustache was chasing me. He cornered me in a motel room and wanted to rape me. I was ready to surrender, but then felt furious. Suddenly, I was outside and a huge tree was swaying in the wind. I was afraid it would fall on me and crush me.

"My father had a moustache," she continued. "And so did my uncle. I was reminded of a trip I took with my father when I was eleven years old. My mother stayed home with my brother. We could get only one motel room, and we had to share the bed together. I remember seeing him exposed and being frightened.

"My neighbor and his wife visited us the other night. Now that I think of it, he also has a moustache. She kept wanting to leave, but he insisted on staying on. He seemed attracted to me. I began to wonder what it would feel like to get involved with him."

Fortunately, the therapist in this hypothetical session did not interrupt the patient's flow of associations (a rather uncommon occurence). He listened and tried to understand what the patient was communicating to him.

Even with so short an excerpt, there are an enormous number of implications to this material. It is humbling to realize the human mind's capability for expressing simultaneously a multitude of messages, each on a different level. When these separate units of multi-meaning messages appear in a collective sequence of this kind, the total number of implications is staggering.

In *The Interpretation of Dreams*, and in a number of his case history reports, Freud attempted to develop a series of techniques for decoding the hidden messages communicated by patients in psychotherapy and psychoanalysis. There is no question whatsoever that every patient involved in a therapeutic relationship is inclined to shift to a mode of communication in which primary process mechanisms play a significant role. Patients' therapeutic needs prompt them to communicate, consciously and unconsciously, with a high level of combined meaning and defense.

At issue, then, is not the question of whether patients will express themselves in this fashion in treatment situations. Instead, the question is whether a therapist is interested in unconscious communication, whether he or she believes in its importance in understanding a patient's emotional difficulty, and further, whether he or she is convinced that a decoding of the unconscious messages that are the foundation for neurosis is the best means of curing or alleviating this particular type of human suffering. Because of this, psychotherapeutic techniques differ considerably in regard to whether they are designed to make accessible and identify the underlying basis or unconscious truths on which a patient's emotional disturbance is founded.

Those treatment approaches that tend to facilitate the patient's free and open communication (the use of free association) are designed with relatively little interference from the therapist in the patient's pursuit of encoded meaning. Quite importantly, they involve the establishment of a specific set of conditions under which unencumbered communication is safe and advisable. Thus such an approach involves not only the relative silence of the therapist, but also the establishment of a secure and private therapeutic setting and relationship, with a stable set of conditions that genuinely foster a sense of trust and safety in the patient. Any compromise in these conditions is quite likely to interfere with the patient's communicative openness, both consciously and unconsciously—on the surface and in terms of encoded expression.

Most therapeutic modalities are based on a therapist's disinterest in or inability to truly fathom the unconscious basis of the patient's emotional disturbance. Instead the focus is on the surface or on some other means of cure or relief. Therefore conditions are *not* established for the patient's free and open communication, and listening does *not* involve attention to the patient's encoded messages (i.e., his or her *derivative* or unconscious expressions). Further, many such treatment efforts are actually designed to obliterate, destroy, and even falsify the unconscious foundation for the patient's emotional disturbance. Remarkably, as has already been shown, such measures may nonetheless provide the patient with the symptom relief that he or she is seeking. The last part of this volume will show just how this type of lie-barrier cure takes effect.

Freud used the term *derivative* for any manifest expression that contains within it a latent or hidden message. The term is meant to imply that the manifest association, dream element, or whatever is *derived from* (and therefore a *derivative of*) a latent raw message. The manifest communication is therefore a disguised version of the latent content. It is derived from that latent content, and in return, through proper decoding procedures, the latent content itself can be derived from the manifest association. Thus, while these manifest elements have their surface meanings in terms of logic and other secondary process considerations, they may also serve as a vehicle for encoded messages or latent meaning—as derivatives. Whenever one attempts to decode a manifest message, one must treat it as a derivative. To understand the hidden messages contained in the opening segment of material reported to Dr. Baker by Mrs. Able, each manifest element of the patient's associations must be taken and treated as an encoded message. Several interrelated measures are available.

Decoding may begin with *a study of the manifest contents*. This involves a meaningful reading of the surface of the patient's associations, sometimes with consideration of the sequence of communicative elements and often with selected accents and emphasis. With regard to the vignette, for example, it might be suggested that Mrs. Able is concerned about being trapped and raped. She is conflicted about such a possibility in that she is prepared to surrender and is yet enraged. She seems frightened as well of being harmed. All of this is connected in some way to a childhood incident during which she shared a bed with her father and to a recent feeling that a neighbor was attracted to her. Her own response to this last possibility was to give it some kind of consideration.

This kind of reading of the surface of material from patients, which may be applied to a great deal of daily conversation, tends to simply echo the patient's manifest messages, though there is in addition some slight shading into possible but relatively transparent *implications* of these surface communications. Possible hidden meanings are also detected through the evident sequence of associations; here, the shift from the dream to the childhood incident to the experience with the neighbor.

An additional form of this type of decoding is carried out by identifying general surface themes. Thus the dream element of the man trying to corner the patient could be read as implying some kind of fear of entrapment. The fear that the tree might fall on her could imply some sense of anxiety regarding bodily harm. This type of reading of manifest content shades into the second form of decoding, through which more extensive inferences are made from the patient's surface associations.

Surprisingly, both psychoanalysts and insight-oriented psychotherapists concentrate a large part of their efforts on understanding the communications from their patients on the manifest content level, making use of a minimum degree of inference. Such therapists might suggest to Mrs. Able that she was concerned about entrapment or rape. They might even point out that she seemed divided in her feelings about such experiences: prepared to surrender and yet infuriated. They might add that she appeared concerned as well with some type of bodily harm. Since these statements seem heavily loaded with possible meaning, both patient and therapist would be inclined to believe that some important *unconscious* source of the patient's emotional disturbance had been recognized in this way. The postulate would be to the effect that Mrs. Able's dream had directly revealed her unconscious concerns or fantasies. It would go unnoticed that no decoding process had been used. Instead, the belief would be maintained that Mrs. Able's unconscious had spoken directly to her therapist through her dream.

In actuality, this postulate is false. Individuals, patients or otherwise, do not communicate encoded messages without encoding them. Even when there is an apparent breakthrough of a previously hidden message, the new message serves in some way as a derivative or encoded expression for still another message, which remains unconscious.

Both patients and therapists alike have been seduced by seemingly loaded (instinctual-drive laden) material into believing that the so-called unconscious has expressed itself directly, or that a patient has now communicated without defense. To the contrary, individuals are never without their defenses and compromises. The most blatant message, if it is truly meaningful in psychotherapy, has both manifest and latent, direct and encoded, implications.

Many so-called interpretive and noninterpretive forms of treatment, if they deal at all with the patient's associations, do so in this kind of straightforward fashion. The formulations involved *seem* meaningful, but are *functionally false*. That is, they are statements of apparent understanding that serve to avoid the actual basis of a patient's emotional disturbance. It is tantamount to stating that the sun rises in the east, as if this explained the patient's psychological symptoms. A true statement has been used to provide a false and unfounded explanation. When the statement itself is couched in dynamic and theoretically important language, both patients and therapists have considerable difficulty in recognizing that their formulations actually serve to mislead rather than to promote insight. The key to their falseness lies, of course, in the absence of any type of decoding effort.

And yet, since encoded messages involve raw perceptions and fantasies of considerable threat, their avoidance through seemingly meaningful though actually false statements is quite attractive and somewhat protective for all concerned. The true underlying message is sealed off, and a piece of fiction, directly stated, is offered in its place. Both patient and therapist are then spared the painful work necessary to modify the patient's defenses and to decode his or her messages to the point where the underlying and threatening raw perception or fantasy would be recognized. Staying on the surface tends to be easy, protective, immediate, attractively simple, and far less threatening than attempting to delve into the depths. Manifest content therapy is in wide use, extremely popular, and undoubtedly will always have a notable following. This is especially true because the fictions, lies, and barriers involved in pretending that the patient's surface communications reveal the hidden depths may sometimes offer both parties to therapy a sense of relief from their emotional struggles.

In sum, then, the first form of supposed decoding involves (1) no decoding whatsoever, but simply a reading of the patient's manifest associations, and (2) the development of self-evident inferences derived from understanding the general themes of the manifest material and the clues provided in a sequence of associations. Because of its simplicity, defensive utility, and immediacy, most patients and therapists are inherently drawn to this level of understanding. Nonetheless, it in no way serves as a means for comprehending the hidden or unconscious basis of a neurosis or a patient's encoded commentaries on the state of his or her therapeutic interaction with a therapist.

Most therapists who are committed to some type of decoding endeavor, will attempt to examine a patient's associations for evident inferences, for implications contained in the sequence of associations, for possible symbolic representations, and for other types of isolated and yet disguised products of the patient's imagination. Little differentiation will be made between intellectualized inferences and specific encoded daydreams and memories— between a flat *inference derivative* and a rich *image derivative* (the true language of unconscious expression). Image derivatives, in the form of unconscious fantasies and unconscious perceptions, constitute the hidden basis of emotional disturbance. Inference derivatives are imposed upon the patient's material by a therapist familiar with symbolism, psychosexual development, self-psychology, and other aspects of psychoanalytic theory. They do not serve true understanding.

This type of *isolated decoding* is based on a belief in the existence of relatively isolated intrapsychic struggles within the patient, some of them almost coincidentally set off by relatively inconsequential present and past experiences. The day residues or stimuli (precipitants or triggers) for these struggles are of relatively minor importance. The overriding focus is on the patient's intrapsychic, internal conflicts and struggles, and the fantasies and memories on which they are based. In particular, this type of decoding only rarely takes into consideration triggers derived from the interventions of the therapist. Furthermore, when it does so, it approaches these stimuli in terms of their surface attributes and in rather naive terms.

The therapist who makes use of inference decoding might suggest to Mrs. Able that she not only was concerned about being seduced or raped, but that unconsciously, she had *wishes* for this very occurrence. As evidence, the therapist would note that she had dreamt of someone who wanted to rape her, adding that dreams always reflect hidden wishes. Through displacement, the therapist would propose that Mrs. Able's own secret wish has been expressed as a desire belonging to someone else—the man with the moustache. As further evidence, Mrs. Able's preparedness to surrender to the man would be cited in support of this thesis, though some ambivalence (mixed wishes and feelings) would also be noted in that she also responded with fury.

The inference-derivative therapist might then proceed to connect the dream to the incident of sleeping in a motel bed with her father. The fact that this experience was recalled as the first association to the dream would be seen as strong testimony in favor of this postulate. It could then be proposed to the patient that she both feared and wished to be seduced or raped by her father on that occasion. Furthermore, the wishes aroused at that time still exist within Mrs. Able in powerful form. The wish corresponds to an Oedipal triumph in that the patient imagined possessing her father sexually in the absence of her mother. All of this is quite attractive and, though candid, somewhat disarming.

Making use of symbolic decoding, this therapist might well suggest further that Mrs. Able's fear in her dream that a huge tree might fall on her probably represented her fear of her father's phallus. The tree symbol suggests an image of his penis as huge and physically destructive. If Mrs. Able were suffering from frigidity, such a therapist might then suggest to her that she is unable to enjoy herself sexually because of an unconscious fantasy that her husband's penis is also a huge organ of destruction. The problem would be thought to have been further aggravated because her husband is still linked unconsciously in some way to her father, thereby affording incestuous meaning to intercourse with her husband. In an effort to defend herself against these incestuous wishes and also against the seemingly evident masochistic rape fantasies, it would be proposed that Mrs. Able is frigid as a way of unconsciously denying her participation and pleasure in the sexual experience, colored as it is with all of these hidden and forbidden meanings.

To complete his or her discourse, the inference therapist could then suggest that Mrs. Able's sense that her neighbor was attracted to her was the day residue or stimulus for both her dream and her childhood recollection. The interest shown by her neighbor, who happened to share a physical attribute with her father, reignited Mrs. Able's masochistic incestuous fantasies and memories. The aroused wishes then appeared in her dream and received their genetic meaning from the childhood incident with her father.

Therapists appear to divide into two groups: those who wish to obliterate dynamic-genetic (childhood connection) formulations and those who engage extensively and often with enormous pleasure and excitement in generating elaborate postulates of this kind. Among the latter group of therapists, there is a powerful attraction to developing the dynamic and genetic implications of the patient's material as they pertain to the hidden emotional life of the patient. Such formulations tend to be generated with great ease and abundance. Careful attention to patients in psychotherapy reveals that there are many who are themselves well versed in symbols and psychoanalytic theory and who can carry out this type of isolated decoding with great facility. Freud's psychoanalytic theory was founded on this type of decoding, and virtually all of classical psychoanalysis remains committed to this kind of approach.

Where then lies the flaw? Everything seems to fit together quite neatly. Regarding those who object to this type of highly intellectualized means of formulating, it would be suggested that their protest is based on their own fear of these threatening and sometimes primitive unconscious fantasies and memories. Their lack of understanding would be said to be based on techniques and procedures, of the kind alluded to in Chapters 3 and 4, that are designed to preclude the production of encoded expressions from patients. It is their fear alone that turns them against insight therapy of this kind.

Here too there has been a battle without content. Those who have criticized the psychoanalytic approach have defended themselves by stating that none of this kind of understanding, if it is in any way valid or meaningful, is necessary to resolve a neurosis. "Much ado about nothing" is the essence of their rejoinder. Those who have tried to be critical of these efforts at decoding have not been able to identify the basic problem in these endeavors. Besides suggesting that these unconscious memories and fantasies are insignificant (if they exist at all!), these critics simply propose in addition that classical psychoanalytic theory overlooks one or another aspect of emotional disturbance—it has paid insufficient attention to the area of narcissism or to existential crises. It ignores the family and culture and becomes mired down in the patient's unbridled fantasy life in a way that takes him or her away from reality rather than enabling him or her to cope. There are almost as many theories on the basis for emotional disturbance as there are forms of therapy. Lacking a means of resolving these disputes, lacking a methodology that could permit investigation and then provide evidence and answers, these discussions have proved entirely inconclusive.

However, one problem with the intrapsychic or closed-system decoding process described here and in current use by many psychoanalysts can be quickly identified. Oddly enough, in the usual case report, there would be no way of discovering this basic flaw. The session as reported here does not reveal its presence because this involves a particular fact that most therapists would overlook.

In the situation between Mrs. Able and Dr. Baker, this fact is that, at the time of the previous session, Dr. Baker had inadvertently extended Mrs. Able's 50-minute hour to a full 60 minutes. Since she was his last patient for the day, he realized his error only on his way home. Of course, neither he nor Mrs. Able had mentioned the extension of the time at the beginning of this session. There are strong reasons to believe that this particular day residue—a ground-rule issue—had in some way triggered Mrs. Able's dream.

This interpretation is an example of the third and final means through which dreams and other associations of patients, and primary process-dominated communications in general, can be decoded—*trigger decoding* (synonyms: day residue decoding, precipitant decoding, stimulus decoding, context decoding, or adaptation-evoking context decoding). This effort is carried out by using the implications of the critical stimulus for the patient's communications as the key through which the decoding process is carried out. Instead of an arbitrary reading of inferences, images, and symbols, trigger decoding begins with a careful analysis of the nature of the day residue. Once its main attributes (manifest and latent) have been determined, they are used as a basis for the detection of activated hidden meanings in the patient's associations.

Trigger decoding immediately introduces interaction. It is modeled on the basic concept of stimulus and response. It postulates an open system with inputs from an outside individual and contributions from within the communicator. It is based on a realization of the presence of a continuous and spiraling communicative interaction between a given person and those of importance to him or her. It recognizes communicative exchanges with manifest and latent implications on both sides, in respect to both sender and receiver. It studies all messages as part of communicative exchanges with manifest and encoded meanings on both sides.

Specifically, in psychotherapy, trigger decoding requires an understanding of the conscious and unconscious communications from both patient and therapist alike. Such an approach immediately belies the silent assumption in psychoanalysis and psychoanalytic psychotherapy that therapists say what they mean and mean what they say, expressing themselves manifestly and logically without significant unconscious meaning. This hypothesis stands in contrast to the usual view of patients as people who do not mean what they say and say much whose meaning they do not recognize.

The closed-system arrangement is a rather neat one for the therapist. He or she expresses himself or herself directly and means nothing more or less. If the patient senses a hidden implication, it is his or her distortion. The patient, in contrast, is mainly communicating through encoded messages that derive primarily from unconscious fantasies and memories. The surface of his or her associations is of little consequence; instead, the hidden messages are what matter. Thus the therapist is supposed to be lacking in unconscious expression, while the patient's communications have little manifest meaning. There is an inequity and distortion here that cannot be substantiated through careful clinical observation. Still, it forms the foundation for much of the psychoanalytic conspiracy between patients and therapists.

Inference decoding tends to be highly intellectualized and arbitrary. Without a guide by which a therapist can determine which of several associations have the greatest meaning, or which of several figures condensed into one image is most important, he or she soon becomes involved in rather biased attempts at selection. The consequent interpretations have an arbitrary ring to them, and in actuality they are often refuted by the patient. In addition, hypothetical clichés abound in such work, giving a false and suspicious tone to the therapist's efforts.

By contrast, trigger decoding always entails the search for specific, underlying raw images—narratives, symbols, imaginary daydreams, clearly defined perceptions, and the like. Further, once the nature of the trigger for a dream is well understood, the decoding process takes on a very definitive quality. It is the trigger that gives special and specific meaning to the patient's encoded messages. Dynamically active issues are involved as well, most of them concerning the therapeutic interaction. As a result, clichés are rare, and lively formulations are common.

CHAPTER 18

TRIGGER DECODING

According to clinical research the therapist is the most critical trigger for the communications from patients as these expressions pertain to the unconscious bases of patients' emotional disturbances. From the very first moment a patient considers entering psychotherapy, the therapist becomes an exceedingly important figure. The therapeutic relationship and interaction is quickly established as the main arena within which the battle against the patient's neurosis is carried out. Experiences with figures outside of treatment, while they remain important in the patient's real life, are virtually never the basis on which an analysis of the unconscious factors in the patient's neurosis can be undertaken. Most often such experiences serve as disguised and encoded means through which the patient unconsciously expresses perceptions of, and fantasies about, the therapist.

An entirely new level of meaning emerges when the material from Mrs. Able's session is decoded in light of the key trigger—that Dr. Baker had extended her previous hour. In trigger decoding, one always begins with an analysis of the stimulus itself. Following that, the patient's dream or associations are decoded, with these revelations (implications) as a guide.

There are two possible approaches to the decoding of the

trigger or stimulus for this material: (1) a reading of Mrs. Able's dream and associations in an effort to use her own encoded messages (primarily perceptions, though possibly some measure of fantasy) regarding the nature of the stimulus from the therapist; or (2) an independent evaluation by the therapist of the attributes of the trigger, its manifest latent meanings and functions.

Here it seems best to attempt, through self-analysis and self-awareness, to define the most important meanings of the therapist's error. This is very much how a conscientious therapist would work under these conditions. Thus, it would be proposed that on the surface the manifest message was the wish to detain the patient in her session for a longer period than agreed upon. The most evident implications would involve wishing to delay the patient, to hold or possess her, and to keep her in the office longer than necessary. Also evident is the therapist's wish to give a gift to the patient—to offer her some of his time without an additional fee.

Since one is dealing here with an action, and the therapist's private associations are not available, further formulations, even as they move toward latent contents, will of necessity be rather limited. From the therapist's behavior, one could speculate a wish to be especially close to the patient or a defensive reaction against an impulse to be rid of her. Perhaps there is a rather seductive quality to what he has done, and a loss of control. The boundaries of the therapeutic relationship have been rendered unclear, and in a way, the error could well disturb the patient's contact with reality—this session did not end at the expected time.

These appear to be the main qualities of the therapist's error. They are contained implicitly and unconsciously in his behavior. The formulations state actual (real) unconscious implications of what the therapist has done. One would expect the patient, either consciously or unconsciously, to be aware of these meanings in the therapist's act. Such responses would constitute valid conscious and unconscious perceptions of his mistake. The patient could in addition readily add her own reactions, elaborations, and fantasies.

However, the patient might well avoid a direct confrontation with the therapist regarding his error. The qualities of his mistake make him a dangerous and untrustworthy figure. Thus the raw perception (the raw message) would in all likelihood be encoded and expressed through disguise and derivative. It is well to recall that the primary process mechanisms do not influence the nature of a raw perception or fantasy, but instead operate in the transformation of these unregistered or unconscious images into conscious mentation or experience. The conscious product is the result of condensation, displacement, symbolization, concern for representability, and secondary revision. Freud called this the *dream work*, and more broadly it may be understood as the *encoding work*—the means by which patients disguise (avoid and yet express) dangerous raw images.

When a trigger from the therapist involves an error and countertransference and is likely to disturb the patient, the connections to past figures must be understood as having a special meaning; i.e., under these conditions it is quite likely that the therapist's behavior will remind the patient of some seductive and threatening behavior on the part of a parental or other important early figure. Such a connection is based on a legitimate resemblance (nontransference), rather than being inappropriate and a sign of pathological wishing within the patient (transference).

For the therapist it would also be helpful if he were aware of the personal triggers for his error. If, for example, he was in the throes of getting divorced, he would be quick to recognize that he had acted out some type of wish to be unusually and inappropriately close to this patient. If, on the other hand, he had recently cancelled a session with this patient, his behavior would reflect an unconscious wish to make up for the lost time. If he had increased Mrs. Able's fee, the action could reflect guilt over the new charge and a wish to make amends. If he had instead decreased her fee, his behavior could reflect a need to bring out the unconscious and seductive aspects of this particular measure.

Clearly, each of these triggers gives a somewhat different meaning or accent to the specific implications of the therapist's mistake. Triggers form the context and stimuli for the patient's communications, and as contexts change, the implications of identical associations will similarly change. In like fashion, a specific behavior or error of a therapist will reflect a series of definitive meanings depending on the stimulus that triggered the therapist's own behavior. In turn, as noted, the specific nature of the therapist's error in the context of the total and immediate therapeutic relationship and interaction will create a series of definitive meanings for the patient's associations (as in the session described above).

There is always a universal meaning for a trigger, one that is shared by all. Here, for example, it would be unimaginable that a patient would fail to notice the overindulgent and seductive aspects of the extension of the hour. However, patients tend to select from the multiple implications of a stimulus those meanings that are most pertinent for themselves. In addition, depending on the patient's own past history and inner mental life, a particular trigger may have a very special meaning.

When the trigger is known and appreciated in depth, hidden meanings in the patient's communications are often very easily identified. It is striking now that Mrs. Able's dream began with a man trying to corner her. There can be little doubt that this is a valid unconscious perception of one implication of Dr. Baker's error. He was indeed attempting to entrap his patient, even if momentarily and unconsciously. Nor is it unexpected that this effort at trigger decoding first revealed an unconscious *perception* rather than an unconscious fantasy or memory. It cannot be overstressed that patients very often find it necessary to encode their perceptions of their therapists, largely because of the dangerous nature of the interventions involved.

The dream element begins with a raw unconscious perception: in this case, the therapist's extension of Mrs. Able's hour. (Later in the session it emerged that Mrs. Able had been quite unconscious of the fact that Dr. Baker had extended her session until she arrived at home some ten minutes later than usual. Only then did it suddenly occur to her that she had noticed in passing, but had not consciously registered, the later time at which the session had been terminated. With a laugh, she had brushed the incident aside. Dr. Baker was sometimes forgetful, and he had made an amusing mistake. To her knowledge, she had no further conscious thoughts about the incident.) The raw perception, then, partly conscious and partly unconscious, took on an immediate coloring: Dr. Baker had a need to detain and thereby entrap Mrs. Able. Based in part on a fear of confronting her therapist with his error and its implications, and in part on her own frightening reaction, it was necessary for Mrs. Able to repress (obliterate) any direct awareness of the time at which her hour had ended until she had arrived at home. Even then, it was necessary for further reasons of defense to set the matter aside and to afford it little evident meaning.

While the incident was thereby disposed of on a conscious level, Mrs. Able nonetheless had a need to work over and adapt to the experience. Feeling a sense of endangerment from both external (Dr. Baker) and internal (perceptive and fantasied) sources, she responded by creating her dream. The day residue for the dream is, of course, Dr. Baker's extension of Mrs. Able's session. With this as a guide, the elements of the dream may now be properly decoded.

Thus the image of a man with a moustache trying to corner her represents in encoded form her unconscious perception of one meaning of Dr. Baker's error. The raw perception of his detaining her in his office is changed in the following ways: through *displacement*, the dream is about a man with a moustache rather than Dr. Baker. The scene is a room in a motel rather than the therapist's office—again, *displacement* is operative. Some *symbolic representation* is also at work, in that the original stimulus was an extension of the patient's hour, while the dream image involves entrapment. In a way, the dream image actually works in the reverse direction of the usual symbolic process: it takes a symbolic act (the extension of the time) and exposes one of its unconscious meanings (the wish to entrap).

Parenthetically, one may note too the patient's use of *condensation*, in that the image of entrapment combines the patient's accurate perception of the therapist's error with a valid perception of seductive wishes in the patient's father (borne out in other sessions). The same image also portrays a similarly valid perception of the neighbor (also borne out through later material). A series of threatening, raw, conscious and unconscious perceptions are encoded into a single dream element in a manner that, unfortunately for Mrs. Able, does not sufficiently disguise the perceived threat to a point where it alleviates her own sense of anxiety.

It is important not to lose the focus in one's efforts at trigger decoding. In psychotherapy, since the triggers stem from the therapist and frequently reflect pathological needs and wishes of which he or she is unaware, this type of decoding meets with great conspiratorial resistance. Nonetheless, trigger decoding reveals a particular level of meaning in the material from patients that must be formulated in order to determine the true source of their emotional difficulties and to generate valid statements on the nature of the therapeutic interaction.

The next element in Mrs. Able's dream is that the man wanted to seduce or rape her. Based on knowledge of the precipitant, it seems fair to state that this particular manifest element encodes a mixture of a valid unconscious perception of Dr. Baker and a measure of the patient's own fantasied response. Thus Dr. Baker did not make any kind of sexual overture to his patient. He did not attempt manifestly to seduce or rape her. Nonetheless, by extending the hour, he did behave in a seductive and even somewhat entrapping, forceful manner. He did not permit the patient to leave until he dismissed her. There were therefore certain seductive and intrusive qualities to his error. Nonetheless, to characterize it as an attempt at rape seems to extend to some degree the qualities of his intervention.

Whenever a ground rule is modified, trigger decoding will involve a difficulty of this kind. The patient unconsciously recognizes the highly sexual, and sometimes quite aggressive, implications of the therapist's modification of the ground rules. At the same time, based on his or her own inner needs, fantasies, and memories, the patient will tend to add something from his or her own inner mental world to these valid perceptions. Mrs. Able's characterization of the extension of the time as a kind of rape reflects not only a reasonable reading of the therapist's unconscious message, but also her own involvement in self-punitive rape fantasies, which she tended to act out on some level in her daily relationships.

When unconscious perception is involved, the symbolic meanings of the therapist's behaviors are clearly perceived. The extension of the hour may indeed clearly symbolize an attempt at entrapment and therefore at rape. The important distinction here lies in the fact that the therapist did not physically assault the patient and confined himself to a symbolic activity. The actual means by which an underlying wish or fantasy is expressed—the form of the communication—offers an important perspective on the situation.

It must be noted too that the interaction was continuous and spiraling. Dr. Baker's extension of the hour had been prompted in part by several provocative attacks to which Mrs. Able had subjected him. While it is indeed his responsibility to control and manage the feelings, fantasies, and perceptions that his patient's behaviors arouse in him, it is nonetheless important to recognize that the therapist's interventions are triggered by the patient's material, just as the patient's material is triggered by the therapist's interventions. In psychotherapy, although it proves most useful as a rule to begin with the therapist's interventions as a way of understanding the patient's associations or behaviors, the analysis of the trigger does indeed involve an understanding of the material from the patient that stimulated the therapist's intervention.

Even though Mrs. Able was a provocative woman with both her husband and therapist, the therapist must always take full responsibility for his countertransferences and errors. Unfortunately, these provide the patient with a measure of pathological satisfaction that reinforces her own emotional illness. Here, for example, the extension of the hour did indeed gratify certain rape fantasies entertained by Mrs. Able. The satisfactions involved are an important component to this type of psychotherapeutic conspiracy, in which the pathological needs and fantasies of both patient and therapist find mutual satisfaction.

Trigger decoding tends to emphasize first the *action* qualities of the therapist's intervention, here the entrapping and seductive aspects of the extended hour. This approach does not simply assume that dreams are entirely figments of the patient's imagination and the product of unconscious wishes and fantasies. It recognizes an important source of dreams in threatening unconscious perceptions of others. Typically, patients will incorporate or take into themselves the traumatic qualities perceived in others, and they will often then dream about carrying out such behaviors on their own. Many important encoded messages about therapists are conveyed in dreams and associations that refer manifestly to the patient. Such allusions are undoubtedly among the best means of disguising perceptions of, and reactions to, the therapist.

Trigger decoding provides a far more balanced view of the therapeutic situation, and of the patient and his or her illness and associative material. It allows room for both valid and sensible unconscious and encoded perceptions, as well as highly distorted representations of unconscious memories and fantasies. The decision as to which quality is uppermost in a particular image always depends on an appreciation of the implications of the trigger.

The next dream elements, Mrs. Able's wish to surrender and yet her rage, and her fear of the huge tree that might fall on her, derive mainly from another source in the therapeutic interaction. Dr. Baker tended to alternate between sitting back while quietly listening, and the use of rather intrusive, hostile interventions. There was a distinctly phallic cast to his thrusts, though he never became involved in direct physical or sexual attack toward his patient. These unconscious perceptions are also encoded in the dream.

The recollection of the childhood seduction by Mrs. Able's father can be decoded in light of the trigger from the therapist as the patient's unconscious perception that once again she was faced with a forbidden (incestuous) man who wished to seduce her. The therapist's extension of her hour was a repetition of her father's invitation to join him in bed. Mrs. Able rightly perceived unconscious seductive and incestuous wishes in both figures. This relatively neglected aspect requires clear definition before alluding to Mrs. Able's own complementary wishes to be seduced.

Similarly, it is quite evident that Mrs. Able's allusion to her seductive neighbor was an ingenious means through which, with notable disguise, she could both represent and avoid the incident with her therapist. The perception that Dr. Baker had extended her hour is represented in disguised form by the reference to how the neighbor stayed late at Mrs. Able's house. Here displacement and symbolic representation are at play. The neighbor's attraction to Mrs. Able is an encoded representation of an unconscious perception of some attraction in the therapist toward his patient. Once he had analyzed this particular error within himself, Dr. Baker readily verified his patient's belief that he was attracted to her. He did indeed find her a most interesting and fascinating patient. His error reflected his undue attachment toward her.

Simultaneously through condensation (as later material bore out), the reference to the neighbor who was attracted to Mrs. Able represented her own attraction to her therapist. This too played a role in this material. However, in light of the trigger, a solid understanding of Mrs. Able's associations would have to focus first on her unconscious perceptions of her therapist, and then only secondarily on her reactions to these perceptions.

In *The Interpretation of Dreams*, Freud (1900) attempted to demonstrate that primary process thinking dominates our dreams and forms the basis of emotional disturbances. Therapists, however, have paid little attention to the question of which type of thinking and functioning dominates the therapeutic interaction. Those who are psychoanalytically oriented have attempted to listen to the

material from their patients with the two types of thinking in mind.
They have attempted to understand both manifest and latent messages. However, they have treated these communications entirely
as isolated messages reflecting the inner or intrapsychic state of the
sender. They have neglected to study the ways in which their own
interventions have helped to shape these messages. Furthermore,
they have tended to ignore the ways in which these messages
pertain to the very state of the therapeutic interaction. They have
treated these communications as products of the patient's imagination rather than as a living consequence of the ongoing therapeutic
interaction. They have thought of these messages as reflecting the
inner mental world of the patient. They have not considered how
these messages reflect their own inner mental worlds and the
various levels of communicative interaction between themselves
and their clients.

The use of a relatively naive approach to their own messages and
to the messages of their patients has served an enormously protective function for therapists. Some therapists basically ignore or
obliterate the messages from their patients. Some lock in the
manifest communications and seal off any possible unconscious
implication. Other therapists will elaborate upon a particular element in a message while totally ignoring all other components. Few
if any attempt to understand the context of a message in order to
decode its actual *functional* meaning.

Suppose a patient says to a therapist, "I remember my mother
forcing food down my throat." Manifestly, this is a message about
the patient's past. It is a recollection that is either valid or falsified.
Some therapists would attempt to investigate this issue. They
would try to clarify the veracity of the recall as a way of establishing a dimension of the patient's relationship with his or her mother.
For some patients, this type of clarification would seem illuminating
and helpful. It would lead to conscious realizations that they had
not experienced previously. For others it might seem pointless and
empty. Nevertheless, it is the manifest encouragement from patients
who believe that some aspect of their lives has been clarified that has
led therapists to adopt this type of exploratory technique.

Therapists who are more analytically inclined would wonder
about issues of dependency, autonomy, and orality. They might
propose that the patient had recalled this memory as a way of
expressing an oral-rape fantasy. If the patient were a woman, the

presence of unconscious homosexual fantasies and conflicts might be discussed. With a male patient, such a therapist might hypothesize an image of a phallic woman capable of penetrating a man and a complementary image of the man as a passive-feminine victim. The patient would be seen as making use of his mouth symbolically to represent an unconscious fantasy that he possesses a vagina.

For therapists seeking to do their job while simultaneously maintaining themselves in a state of relatively stable emotional equilibrium, there are strong pressures to respond to such associations with either some form of obliterating mechanism (repression and/or denial) or by engaging in highly stimulating formulations regarding the fantasy life of the patient. Therapists find considerable gratification in such meanderings and speculation. They satisfy defensive needs in avoiding entirely any way in which this particular kind of message could be an encoded perception of themselves. Some who are a bit braver might suggest that the association involves what is called a *transference fantasy*, that the therapist is in some way forcing something upon the patient. Still, this fantasy would be seen as quite distorted and as based on an earlier experience with the mother rather than on any actuality with the therapist. While connected to the therapist, messages of this kind are seen entirely as products of the patient's fanciful imagination.

When trigger decoding is employed, it is recognized that no message exists in isolation. A message is always a response to a stimulus, another message; it always has a context. It always contains meaning on a manifest and latent level. Then too, it always involves both conscious and unconscious communication.

Without knowledge of the trigger, the latent meaning of a message is a matter of sheer speculation. The fact that a therapist can assign a hidden meaning to a particular message has been mistaken by patients, at least consciously, as a sign of brilliance and perceptiveness. A statement of a second meaning for a manifest (direct) message has rather consistently been accepted as inherently wise and pertinent. The fact that therapists could develop their formulations entirely in terms of their own fantasies and beliefs has seldom been pointed out. The possibility of error is virtually ignored. Most of the time this argument arises from skeptics and those who intend to defame psychoanalysis. Because of the sources, it has been easy for analysts to ignore such considerations.

Some patients will actually accept a therapist's statement of decoding with utmost blind faith even when the decoded product bears little resemblance to the original message. For example, it is not beyond possibility for an analyst to tell a patient that his memory of his mother forcing him to eat is actually a fantasy based on a primal scene (parental bedroom) observation of fellatio when he was 15 months of age. Another analyst might propose that the patient seems to confuse his mouth with his anus, and that he sees sexuality as an incestuous rape from his mother. Or it might be suggested that the memory reflects a cannibalistic fantasy of devouring the mother and eliminating her as a fecal mass. Using another tack, an analyst might propose that the memory reflects an omnipotent fantasy of devouring the universe.

Patients have accepted and fancifully elaborated upon formulations of this kind many times over in the first 100 years of psychoanalysis. It has proven difficult to refute these formulations, though many therapists will have nothing to do with them. To some, they seem to resemble the ravings of a mad person. To others, they are brilliant psychological formulations of unconscious contents and processes. The debate rages on without resolution.

The presence of some measure of possible psychological truth in formulations of this kind has helped to maintain their use in psychoanalytic practice. Nonetheless, it is possible for a therapist to make use of a statement that is truthful in one context in a manner that is false in light of a different framework. This book has already presented many illustrations of how this can take place.

Many of these therapeutic procedures are carried out by therapists who are divided and split emotionally and are accepted by patients who are in a similar state. In the dream of the first therapist-supervisee (see Chapter 3) and in Freud's Irma dream, splitting of this kind was evident in two rather different therapists. Both adhered manifestly to therapeutic procedures for which they had a deep commitment. Yet both revealed through their dreams another level of thinking and feeling, much of it encoded and primary-process dominated, and fraught with doubts, uncertainty, self-criticism, and even self-condemnation.

Similar communications are also common from patients. Typically, they ask on the surface for highly uninsightful and over-indulgent forms of therapy, while their encoded communications are extremely critical of such approaches. Whatever its protective value, then, splitting is an important factor in all forms of therapeutic conspiracy. When we have completed decoding the patient's image of his mother forcing food down his throat, it will be possible to consider this mechanism in more detail.

There are several possible triggers for this image. Each precipitant is a stimulus that derived from an intervention from the therapist, shaping and providing a context for the patient's message. And it is always the stimulus that points to the most meaningful unconscious implications involved.

Suppose that the therapist had been very active in this session. After each sentence from the patient, the therapist had been confrontational or proposed a dynamic formulation and meaning for the material. When the patient became confused and raised objections, the therapist insisted that the patient was becoming resistant and unduly obstinate and relentlessly pressed on with his formulations, insistent upon their validity. In this context, the memory conjured up by the patient of his mother forcing him to eat would be decoded to contain a raw unconscious message to the therapist: "You are forcing yourself upon me, trying to stuff your formulations and interventions into me. Your pressure reminds me of earlier experiences with my mother who forced me to eat. On some unconscious level, you are trying to force-feed or stuff your ideas into me."

Suppose instead that the patient had complained in the session that he was having financial difficulties. He felt that he could no longer maintain twice-weekly therapy because of the cost. At that point, the therapist proposed a reduction in his fee from $75 to $50 so the patient could continue twice-weekly therapy. In response, the patient remembered his mother forcing him to eat. This manifest message-memory would then be seen to contain within it an encoded and unconscious perception of the therapist as forcing undue gratification on the patient. The memory would imply something inappropriate and destructive in the therapist's intervention, and rightly so. From the patient's side, the use of the feeding idiom would derive in part from actual experiences with the mother and from his consequent fantasy life, though also from the nature of the stimulus that itself has unconscious feeding qualities.

Finally, suppose that the therapist had announced his vacation during this session. In the previous hour he had been silent, and an analysis of the session indicated that there was no reason for him to have intervened. After alluding to his vacation, the therapist fell silent. The patient then responded with the memory of his mother forcing him to eat. Here the image of being forced to eat would appear to be a fantasy-wish within the patient: faced with the loss of the therapist and a measure of deprivation, the patient conjures up a memory of forced gratification. Perhaps the association would also reveal a hostile need within the patient directed toward the therapist: he may wish to now force something down the therapist's throat in a manner not unlike the patient's experience of the therapist's announcement of his vacation.

The human mind works automatically toward self-protection, simplification, and immediate gratification. Both patients and therapists prefer to consider only the manifest meanings of their communications to each other. Based on a humanly necessary conspiracy, both patients and therapists have granted only a small measure of leeway to these manifest preoccupations. Under some conditions of treatment, there will be a search for latent meanings. However, many treatment modalities never search the therapist's interventions, and investigate the patient's associations solely in terms of fantasies and wishes.

Because of the needs satisfied in both participants to treatment through this collusion, it has been difficult to get therapists to realize that messages do not exist as such in isolation, that they are never simply expressions of intrapsychic fantasies in their patients, and that they are always communicated in the context of the ongoing therapeutic interaction. To do so would bring the therapist full force into the therapeutic experience. And with his or her presence, would come a full measure of pathology—whatever else might be constructive. As a result, the therapist would of necessity have to know himself or herself and the nature of his or her inputs into the treatment process. There is strong evidence that such a prospect is far too painful for those who practice psychotherapy in any form whatsoever, including psychoanalysis. The threatening aspects are split off and denied.

In order to understand the therapeutic interaction, then, one must surrender the protective notion that the patient's material can be understood entirely in terms of manifest meaning and fanciful implication. One must recognize that it is entirely possible for therapists to be quite in error in an effort at decoding the communications from their patients. While formulations developed by therapists are often clever and attractive, they may have little to do with the intended meanings of the patient. Therapists must also be prepared to examine and decode their own messages to their patients in light of the adaptation-evoking contexts that derive from their clients' communications.

Psychotherapy, since it should deal primarily with the emotional problems of the patient, always involves conscious and unconscious communicative exchanges between patients and therapists. Certainly, it is possible for a therapist to behave in a fashion that discourages openness and the expression of meaningful material. A therapist may keep his or her patients so focused on the surface of their communicative exchanges that little unconscious meaning is discernible. Then too, the therapist may respond to a patient's associations in a fashion that falsifies their meaning, obliterates their intended implications, and substitutes something far different from that which the patient had expressed.

Psychotherapy involves a spiraling conscious and unconscious communicative interaction. The patient's neurosis becomes an inherent part of this communicative interplay. Symptoms themselves become a communicative expression in light of the stimuli of the treatment experience. If a therapist wishes to understand the unconscious basis of a symptom, he or she must establish a formulation in terms of the ongoing communicative interaction. The true and currently active unconscious meaning of the patient's emotional disturbance can be established only in light of the stimuli from the therapist and their implications. A therapist may choose to help a patient resolve his or her symptoms by either defining their immediate (functional) unconscious basis (the truth) or through some other means. Communicative truths may be falsified, set aside, or appreciated only in part. These barriers to the truth may also provide the patient with some measure of symptom relief.

Trigger decoding requires of the therapist a capacity for self-knowledge and self-awareness that is difficult to achieve and even harder to maintain. The belief that therapists work and express themselves almost entirely on a manifest and conscious level is a myth designed to protect them from the painful awareness of many disturbing and disruptive unconscious implications of their efforts. Trigger decoding requires of therapists a full analysis of their silences and interventions with their patients. It follows, then, that a full and truthful appreciation of the basis of an emotional disturbance in a patient (and of the therapeutic interaction itself) can be ascertained only in light of a thorough and sound measure of self-understanding in a therapist. Only those therapists who know themselves well can know the truth about their patients' communications and emotional disorders.

In the clinical example, the frigidity experienced by Mrs. Able would stem partly from her valid unconscious perceptions of Dr. Baker's seductiveness. The communicative meanings of the frigidity, upon analysis, would involve, first, a corrective *model* to Dr. Baker that he should be better able to manage and even to desexualize his pathological erotic wishes toward his patient. The encoded message contained in the symptom of frigidity (and all symptoms are indeed a form of unconscious communication) would be stated in raw form, "You are too aroused sexually, Dr. Baker; try to be less sexually active." There is certainly a pathological element in expressing a message of this kind through a symptom, and the advice is somewhat overstated. Nonetheless, this would indeed be one hidden and symbolized meaning to Mrs. Able's problem.

In light of the triggers from Dr. Able, a second meaning would involve an unconscious defensive reaction designed to protect Mrs. Able against her therapist's inappropriate seductiveness, as well as against her own incestuously tinged unconscious wishes toward her therapist. Any attempt to explain this symptom without a full consideration of the inputs from the therapist would neglect and even falsify a major input into the patient's emotional disturbance. A sound and truthful measure of therapeutic understanding can evolve only when the inputs from the therapist, conscious and unconscious, are given their full due. Cure could follow only if Dr. Baker actually corrected his ways (*rectification*) and then offered Mrs. Able a valid interpretation. All else would be quite conspiratorial.

Trigger decoding may be used in our daily lives as a way to better understand our own reactions to others and their reactions to us. Identifying the stimulus for a particular outburst or strange piece of behavior often reveals in a flash its hidden meanings.

In psychotherapy, an understanding of trigger decoding leads to a basic postulate that therapy can be carried out in only one of two basic ways: (1) by attempting to arrive at the truth of the patient's neurosis in light of the ongoing therapeutic and communicative interaction between the patient and therapist—*truth therapy*; or (2) by avoiding, falsifying, covering over, or otherwise defending against these fundamental truths—*lie or lie-barrier therapy*.

In these terms, there can be only one form of truth therapy and only one comprehensive truth to the hidden and presently active structure of a patient's neurosis. On the other hand, there can be an unlimited number of lie therapies, an endless variety of ways in which the truth can be distorted, covered over, or falsified. Further, the truth, when it comes to the basis of an emotional disturbance, is always painful and threatening, though its recognition can lead to considerable maturation and coping capacity. It is therefore welcomed by those who can tolerate its pain and those who can comprehend its complexities. On the other hand, lies tend to bring with them an immediate sense of relief, though they are quite restricted as a means of coping. One lie begets another and requires further lies for backup. Lies also involve false relationships. True growth and maturation are impossible, though relief may occur. Thus, truth therapy and lie therapy each offer something quite different to patients and therapists alike.

PART IV
TRUTH THERAPY, LIE THERAPY

CHAPTER 19

SPLITTING AND THE GROUND RULES OF THERAPY

Emotionally, we are virtually always divided. We wish to deal with a problem, but we prefer to avoid it. We want to know ourselves, but we'd rather not. We want to help people, but then again we'd like to hurt them. We feel love, but it is marred by hostility. We opt for one solution to a conflict, but it poses problems. We wish to communicate, but fear to do so.

During the first 100 years of psychoanalysis, *repression* has stood as the model and key defense. When faced with a source of anxiety, we respond by obliterating its existence. We forget about it. We are not aware it is there. Should something happen to remind us of its presence, we assign it little in the way of importance.

For some time now, *denial* has also been treated as an important mental mechanism. In repression there is a memory or fantasy that we disguise and fail to recall directly; in denial there is a reality or actuality whose existence is completely ignored. We fail to perceive a reality of which others are readily aware. We deny its existence.

Both repression and denial can be used as healthy defenses or in pathological, maladaptive ways. We make sound use of repression when we are able to forget a highly painful trauma. As long as we do not react to other situations inappropriately because of the influence of the forgotten memories, we are able to manage fairly well. We do so in part because we spare ourselves repeated reminders of a painful experience. Similarly, we are made more comfortable by quietly denying the inevitability of our death. However, were we to deny our inability to fly and step off a high ledge, the defense would be highly maladaptive and lead to serious injury or even death.

Among the many psychological and interpersonal defenses that we use in our daily lives, psychoanalysts have recently paid a good deal of attention to a mechanism called *splitting* (Grotstein 1981). The concept that we may divide up (split) our perceptions, our reactions to stimuli, and our state of mind goes as far back as *Studies on Hysteria* (1893–95), where Breuer and Freud described the splitting of consciousness into a hypnoid state and a normal state.

Toward the end of his writings, Freud (1927, 1940) described splitting as a mechanism used by fetishists. Such individuals include men who make a special object (fetish) of a woman's shoe, using it symbolically to represent the imagined (fantasied) female phallus. With one part of their mind they recognize that women have no penises; with another part, they use this fetish to maintain the belief that this is not at all the case. Mentally they are divided—split. Each part of the mind is organized around a constellation of related conscious and unconscious fantasies and perceptions. Through splitting, strikingly contradictory attitudes, beliefs, and fantasy and perception constellations can be maintained side by side.

Prodded by the Kleinian school of psychoanalysts in England, therapists have afforded a growing measure of attention to the mechanism of splitting. Recent investigations indicate the need to understand this defense in order to clarify the true nature of the therapeutic experience and conspiracy.

Splitting plays an important role in the psychotherapeutic experience, much of it inadvertent. Virtually all psychotherapy in existence today involves splits in patients as well as in therapists. Patients enter treatment divided in their basic wish to be rid of their emotional disturbances as opposed to the wish to maintain their illnesses. They are divided too, quite unconsciously, in their intentions concerning their therapists. They wish to be helped by them as much as they wish not to obtain such help. However, many patients also unconsciously intend to do harm to their therapists if need be. At the same time, these patients are also prepared to be helpful and even curative if their therapists need such help. By and large, as long as a therapist expresses his or her therapeutic needs unconsciously, the patient will respond in curative fashion. If the therapist abrogates the patient's position and asks directly for treatment, the patient's response may be quite different and rather antagonistic.

The therapist too is divided, often quite badly. Most therapists consciously wish to be of help to their patients, though some even lack this level of commitment and concern. Their unconscious intentions are quite another matter. A split is in evidence: on the one hand, they wish to make their patients well, while on the other, they strive to make the patient sicker. In some ways, it is often necessary to make the patient more ill in order to make him or her well. Still, some of these destructive wishes toward the patient are entirely in the service of pathological needs within the therapist.

The structure of virtually every form of psychotherapy reflects this split in the therapist. While treatment should be designed entirely for the therapeutic needs of the patient, and for those satisfactions that the therapist can accrue within such confines, this is seldom the case. Therapists deviate from the ideal ground rules and boundaries of the treatment relationship for pathological reasons of their own. Based on such needs, they intervene non-interpretively and often without attempting to understand the patient.

It would appear that even insight-oriented psychotherapy and psychoanalysis have been shaped in part by the pathological needs of therapists. The very structure of the therapy enables therapists to enter the treatment relationship with a significant measure of conspiracy. The patient is told that the treatment is designed to alleviate his or her emotional disturbance, but the treatment is structured in such a way that the therapist intervenes in a fashion that inherently expresses aspects of his or her own emotional difficulties. Accepted techniques permit such expressions and create a situation in which the therapist unconsciously functions as a patient, hoping that the patient will unconsciously function as a therapist.

In order to maintain this level of collusion, therapists have ignored many of their own messages to patients. Selectively, such as when they offer a so-called interpretation, they will acknowledge the manifest implications of their communication to the patient. Even then, however, they will deny the unconscious implications of their interventions or ignore such ramifications.

Furthermore, therapists make many interventions whose messages and impact on the patient are given virtually no consideration whatsoever. This is commonly seen when a therapist changes an hour, offers advice, raises or lowers his or her fee, or otherwise modifies the ground rules of psychotherapy or psychoanalysis. Such communications are viewed by therapists as inconsequential. This attitude is supported by attending to the patients' material entirely on a manifest level.

Were the therapist to shift to trigger decoding, he or she would very quickly discover that all of his or her responses to patients, from silence to any kind of active expression, are filled with conscious and unconscious meaning. Furthermore, patients are highly sensitive to the unconscious implications of everything that the therapist does. They respond, however, mainly through encoded messages of their own to these encoded messages from their healers. Since patients are seldom direct in this regard, the conspiracy continues quite unnoticed.

The split in the therapist involves his or her stated intentions toward the patient and the actual implications of his or her messages. Therapists profess one intention and unconsciously carry out another. They propose to heal patients, and instead attempt to heal themselves. They propose a set of conditions supposedly designed to bring out patients' emotional disturbances and their underlying bases. Instead, therapists offer conditions designed to create barriers to such expression and to limit the measure of meaning in the patients' associations. Patients are quick to unconsciously detect such splits. They react in divided fashion themselves, exploiting the therapist's difficulty to some extent and attempting to resolve it as well.

Another split in therapists is reflected in the nature of their interventions. While interventions are consciously designed to explain to the patient the basis for his or her emotional illness, their actual unconscious function more often is to express a series of fictions that reveal more of the therapist's own inner fantasy life and pathology than the truth of the basis of the patient's emotional difficulty. Therapists claim to offer interpretations designed to help the patients understand themselves, while in actuality their interventions do not provide such insight. They intend consciously to cure through understanding, while their interventions are often designed unconsciously to be hurtful, uninsightful, or noncurative.

Suppose that the patient who remembered his mother forcing him to eat developed heartburn or vomiting or an aversion to food. Some therapists would immediately suggest that the symptom was based on a repudiation of his mother's pressures and a reaction against the early memory of being forced to eat. The more fanciful analyst would propose that the patient was struggling with cannibalistic fantasies toward his mother, which he must then defend himself against.

Only the communicative therapist, the therapist who is aware of the main trigger for the patient's association, would be in a position to suggest that his own previously false and forceful interventions had conjured up the patient's memory of being forced to eat by his mother. He would then be able to suggest to the patient that his heartburn was a reaction to the therapist's own interventions, which were reminiscent of his mother's behavior.

This last would be a truthful interpretation of the essential (activated) unconscious basis for the patient's emotional disorder. It would accept the patient's valid unconscious perception that the therapist had indeed been pressuring the patient to accept his comments. It would accept too that the therapist had intervened in a manner that, on some unconscious level, implied a need to force-feed the patient, the presence of a hostile feeding act. It would fully accept the existence of unconscious needs, fantasies, and perceptions in the therapist. It would also eventually account for the patient's symptom through an understanding of additional contributions from within the patient's imagination. However, every possible valid unconscious reading of the implications of the therapist's prior intervention would be accepted as nondistorted and nonpathological. The presence of distortion and pathological fantasy would be proposed only when the stimulus from the therapist would in no way, consciously or unconsciously, justify the patient's encoded perception and response.

The therapist who proposes that the patient is having an eating difficulty based on cannibalistic fantasies toward his mother is attempting to be helpful and curative. Still, his intervention is designed primarily to avoid the therapeutic interaction. It has been created as a dynamic fiction shaped by the material from the patient, but designed functionally to avoid an unconscious perception of the therapist himself. It involves the use of a statement with some general measure of truth designed as a barrier to the realization of the patient's actual experience of the therapeutic interaction and of the therapist's intervention.

It is a fact that forceful, pressing, and repetitive interventions symbolically cannibalize and devour the patient. Because of this, a more truthful interpretation would have been to the effect that the patient's memory of eating is a reflection of the devouring qualities of the therapist's comments . The memory reveals (encodes) a valid perception of the therapist far more than it reveals any wild imagination on the part of the patient.

The therapist who proposes the presence of a cannibalistic fantasy in his or her patient under these conditions is actually expressing aspects of the therapist's own primitive fantasy life far more than touching upon primitive fantasies within the patient. It is the therapist who introduces cannibalism or sexual confusion or the symbolic use of the mouth as a vagina. It is the therapist who denies that the image could contain a sound unconscious perception of himself or herself, and who locates his or her own problem in the client. In this way, such a therapist introduces aspects of his or her own psychopathology for the patient to incorporate and respond to consciously and unconsciously.

Collusion between patient and therapist also relies on the splitting mechanisms used by patients. Consciously, patients state to their therapists that they wish to be rid of their emotional illnesses. When offered insight-oriented therapy, they agree to strive to understand themselves. They clamour for insight and for psychoanalytic interpretation. They aver directly that they are seeking out the conditions under which such insight may be achieved.

Patients are quite concerned with the conditions of treatment. Early in psychotherapy, most patients address and test out the ground rules of therapy. Their conscious intention is to have a set of conditions under which they can work toward insight and symptom relief. However, they are quick to propose ground rules and conditions that will virtually preclude such an outcome. They ask to be excused from sessions, not to be responsible for hours missed because of illness or business, to be allowed freely to change the time of their sessions and to have additional appointments if they feel the need. Consciously, they implore and entreat their therapists to be flexible, giving, and lax. Unconsciously, however, should the therapist accede to such deviant conditions, the patient will be enraged and will produce encoded messages of reprimand and recrimination. Typically, the fuss is displaced and directed toward someone else and virtually never toward the therapist.

If, on the other hand, the therapist attempts to secure an ideal set of conditions (framework) for insightful treatment—ground rules under which the unconscious truths of the patient's neurosis can emerge for interpretation—many patients will object and take issue. They will demand changes in the therapeutic contract and protest loudly when these are not accepted. Nonetheless, attention to their encoded messages reveals a deep sense of appreciation and trust for the therapist who has the capacity to maintain the frame. These encoded messages indicate that the patient feels safe and secure, though he or she is deeply frightened of what will emerge. And certainly, the patient under these conditions has every reason to be anxious, since these are the circumstances under which the painful and terrifying truths of his or her emotional sickness will be revealed.

Consciously then, patients clamour for deviations in basic ground rules and for deviant conditions of treatment. Unconsciously, every patient appears to know something of the ideal conditions of treatment and of the kinds of interpretations that actually provide true insight. Through encoded messages—and almost always, only in this disguised way—they are prepared to guide the therapist in structuring a proper treatment situation and in offering sound interventions. Yet, the split in patients is such that when the therapist does just that, many will protest loudly on a conscious level, while nonetheless expressing gratitude in their unconscious expressions.

The insight-oriented psychotherapeutic conspiracies have developed because therapists have created their techniques on the basis of their patients' conscious communications—if they consider the patient at all. The second level of expression, the latent and encoded level, has been almost entirely ignored. Because of this, the split in the patient has not been recognized.

A treatment experience designed on the basis of the patient's conscious associations will have rather different attributes compared to one created on the basis of the patient's encoded communications. As a rule the two are quite opposite in their nature.

And since the patient will only, as a rule, express appreciation and the wish for a truly insightful treatment experience on an encoded and unconscious level, it is only through attention to these derivative expressions that therapists could create those necessary conditions. Because of their own inappropriate needs, therapists have not listened to the patient's derivative commentaries on the conditions of treatment and on the implications of their own interventions. Instead, they have followed the patient's manifest thoughts and reactions. They have accepted the patient's pathological needs and used them as their own guides. They have created a form of unconscious collusion based on conscious exchanges, creating conditions under which a far different set of transactions take place on the unconscious level.

A CLINICAL VIGNETTE

Mr. Call arranged for a consultation with Dr. Daniels, a psychotherapist. In the session, he told the therapist that he was having considerable difficulty in his life because he drank too much. He tended to show extreme swings of weight, becoming obese through excessive overeating in binges, after which he would go on crash diets. His marriage was stormy, and he was involved in a number of affairs that were not especially satisfying. He felt guilty for betraying his wife.

Dr. Daniels listened for a while and then recommended twice-weekly therapy. Mr. Call said that he was prepared to agree, but he had to be sure that he would not be charged for missed sessions. Because of his job, he had to travel from time to time. Certainly, it would not be fair to charge him for these sessions. His schedule was a tight one, so it seemed likely that the hours could not be made up. He would do what he could to keep it to a minimum, but he wasn't going to get involved in a treatment situation where he would be penalized because of the nature of his work.

Before Dr. Daniels could respond, Mr. Call said that he somehow now thought about his mother. When he was a child, she had this overindulgent attitude. There was nothing he wanted that she wouldn't find a way of getting for him. She spoiled him rotten. Maybe that had something to do with how he became an alcoholic. Well, he asked, what about arranging therapy? If it could be done fair and square, Mr. Call was ready to get started.

Dr. Daniels indicated that he wanted to get treatment going in a way that would make Mr. Call feel comfortable. After all, Mr. Call would have to trust him and, certainly, if he imposed hurtful conditions on his patient at the outset, it was bound to create complications. Mr. Call corrected Dr. Daniels and said that, to the contrary, there would be no therapy at all. Dr. Daniels agreed, and said that as long as Mr. Call was prepared to explore the meanings of excused sessions and to keep them within limits, he would agree to seeing him under the conditions he proposed. Mr. Call was very grateful, told Dr. Daniels he seemed like a very understanding person, and agreed to twice-weekly therapy.

Treatment has not yet begun, yet already there is evidence of a split in both Dr. Daniels and Mr. Call. The former indicates that he wants to create the best and most trusting conditions possible for his patient, but then agrees to forego his fee when his patient must be out of town for a business trip. Mr. Call himself indicates that he too wants the best conditions possible for his psychotherapy, though he proposes a stipulation that must be met by Dr. Daniels if treatment is to be undertaken. The conscious contract is agreed upon to the mutual conscious satisfaction of both. In fact, Mr. Call is filled with praise for Dr. Daniels for his flexibility and kindness.

Overlooked, of course, is the segment of associations from Mr. Call that followed his request. There, images of his mother's self-sacrificing and overindulgent attitude appeared. Mr. Call spoke of her kindness, and yet he held her responsible for his present emotional problems. In light of the trigger—Mr. Call's anticipation that the therapist would agree to his request to be excused from the responsibility for some of his sessions (to be an exception)—it seems highly likely that this particular association was designed as an encoded warning to Dr. Daniels: "If you make this exception for me, you will be overindulgent and sacrificing yourself for me in a manner similar to my mother in my childhood, and in a fashion that contributed to my sickness."

Dr. Daniels simply took this piece of information as a bit of the patient's history. It never dawned on him that it could be a vehicle for a critical encoded message and indirectly contain an unconscious meaning of the contract proposed by his patient. In fact, he believed this particular comment to be a reflection of a strong sense of psychological-mindedness in his patient and took the speculation as a sign of a good prognosis. Thus it seemed to Dr. Daniels that his patient tended to reflect on psychological causes and to have some sensitivity to their presence.

Dr. Daniels did not realize that whatever clichéd (and therefore functionally meaningless) truth there might have been to the patient's conscious insight, the most important implication of that particular message involved the current therapeutic interaction: it was a disguised but valid reading of the meanings and functions of the set of conditions to treatment proposed by the patient.

Had Dr. Daniels understood this, he might well have responded with an interpretation rather than with acquiescence. Had he done so, the patient consciously might have been quite enraged. However, if Mr. Call was prepared to seek insight, he would have understood unconsciously that the condition he proposed for his therapy would preclude insight and substitute in its place a pathological interaction that duplicated the relationship with his mother that had formed the soil for his present and past emotional difficulties. While consciously seeking a set of conditions under which he could get well, Mr. Call had proposed a therapeutic contract under which this was impossible through insight. The very basic conditions of treatment, by supporting and gratifying his neurosis, would render all understanding superfluous or give lie to supposed interpretations of factors in Mr. Call's disturbance.

The ground rules of psychotherapy are actualities filled with conscious and unconscious meaning. They determine the basic transactions of treatment, the meanings of the verbal–affective communications, the nature of the relationship between the patient and therapist, and the very mode of cure. If cure is constituted through a deviation that regularly entails some type of action-discharge or pathological satisfaction, understanding will be impossible except in one sphere: the meaning of the deviation that undermines insightful treatment. The patient's manifest associations will contain encoded communications pertinent to these deviations. If the therapist addresses and corrects these flawed conditions, the patient can gain a great deal in a positive and constructive sense. If instead the therapist entirely ignores this level of communication from his patient and the issue itself, his own interventions will be belied by his unconscious collusion with the patient. In addition, the efforts directed at understanding and cure will be a sham, since the therapist has already behaved in a manner designed to support the patient's sickness.

In the following session, Mr. Call began by stating that he was really feeling great—"high." Since the last session he had been flooded by memories. Once his mother actually stole some dresses from a department store and sold them to friends in order to pay for some dental work Mr. Call had needed as a child. He himself remembered stealing from his father's wallet on many occasions. When he was fourteen, he had been seduced by a man who went down on him after promising to give him some money. After that, Mr. Call had been very distrustful of men in particular.

At work, there is a lot of absenteeism in his division. It's the fault of his section head who is something of a fool. He lets people take sick and personal days very freely. He looks away when they take extra days and cheat on him. As a result, none of the work gets done. He really ought to set up some decent work rules and stick to them. The way it is, everyone walks all over him and takes advantage.

Once you develop a sense for trigger decoding, understanding the encoded messages in a session of this kind poses few obstacles. Certainly, there are many therapists who would concentrate on Mr. Call's alcoholism and its roots in his early childhood. Once again, they would point to his mother's overindulgence, to the impulsive stealing from his father, and to the homosexual seduction as factors in Mr. Call's present disturbance. There would be a thin measure of empty truth to these formulations. However, they would merely be intellectualized inferences based on the patient's manifest associations without the use of any type of decoding method. They would propose that the missing or unconscious link in this material is Mr. Call's failure to realize the ways in which these experiences have contributed to his present addiction. They would provide him with what is called a "genetic link," a connection to the past, expecting that he would then resolve his alcoholism based on this kind of understanding.

If in this session, Mr. Call had gone on to describe a fantasy of seducing Dr. Daniels, of performing fellatio on him, of stealing for him or having Dr. Daniels steal for him instead, these therapists would then introduce the concept of transference. They would take these manifest fantasies as a sign of transference, of involvement with the therapist based on Mr. Call's early experiences with his parents. They would suggest, for example, that the homosexual fantasy derived from the homosexual experience in Mr. Call's childhood and perhaps from underlying fantasies Mr. Call entertained toward his own father. The fantasy of having Dr. Daniels steal for him would be traced to Mr. Call's experience with his mother, the occasion when she stole the dresses in order to provide him with dental care. In essence, the proposition would be maintained that these early experiences were now influencing Mr. Call's fantasies toward Dr. Daniels, his transference. Overlooked along the way is the fact that these are all *conscious* fantasies, and transference resides in *unconscious* constellations, which may find expression only via encoded messages.

Conscious fantasies toward a therapist are actually one of the most unlikely ways in which a patient might encode an unconscious fantasy about that very person. Most encoding of fantasies, and of perceptions of the therapist as well, is embedded in messages regarding other persons. This makes sense, since the messages involved, whether perceptions or fantasies, are highly charged and threatening and require considerable disguise because of needs for defense.

Part of the psychoanalytic conspiracy has involved the use of manifest fantasies regarding the therapist in terms of their direct messages and obvious inferences without any effort at decoding. The meanings then assigned to these manifest communications relate entirely to the patient's present fantasies and past-life experiences. Valid unconscious perceptions of the therapist and his or her interventions are not engaged. Instead, massive fictional and lie-barrier systems—self-protective formulations—serve as defenses against the painful details of the actual unconscious communicative interaction between therapists and their clients.

In the present clinical vignette, the therapist's decision to establish a basic ground rule that Mr. Call need not pay for missed sessions when he is absent because of travel commitments related to his job may be taken as the organizing stimulus for these associations. A number of implications of this particular trigger have already been identified: that it is inappropriately indulgent of the patient, a sacrifice by the therapist, a form of seduction, and a reflection of an inability to establish a firm hold with clear boundaries for the treatment relationship. How does Mr. Call himself characterize Dr. Daniels' deviation through his encoded associations and his derivatives?

Mr. Call is consciously happy and even high. He appears to be directly gratified by the deviation. Having already praised Dr. Daniels for his decision, he says nothing more of the arrangement in his direct associations. A manifest content therapist would feel that the ground rule issue had been settled and accepted by his patient. He would have no reason to believe that anything in this second session had a bearing on the basic conditions established for Mr. Call's therapy. Instead, as already formulated, he would be prepared to pursue the unconscious dynamics and genetics of Mr. Call's alcoholic problem and affairs. The therapeutic contract and interaction would be set to the side until the patient did or said something rather manifest and dramatic. Even then, Mr. Call's comment or behavior would be traced to fantasies and memories, not to perceptions of the therapist.

It happened that toward the end of this session, Mr. Call announced that, by the way, next week he would have to miss one of his sessions because of a business trip to Montreal. It is well to keep this addendum in mind as Mr. Call's manifest messages are decoded in light of the adaptive context or trigger of the fee arrangement. It is this added comment, offered almost as an aside, that lends support for the validity of this type of decoding.

The memory of Mr. Call's mother stealing from others in order for him to have dental care can be taken as an encoded message that represents the unconscious realization within this patient that the basic agreement of treatment creates conditions under which he can deprive Dr. Daniels of income to which he is entitled. Mr. Call gives this arrangement a dishonest cast and characterizes it— through derivatives, of course—as a form of stealing from his therapist. In one sense, this is an entirely valid perception of what Dr. Daniels is permitting his patient to do. On another level, the emphasis on the dishonest qualities may stem in part from corrupt needs within Mr. Call and from the dishonesty of his mother. It is rather typical under these conditions to find that the patient's communications decode in a form that allows for *transversal* messages, communications that traverse both perception and fantasy, therapist and patient, valid commentary and some measure of distortion.

The theme of stealing is further reinforced by Mr. Call's memory of stealing from his father. Mr. Call commented in the session on how his father left his wallet in the living room where it was easy to take money from him. His father also seemed to ignore the loss of funds, as if unconsciously promoting the theft. All of this pertains to a valid unconscious perception to the effect that Dr. Daniels was indeed blindly permitting his patient to deprive him of money that would be his due. In psychotherapy, it is almost impossible for a therapist to replace missed hours of this kind, since the therapist sees patients at regular hours. Dr. Daniels was indeed sacrificing his own personal needs for those of his patient.

The memory of being seduced by a man through the offer of money (the homosexual experience) is an encoded derivative perception of the seductive aspects of Dr. Daniels' decision. He is both permitting himself to be seduced by Mr. Call and is seducing Mr. Call in turn. Through this encoded message, Mr. Call captures this particular quality of the basic arrangement for treatment.

The material regarding the situation at work contains less in the way of the underlying instinctual drives that are being gratified on both sides by this arrangement. Rather, it contains a more cognitive working over of the nature of the arrangement and its liabilities. Here, Mr. Call readily portrays Dr. Daniels as ineffectual, as allowing others to cheat and exploit him, as creating conditions where the job will not be done, and as failing but needing to set firm limits and boundaries. Through derivatives, Mr. Call offers Dr. Daniels a clear *model of rectification*—an encoded suggestion that if the work of therapy is to be done, the basic ground rules will have to be changed and solidified.

Once stated, these encoded messages seem self-evident. They reveal a deep split within this patient who consciously wishes for a deviant therapeutic contract while unconsciously indicating its pathological qualities and the ways in which it will undermine effective insight therapy.

Dr. Daniels' behaviors—his own encoded messages—unconsciously repeat versions of the very childhood traumas that contributed to the development of Mr. Call's emotional disturbance. If Dr. Daniels were to suggest that Mr. Call is an alcoholic because his mother overindulged him and his father permitted him to steal from him, these would be empty, hollow words. They would constitute a pretext of trying to understand at a time when Dr. Daniels' actual interventions have created conditions under which such understanding would be inherently contradicted. By overindulging the patient, Dr. Daniels was indicating that he, like Mr. Call's mother, had some pathological need to overgratify his patient. He was conveying as well that he had unconscious homosexual wishes toward his patient, which he had a need to gratify and indulge. He was also indicating that, like Mr. Call's father, he permitted his patient to steal from him. The split between Dr. Daniels' conscious intentions and communications and his unconscious expressions is enormous. It can only serve to intensify the split within his patient.

Each of these encoded messages involve an actual behavior on the part of Dr. Daniels. No words in the universe can contradict or undo the implications of these behaviors. The influence of these messages can be modified in only one way: by changing the basic contract so that Mr. Call is responsible for all of his sessions. Mr. Call offered Dr. Daniels exactly this model of rectification. As long as Dr. Daniels does not understand his patient's encoded message, and as long as he does not rectify this frame, he will be seen unconsciously as a therapist who unconsciously encourages alcoholism, addiction, illicit affairs, and forms of acting out. The behaviorally communicated mode of cure offered by Dr. Daniels is that of action-discharge, interpersonal merger, and exploitation. In this light, efforts at so-called insight are a sham and meaningless.

Such contradictions can provide relief to some patients. Understanding the nature of this relief is the primary task of this book. This becomes an even more compelling task when other treatment modalities are considered. Another therapist might share a hot tub with Mr. Call, thereby blatantly communicating pathological messages directed toward a reinforcement of Mr. Call's pathology. Still another therapist would ask Mr. Call to go back to his memories of stealing from his father, to dig deeply into them, to feel their pain, and to cry out in anguish. The existentialist therapist would tell him to be the father who was stolen from, to be the child who steals. Mr. Call would be directed to be the homosexual seducer or the boss who is ineffectual. The patient would be asked to feel and become what are believed to be split-off parts of himself. All the while he would be acting out split-off parts of his unconscious perceptions of his overindulgent and seductive therapist. At times these techniques drive patients into madness and even suicide. Still, at times they also bring relief.

Mr. Call might be asked directly to steal or to abuse the therapist. He might be asked to make lists of every thought that he has about drinking. He might be asked to pledge to stop drinking or be offered medication. In group therapy, fellow patients would propose all sorts of dynamic interpretations to Mr. Call or even attack him for his failings. The therapist might take one side or another and even propose dynamic interpretations of his own.

All of the 300 forms of therapy have one factor in common: they avoid the truths of the conscious and unconscious communicative interaction between patient and therapist. They work elsewhere, deal with something else. They propose other explanations of the patient's symptoms, but they do not maintain a consistent understanding of the therapeutic interaction. The psychoanalyst has an elaborate fiction system, while the behavior therapist ignores the interaction altogether and attempts to decondition the patient. The varieties are endless.

CHAPTER 20
THE ROLE
OF DUMPING

It is necessary to understand one final mental mechanism in order to fully comprehend the conspiracies of psychotherapy. It is called technically *projective identification*, an awesome sounding term. It may also be called *interactional projection*, which indicates that it is an interpersonal rather than intrapsychic defense. In plain language it is *dumping* (unloading), a term that immediately characterizes its main attribute.

The British psychoanalyst, Melanie Klein (1952), coined this particular term. She first described its use in rather ill schizophrenic patients. Now it is known to be a mechanism used by all individuals, and its use can be normal or pathological, primitive or quite advanced in nature.

Projection is an intrapsychic or internal mental defense in which an individual attributes to someone else that which belongs to himself or herself. The person is angry, but feels instead that others are angry with him or her. Or an individual is sexually aroused and feels that another person is trying to be seductive. The entire experience can take place intrapsychically and nothing need be communicated to the other individual involved. The mechanism has adaptive value in enabling people in their imaginations to disown impulses and fantasies that threaten their self-image and mental equilibrium. Nonetheless, its overuse leads to paranoid forms of suspicion and, sometimes, to a loss of the distinction between oneself and others.

Identification works in the opposite direction as a rule, in that it is a mechanism through which an individual takes in (rather than extrudes) an attribute from someone else. Through identification with others, one incorporates their traits (some adaptive and some maladaptive) into one's own self-image and way of functioning. Here too, within limits, the mechanism can be constructive, though its excessive use leads to a loss of personal identity and to a sense of inner turmoil based on the contradictory elements of identification or introjection involved.

Projective identification is therefore a rather strange term. It implies that a given individual sends outward—or extrudes—impulses and fantasies, or some aspect of his or her own inner state with which he or she is identified. The term *dumping* captures this process, because it implies that a person actually attempts to place into someone else an aspect of his or her own inner mental world.

It must be stressed that dumping is an interpersonal and interactional mechanism. While there may be inner fantasies of projective identification, its true essence involves actualized efforts to psychologically dump or put into someone else some aspects of one's own inner state. To do so, the target person must be present and there must be an actual interactional thrust.

The most common purpose of dumping is to get rid of unwanted and threatening inner conflicts, perceptions, and fantasies by attempting to establish them in another person. The goal is to have this other person either serve as a receptacle for the extruded material or, instead, to take in the qualities that have been extruded and deal with them in some better fashion than the original person. Eventually, this more effective capacity to manage may be incorporated in return by the original dumper. Thus interactional projection is a riddance mechanism as well as an interpersonal appeal for help in managing one's own inner state by actualizing it in another individual.

From the many examples already cited, it is evident that projective identification or dumping plays a strikingly significant role in most psychotherapeutic conspiracies. By and large, virtually every form of present-day psychotherapy is designed unconsciously as a way of enabling therapists to dump many aspects of their own inner problems into their patients. This is one of the ways in which therapists operate as *functional patients*, placing their sickness into their *designated patients* and hoping that the latter will be able to contain and better handle whatever has been extruded (i.e., will serve as a *functional therapist* to the *designated therapist*).

The recipient of an interactional projection tends to incorporate the extruded contents or experience. Following another British analyst, Wilfred Bion (1962), projected contents are called the *contained* and the recipient of such contents is referred to as the *container*. In psychotherapy, it is expected that a patient will dump aspects of his or her pathology into the therapist. It is the therapist's responsibility to contain these extruded contents and to work them over or *metabolize* them into an understanding of the patient. Bion suggested the term *reverie* for both mothers and therapists who are adept at containing and metabolizing projective identifications.

On the other hand, patients have every right to expect therapists to function as containers for whatever it is necessary for them to extrude. They do not expect their therapists to dump aspects of their problems into the patient, however. It is conspiratorial when this kind of dumping is accepted.

There are dumping qualities to virtually every therapeutic intervention described in this book. The paradigmatic therapist was dumping her own (and her supervisor's) inner aggression into her patient, who in turn reacted rather violently. Directive and assaultive Gestalt and other therapists also dump highly aggressive inner contents into their patients. Sex therapists dump their unresolved sexual pathology into their clients, while psychoanalysts tend to dump their pathological fantasies.

A great deal of dumping is involved in all modifications of the basic conditions of treatment, each with a specific quality in keeping with the nature of the deviation. An increase in fee dumps the therapist's greed into the patient, while a reduction in fee offered in the face of a threat that a patient may terminate dumps the therapist's own separation anxieties and overindulgent tendencies. Ruptures in confidentiality tend to dump highly aggressive forms of betrayal into the patient, who is then under some pressure interactionally to work over the extruded contents.

Projective identification is a major factor in all action-discharge types of therapy. This includes abreaction, deconditioning, and all of the confronting types of therapy already observed. Their possible curative potential lies in part in the opportunity afforded patients to dump pathological contents into therapists and to benefit from their responsive interpretations. In a more distorted way, patients sometimes gain relief when they are able to successfully incorporate and contain the pathological projective identifications from their therapists and experience themselves in a state of reverie. However, such patients are often overtaxed in this respect by their therapists, and the consequences, rather than being ameliorative, are rather destructive.

There is evidence that many forms of psychotherapy are basically designed to foster the pathological dumping efforts of the therapist. Since much of this operates unconsciously, therapists who are burdened with many inner conflicts and problems turn avidly to schools of psychotherapy that sanction the use of this type of pathological interactional and interpersonal mechanism. Such treatment modalities are attractive and popular because of this attribute. Often, the dumping tendencies of the therapist sanction similar propensities in the patient. There will be exchanges of projective identifications between patient and therapist that become more and more violent and disruptive because neither participant to treatment is capable of containment and metabolism. Quite often, a patient, in identification with the therapist, will do a great deal of dumping in outside relationships as well. Therapists who have a need to dump their own sickness into their patients will tend to approve of such behaviors, mistakenly viewing them as a sign of emotional health. This forms the basis for many collusive psychotherapeutic cures.

Until now, this book has concentrated on identifying various motives in patients and therapists for the acceptance of a psychotherapeutic conspiracy. Here and there, one or another type of conspiracy has been identified in its motives and basis, but these efforts have been quite scattered. Thus a sense of the problem has been imparted, but not a systematic understanding. The following chapters provide this type of more comprehensive perspective on the collusion between patients and therapists.

CHAPTER 21
LIES AND TRUTHS

Morally, religiously, and ethically, we are taught to idolize and revere the truth. Many persons give lip service to this ideal, even though unconsciously and often quite consciously they make ample use of lies and deceptions. This is yet another common example of mental and psychological dividedness (splitting).

If the truth is approached scientifically and clinically, some rather surprising attributes may be discovered. The actual basis of a person's emotional disturbance involves highly sensitive unconscious perceptions of others and their incorporation (internalization or introjection) into oneself. Highly disturbing unconscious fantasies and memories are also involved. As such, the comprehensive true source of a particular emotional dysfunction involves very threatening, anxiety-provoking realizations. Little wonder many patients and therapists would prefer to set all of this to the side.

Still, knowledge of the true state of things is the only basis through which sound adaptive resources may be developed with which to handle future emotionally traumatic experiences. A foundation of functioning and understanding based on the acceptance of manifest and latent truths is also the sole basis for genuine growth. A mastery of the truth further provides a foundation within which it is possible to integrate valid realizations from others even though they may threaten one's equilibrium on a temporary basis. In the emotional sphere, every new realization, every new insight, and every hard-won bit of understanding, creates a period of temporary chaos and disturbance. It is through the assimilation of threatening truths, however, that we mature in a manner that involves a maximal realization of our inner potential.

When individuals depend on lies and lie-barriers for emotional equilibrium, they must insist upon having others share their lies and defenses. They are intolerant of the truth and actually feel persecuted by it. They are unable to absorb and integrate the truth and can get by only in the presence of others who share their lie-barrier systems. Often, it is necessary for such individuals to attack and destroy the truth-teller lest their own chaos and disequilibrium become unbearable.

Systems of thought and of clinical practice that are founded upon lie-barrier formations cannot integrate new ideas unless they involve falsifications similar to their own. They do not genuinely expand and grow, but instead become involved in an insidious form of proliferation that is self-fulfilling and circular rather than expansive. Those who ascribe to the lie-barrier beliefs strive only to find new elaborations of their central fictions. The *lie hero* is someone who states the familiar in a form that offers a guise of supposed originality. Sameness is the credo, though means are found to provide it with new trappings. Basic revisions are impossible without a cataclysmic catastrophy. Very few lie-barrier systems have shown a capacity to tolerate such an untoward event.

Clinical psychoanalysis and psychoanalytic psychotherapy are founded on a typical lie-barrier system and fiction. Such a constellation is usually built on statements of general truths that are used *functionally* as falsifications and barriers to the activated truths of a given moment. In this way, psychoanalytic statements regarding psychosexual development, narcissism, dynamics, and whatever, are utilized in a way that denies the existence of the communicative interaction between patient and therapist. Transference, a valid concept, is applied to situations where the intrapsychic and interpersonal dynamics offer no justification for its invocation. The conflicts and dynamics of the patient are interpreted at a time when the patient is unconsciously working over and expressing himself or herself in regard to the conflicts and dynamics of the therapist.

Because of its lie-barrier foundation, clinical psychoanalysis has not been able to integrate truly new clinical findings and ideas into the mainstream of its thinking and clinical practices. The entire conceptualization of an active, two-person therapeutic interaction is repudiated out of hand, since it cannot be integrated into present psychoanalytic thinking, which is devoted entirely to the postulated isolated intrapsychic happenings within the patient. A catastrophic moment would occur if a classical psychoanalytic therapist were to acknowledge the existence of his or her own conscious and unconscious communications to the patient and recognize their enormous impact on the client, as well as their infusion with the therapist's own psychopathology.

The analyst's view of the therapeutic experience would be turned on its head. He or she would no longer be a detached observer, healthy and simply prepared to interpret. The analyst's human qualities, vulnerabilities, countertransferences, and active unconscious participation in the therapeutic interaction would have to be acknowledged. There would be the painful realization that a large portion of the patient's communications involve an unconscious working over of the therapist's sickness. Nonetheless, since this is an acknowledgment of the truth of the situation, it would then be feasible to construct a sound form of psychotherapy that takes these actualities into account. It would also be possible to minimize the contributions of the therapist's pathology to the therapeutic interaction by recognizing their many unnoticed sources in present-day clinical work.

There is a confusion of languages among the many schools of psychotherapy, which all adhere to their own unique teminologies. Beyond this surface problem there is, however, a more fundamental difficulty in integrating the various psychotherapeutic approaches into a single valid paradigm. The goal here is not to create a rigid therapeutic model, but instead to develop a model of treatment flexible enough to serve patients with all types of psychopathology, yet firm enough to entail the best possible therapeutic principles.

At present, each form of psychotherapy involves its own unique lie-barrier system. There is some overlap and sharing, so that there are a number of different types of existential or gestalt therapy, just as there are rather different types of psychoanalytic psychotherapy.

The realization that each involves an organized and systematized group of functional lies helps to explain the enormous gaps between the various schools of treatment. No single school can tolerate the other; none can encompass the best of each. The fear of catastrophe renders this impossible. Immutable differences define and protect each distinctive lie-barrier system.

What then are the dangers and anxieties produced by truth therapy? What are the liabilities of the truth system as it pertains to the basis for emotional disturbance? And just what factors impel many patients and therapists to avoid these truths and to seek emotional relief on some other basis?

The situation of certain patients whose past and present lives have qualities of an unending nightmare hints at the answer. These individuals either find some means of getting rid of their inner chaos in their interactions with others—often through dumping— or they suffer from acute psychotic decompensations. If they enter and are able to remain in some form of exploratory psychotherapy, they will on occasion bring together the terrifying elements of their emotional sickness in unforgettable fashion. They are of interest here because much of their story is an open expression of the terrifying truths that exist in some form in each of us. Nonetheless, their surface revelations are still an encoded version of even more painful underlying raw perceptions, fantasies, and memories. Mercifully, every human being, even if psychotic, possesses a capacity for defense that spares him or her the direct onslaught of the most horrendous aspects of inner mental life and life experiences. It is for this reason as well that it is so difficult to describe to the point of experience and conviction the horrifying truths that must be faced if one is to know the actual basis of his or her emotional disturbance and to make peace on such terms.

A CLINICAL VIGNETTE

Ms. Elman was in therapy for some two months with Dr. Farber. He was her fifth therapist. Previously, she had been involved in a mutual seduction with one of her two woman therapists. Eventually, she worked as a surrogate sexual partner for this therapist, functioning sexually with both men and women who suffered from major inhibitions and other sexual disorders. Her relationship with this therapist came to an end after Ms. Elman became pregnant through one of their mutual clients and suffered through a painful and crude abortion arranged by the therapist. Upon her recovery, in a dispute over fees, they fought physically and the patient's nose was broken. In excruciating pain, she experienced a series of encapsulated hallucinations in which her mother fragmented and disintegrated before her eyes.

Prior to the pregnancy, Ms. Elman had been deliriously happy. For a time, she had lived with her former therapist and served as her lover. The morbid anxieties and fits of suicidal depression to which she was prone virtually disappeared. They returned full force after the break-up of the relationship. In despair, she made a suicide attempt with aspirin, though her own hysterical call to a girlfriend brought her the medical treatment that she needed to survive.

Referral to a male psychiatrist brought her little peace. He attempted to create a rather disciplined and clearly defined therapeutic situation, which at first she welcomed. She felt a sense of strength that she had never before experienced. In the sessions, however, she soon began to experience bizarre feelings of lightheadedness and a sense that the walls were caving in on her. There were occasional hallucinations—this time of her father exposing himself to her sexually, echoes of a past real experience. She began to feel that she was insane and attacked her physician verbally for trying to drive her crazy. She demanded medication and, when he attempted to interpret rather than medicate, she stormed out of his consultation room to never return.

Matters had been little better with her first male therapist, who had seen her in treatment along with the man with whom she was living. There the situation deteriorated when the boyfriend's role shifted to that of a procurer and the therapist seemed to side with him in the bitter disputes that she had with her lover in the therapy sessions. During this time she was not experiencing her anxiety attacks, though she did have episodes of depression.

There was one period of relief when the therapist arranged to see her parents and attacked each of them verbally but soundly. He castigated her mother for her erratic thinking and behavior, for the ways in which she would shift her position without warning. Much of this had come up because of a bitter incident in which the patient had been raped by a neighbor. At first the mother, who had witnessed an argument between her daughter and the man who had raped her, had told the police a story that seemed likely to lead to the man's indictment. Quite suddenly, without evident reason, the mother had changed her tale in a way that held her daughter entirely responsible for seducing her seemingly innocent friend. The helpless rage experienced by Ms. Elman had proven unworkable in the treatment sessions. Her therapist called in the parents and viciously attacked the mother for her ways, basing and documenting much of it on what had been reported to him by his patient.

The father too was condemned and abused for his many affairs, involvements he blithely paraded in front of his daughter. He had also been openly seductive with her, highly exhibitionistic, and had attempted some kind of seduction one summer while alone with her at a resort.

Following the session with the parents, Ms. Elman was party to a chaotic screaming and crying scene with her parents. There was some sense of remorse on both sides, though little sense of relief. Soon after, her parents stopped calling her and refused to see her. Strangely, the patient felt a sense of relief that she only recently had begun to question.

Her last previous therapist, also a man, made use of nude marathons and a variety of encounter techniques. For a while, Ms. Elman felt rather good. She quickly established herself as a leader among the patients and was actively sought after by two of the men. Quite uncharacteristically, the day after the threesome had spent the night in bed sharing a wildly uncontrolled series of sexual experiences, Ms. Elman experienced a major anxiety attack that she was unable to bring under control.

Through the man with whom she was living, a bisexual, Ms. Elman was referred to Dr. Farber in a state of desperation. The referring therapist, who had heard a great deal about Ms. Elman from his own patient, described the situation in detail to Dr. Farber. He reported the conversation back to his own patient, who carried it to Ms. Elman prior to her telephone contact with her new therapist. She herself did not make the initial telephone call until she had arranged and completed several contacts as a prostitute, wishing to have sufficient funds to begin treatment. On the telephone, she asked for assurances that Dr. Farber would provide her with medication, insisted upon knowing the fee, and made clear she would agree only to an initial consultation, nothing more. Because of her disputes with her present boyfriend, she also insisted that Dr. Farber be prepared to contact his therapist in order to help them to work out their difficulties. Dr. Farber had responded that he was willing to do whatever would help her with her suffering.

Ms. Elman began the consultation session with a seductive tone, telling Dr. Farber that she had done some hooking and was ready to pay in hard-earned cash any fee he would name. She insisted on being assured that he had no hangups about taking this kind of bread, and he indicated that this was indeed the case. Relieved, though with a sense of near hysteria, she launched into telling her therapist about herself.

She described her suicidal episodes, her depressions, and her anxiety attacks. She said she knew that she was pretty crazy, and she had a feeling a lot of her grief came from the kind of people with whom she associated. They were all just like her, two and three and four of a kind. Her previous therapists were no better—corrupt hustlers like herself. Every man she knew was ready to hop into her pants. There was no hope.

The other day, she said, one of her more hoody friends, a man, came to her with "dirty" money. He wanted to wash it clean by giving it to her in exchange for sexual favors. Contrary to her usual style, she was repulsed by the proposition. She threw him out of her apartment in a fit of rage. Just once in her life, she'd like a man to make her a clean offer.

The session went on in like vein. Based on her hooking activities, Ms. Elman thought she could afford twice-weekly therapy. Dr. Farber arranged the hours and expressed some hope that he could be helpful. These hopes were shattered the following morning when his patient called him in a state of hysteria. She had had a terrifying nightmare the night before and was now feeling spaced out. She was experiencing horrifying images of men with huge sexual organs that changed into steel-bladed knives. They seemed to be coming after her to rape and destroy her.

The very same images had dominated her dream. In her nightmare, she was in an office that wasn't an office, with a doctor who wasn't a doctor. The man was coming toward her prepared to assault her. His genitals kept changing, from a penis to a knife to a vagina to a gaping wound gushing blood from fragments of flesh. Hundred dollar bills were spewing from his mouth. A siren wailed in the background. The earth began to shake like it was coming apart. Ms. Elman felt herself glued to and merged with the earth and about the shatter into millions of tiny particles. She attacked Dr. Farber for forcing her to have that dream. She was convinced that he was more a sorcerer than a therapist. He was evil and mercenary. No way would she return.

Terrifying nightmares of this kind, fantasies and perceptions, abound in the deep recesses of the minds of all of us. Of course, it is a form of emotional disturbance per se when an individual experiences such horrible images in his or her waking life. It may also be a sign of considerable disturbance when they appear in our dreams.

Ms. Elman is the kind of patient who, to some extent, experiences consciously some of what we all harbour unconsciously. From birth onward, we begin an accumulation of onerous and frightening images, mixtures of reality and fantasy that we must put to rest lest we go mad. Fortunately, as we mature, we develop the mental defenses and coping capacities to accomplish this essential task.

First, there is the primitive mind of the child unable to clearly distinguish self from not-self, reality from fantasy, dreaming from waking experience. Provided with the most primitive conceptual tools, his or her experience with the world is fraught with uncertainty, fragmented images, primitive impulses, and horrifying dread. The monsters of fairy tales bear but muted witness to these early mental experiences.

All of this is compounded by inevitable maternal failings. The communication of conscious and unconscious fantasy constellations from mother to child are capable of creating further fragmentation and disturbance. Of course, on the other side, the mother's positive capabilities provide a critical interactional source for the child's stability and contribute to the development of his or her own internal defensive armamentarium and growth.

With each phase of development, internal bodily and fantasy experiences couple with reality to generate highly charged systems of conscious and unconscious fantasy and perception. The greater the stress and level of anxiety, the more primitive the mental and behavioral response.

Then too there are our responses to the traumas that disturb our equilibrium. There are primitive envy and greed, and the refusal to deal with frustration—often with a concomitant tendency to resort to psychotic-like mechanisms through which we attempt to negate that which disturbs us. There are disorganizing rage and aggression toward disturbing circumstances and toward those who frustrate us. There is the use of sexuality, pregenital and even genital, as a means of fusion, revenge, and the enactment of primitive fantasies—in addition to the possibility of mature satisfaction. There are fantasies and acts of vengeance, of self-protection, of narcissism, and of irrationality. There are primitive splits and violent episodes of dumping. The residua form a cauldron of chaos deep within.

Of course, this admixture of instinct, defense, conscience, and such is a basic component of the forces that give us life and stimulation, the wish to live and experience; it is the impetus behind our hard-won accomplishments—creative and otherwise. Typically, again, the very constellation that threatens to annihilate us psychologically is the source of our most gratifying moments and achievements.

Inevitably, then, a deeply unrealistic, agitated, psychotic constellation lies at the core of our mental structure. In order to function in our daily lives without utter fragmentation, we must develop psychological defenses and make use of protective behaviors. Those who are successful in these achievements, and whose psychotic core is not especially primitive and volcanic, function relatively well. If they happen to seek out a psychotherapeutic consultation, they are diagnosed as neurotic or as having only a moderate measure of characterological disturbance. They are, however, a rare breed.

For most, there are defects and flaws. Ideally, we require defenses that permit some measure of expression of inner disturbance in detoxified form. We need some means of expressing our imaginations and of draining off the more disturbing qualities of our inner mental lives. The resultant dreams and fantasies, while containing elements of pathology, are dressed up into usable products of the imagination.

When our defenses fail only minimally, the symptoms are mild and manageable. We may consider such symptoms to be types of compromise defense that combine expressions of our inner turmoil with modulating forces that make the resultant experiences rather bearable. Were Ms. Elman capable of dreaming of a doll with defective insides that she was trying to repair, her inordinate bodily anxieties would have found a form of expression well modulated by defensive operations—the displacement onto the doll, the use of an inanimate object, and the use of an object capable of being repaired. Instead, her nightmare of the bleeding gaping defect in the man coming toward her to assault her rather blatantly expresses a relatively undisguised and primitive version of Ms. Elman's bodily anxieties. Her defensive use of displacement—the shift from herself to the man—serves some protective function, though it proves insufficient to prevent a state of panic from developing. This same image also conveys some of Ms. Elman's violent impulses toward men, her father and therapist among others. Awareness of impulses of this kind can be very troublesome indeed.

In addition to defenses that manage to effect a significant measure of compromise, we erect uncompromising barriers against our own agitated psychotic cores. We obliterate the sources of terror entirely and substitute some form of unrelated lie or fiction in their place. While compromise defenses serve as safety valves and permit some release of the inner disturbance, lie-barrier defenses fail to do so. They serve to obliterate, but the inner chaos remains, pent up and ready to explode. Had Ms. Elman been capable of dreaming of riding with a man on a bicycle built for two, she would have substituted a marvelous fiction of shared effort in place of the enormously disturbing unconscious perceptions that she had developed of Dr. Farber and her own fantasies toward him. Clearly, she lacked a defensive capability for such a transformation.

A listing of the other sources of inner terror, many of them universal, pales in the writing. To really know and experience the truths that make neurotics or psychotics of us all, one must reenter one's own worst nightmare and experience the horrifying feeling of being unable to escape, even by waking up. There is the shattered illusion of blissful symbiosis with the good or bad maternal figure. There is the guilt of incest desired and of wishes to murder the rivalrous parent—the very person upon whom one's survival depends. There is the growing awareness of major spheres of helplessness, and even hopelessness, and of the inevitability of death. There is the realization that death defeats us all, and that our every triumph is but an illusion or even delusion. These are crushing realities that inevitably intermingle with our own fantasy and memory formations.

Finally, there are our own perceptions of others, conscious and unconscious. We experience their failings, their hostilities and seductions, their primitive thrusts, their selfishness and greed, and an endless array of highly threatening and disappointing traits and impulses. When extreme, we fear for our lives and are flooded with mistrust. To this terrible array we must add the unexpected traumas that life can create, experiences that remind us of our vulnerabilities, which brings us full circle in this nightmare of dangers that threaten to strangle us all.

With this as but a sampling, one may nonetheless sense the powerful reasons and motives within patients and therapists for attempting to deal with emotional disturbances through some other means than facing their sources and roots. Automatically, almost instinctively, the individual erects compromised and uncompromised defenses and seeks out some form of unknowledgeable immediate relief. Sometimes he or she even attempts to believe or act as if the entire problem is nonexistent. Still, oddly enough, most human beings are highly divided (split) in their attitude toward this struggle: on the one hand, they seek immediate resolution in a manner that entirely bypasses the truths involved; on the other, almost instinctively too, they are impelled to express and deal with these truths.

For reasons that remain to be clarified, there are, however, some individuals more committed to a search for this kind of truth than others. In response to disturbing adaptation-evoking stimuli, some will express in encoded form, through derivatives, their underlying plight. In contrast, others ignore or obliterate these adaptive stimuli and respond with lie-barrier systems that seal off virtually everything that exists in the chaos below.

Those who fall into the first group can be called *truth tellers*. Those in the second, *liars*. The terms are used without a shred of moral implication and, further, have little to do with conscious or deliberate lying. They are descriptions of how we deal *communicatively* and *unconsciously* with emotional stimuli. A conscious lie may express an encoded truth or function as an unconscious lie-barrier system. Often, however, it is indeed a means through which an individual attempts to falsify reality in order not to deal with perceived truths. Because of this, there is usually a barrier element to a deliberate lie, whatever else it may contain in latent form.

The truth-teller must be capable of tolerating expressions of his or her inner nightmares. The potential rewards include adaptive resolution, the development of sound coping capacities, the solution of unconscious and hidden conflicts, the modulation of primitive inner fantasies and perceptions, and the development of constructive ways of coming to terms with the inevitabilities of life and death. Still, all of this takes place through a sequence of experiences that are inevitably horrifying and chaotic. It is necessary to tolerate and cope with major experiences of disequilibrium, including temporary fragmentations of one's sense of self, identity, and contact with reality. With reintegration, however, there comes a new set of capacities, a firmer sense of identity and self, a greater ability to cope, and a form of genuine growth and maturation feasible by no other means.

Ms. Elman is the kind of patient for whom both reality and inner fantasy are so overwhelming as to be virtually unmanageable. In her session and through her dream she expressed a series of emotional truths of rather terrible proportions. It is a moot question as to whether she would have proven capable of analyzing, understanding, and working through the truths with which she had to deal had she been given a sound therapeutic opportunity. The more terrifying the activated truths and the weaker the individual's (ego's) resources, the more likely it is that a person will resort to primitive attempts to split himself or herself apart, attempting in some violent and psychological manner to divorce himself or herself from the underlying catastrophic disturbance. This type of splitting is a form of action-discharge designed for immediate relief; it does not permit a recognition and working over of the chaos. Often, it is supplemented by violent efforts at dumping, used as a further means of evacuation and riddance.

In a small way, Ms. Elman attempted to use these mechanisms in her telephone call to Dr. Farber. In attacking her therapist, she was attempting to get rid of the violence inside of herself. Some of this, as shall soon be seen, came about because Dr. Farber in his own way had done violence to her. His less primitive dumping evoked a far more primitive type of projective identification from his patient.

In fact, Ms. Elman's violent efforts at dumping did not stop with her telephone call to Dr. Farber. Later that day she called her parents in a manifest effort to engage their help. However, her split-off unconscious wish was to do violence to them. Quite soon in the conversation, she attacked each of their helpful suggestions, and soon launched into a violent tirade against each of them. Inevitably, they experienced the sense of hopeless frustration and fragmentation inside of their daughter, though their own only available means of coping proved to be hanging up on their child. They too of course had dumped much of their own inner turmoil and violence into their offspring at one time. It is in this way that unconscious vicious circles with violent exchanges of projective identifications plague many family interactions, as well as many therapeutic conspiracies.

In reporting her dream to Dr. Farber on the telephone, Ms. Elman was also attempting to split off these disturbing experiences and to dump them into her therapist. Her abrupt termination, which left her therapist without recourse, was a behavioral and interactional way of having him experience her own sense of utter helplessness. Dr. Farber did indeed feel dumped into, angry, perplexed, victimized, and without recourse. He wrote off these feelings to his patient's primitive psychopathology, learning little from the experience. His own lie-barrier systems and defenses precluded any possible comprehension and benefit. Quite soon, he himself split off the entire interlude and allowed it to descend into the oblivion of unfortunate outcome unremembered.

With trigger decoding, it is possible (however painful) to recognize that Dr. Farber had all too quickly failed his patient, as had her previous therapists. Even though his failings were not as substantial as those of his predecessors, they were unconsciously perceived and contributed to the abrupt termination of the therapy. It seems likely that the distinctly mixed and split image that Dr. Farber communicated—concerned and dedicated on the one hand, and yet deeply flawed on the other—was a significant factor in the quick demise of this therapy. Clinical experience has shown that patients of this kind will remain with a therapist only if he or she is almost entirely ("purely") corrupted or, in contrast, remarkably strong and capable of offering a sound therapeutic holding relationship.

There are many encoded messages in Ms. Elman's communications in her first hour and on the telephone to Dr. Farber. Their most cogent meanings are revealed in light of the adaptation-evoking stimuli (triggers) from the therapist. Among these, his readiness to medicate this patient and, most importantly, the acceptance of a cash payment drawn from prostitution activities as compensation for his services, appear to have been most devastating for this patient.

The latter trigger (the money) is revealed in the patient's material to be perceived unconsciously as a form of sexual abuse, greed, and as an expression of shared corruption and prostitution. Perceiving her therapist in important respects as no different from herself—as equally damaged and assaulted—Ms. Elman's defenses collapsed and her nightmare ensued. Having no sound basis for trusting Dr. Farber, she fled the scene.

Had the balances been just a bit different, Ms. Elman might have stayed on for some time. The discovery that her own therapist was in some way a prostitute much as herself might have given her a measure of devious unconscious reassurance. Finding in him an assaultive attitude not unlike her father's, and inconsistencies not very different from those in her mother, she might have felt less enraged toward her parents and toward those aspects of herself that resembled them. After all, even a highly experienced psychoanalyst is just as sick as they are on some level. These, of course, are some of the strange means through which lie-barrier therapists bring relief to their patients.

These "curative" factors correspond to another type of behavioral or interpersonal defense that many individuals utilize as a way of either ridding themselves of part of their own inner psychosis or of finding relief from its pressures—the *camouflage defense*. It operates by seeking out or finding oneself in a situation and set of relationships that are inherently disturbed and even insane. The other persons involved are quite often as sick, and usually even sicker than the patient. Their very lifestyles and fundamental ways of functioning are replete with evident disturbance and psychopathology. In such surroundings and in the midst of such relationships, however, the patient quickly feels that his or her own inner difficulties are of little significance. There is a strong sense of sickness in the air, so to speak, but of sickness which belongs to someone else. Involved here is a more elaborate version of the cure through *nefarious comparison*. There is also a measure of *cure through sanction,* with a strong acceptance by the group not only of severe emotional sickness, but also of action-discharge, dumping, pathological fusion, and other forms of immediate relief.

The paradoxical and unexpected ways in which truth-avoiding therapists bring relief to their patients are studied more carefully in Chapters 25–28. First, however, a specimen of truth therapy is offered so that the reader may sense its positive qualities as well as its liabilities.

CHAPTER 22

THE NATURE OF TRUTH THERAPY

No one can tolerate too large a dose of the basic truths to emotional illness. With those rare therapists who actually practice truth therapy, moments of concentrated and valid understanding are quite rare. Much of the therapeutic work is directed toward the defenses that obliterate or compromise these truths.

There are also moderate to long periods during which these truths are not actively expressed and the patient instead lies fallow. He or she then engages in a modified form of self-analysis, in which benign or healthy lie-therapy mechanisms predominate. This effort is highly constructive largely because of the presence of the therapist, who offers a safe holding relationship within which the patient, on his or her own, can modify his or her pathological defenses. This is far different from the usual lie-therapy situation in which therapists tend to impose their own lie-barrier formations and defenses on the patients, who may or may not find them useful in their own inner struggles.

In psychotherapy, there are two ways in which the underlying truths of a neurosis can be probed, understood, and mastered. Both require a therapist willing to create a space and relationship in which the patient has a significant measure of freedom of expression. This is virtually impossible in clinical situations where free association is restricted or over-shadowed by the activities of the therapist. Even then, in settings where the patient is permitted to lead the way communicatively, the therapist must also have the proper listening tools in order to correctly understand the implications of the patient's material.

Under the latter conditions, patients will react to the ideal or secure set of ground rules for psychotherapy with a strikingly mixed (split) response: on the one hand, there is a positive response to the sense of safety and to the trustful image of the therapist, conveyed unconsciously through his or her capacity to establish for the patient a truly safe setting and mode of relatedness; on the other hand, there are anxieties related to fears of entrapment and persecution that arise because of the restrictions imposed on the patient under these conditions and because of the dreaded emergence of his or her own underlying sickness.

Phobic (entrapment) and persecutory anxieties and fantasies of this kind, basically distorted, and forms of true transference (reactions based on earlier life experiences and inappropriate to the communications and behaviors of the therapist) provide the motive force for a *secure-framework therapy*. These same anxieties, however, also move patients and therapists to establish deviant conditions to treatment as a way of sparing both participants the experience and working through of this type of disturbance.

While the combination of a secure hold and the emergence of the patient's primitive fantasies and anxieties is actually optimal for the truth-therapy experience, it is nonetheless enormously feared. It is quite easy to understand why the patient wishes to be spared this kind of pain and prefers a setting within which it will not be experienced. As a bonus, the creation of a deviant setting is in itself an expression of some inner disturbance of the therapist. It is here that the unconscious pathological needs of both participants to therapy find joint satisfaction: the patient is temporarily relieved of his or her own inner sense of disturbance and there is a lessening of the pressures within himself or herself to express his or her psycho-pathology. Simultaneously, the therapist has an opportunity un-consciously to express his or her neurosis so the patient may unconsciously work over those inputs. Further, in unconsciously experiencing the pathology of the therapist, the patient finds a measure of immediate reassurance.

Under conditions of a secure therapeutic contract, the therapist expresses little in the way of his or her own inner disturbance. The therapist maintains a level of control, renunciation, and necessary sacrifice sufficient to hold the patient safely and securely; this occurs without any noticeable danger that the therapist will traumatize the patient with his or her own pathological needs and their expression. Given the absence of pathological inputs from the therapist, and the presence of a safe relationship and hold, the patient will tend to express his or her own psychopathology, which can then become the subject of the therapeutic work. In light of the alternative, in which the therapist's disturbance is actually the hidden agenda, truth therapy of this kind is in many ways a far from welcome treatment modality for a large number of patients.

With a therapist who establishes a largely sound contract, moments of inevitable lapse become major therapeutic opportunities for the patient, and for the therapist as well. A sudden alteration in the ground rules, a break in the frame, an interpretive error, or a shift to a noninterpretive intervention constitutes a therapeutic failure by the therapist and creates a rare moment in which he or she actively expresses an aspect of his or her own inner disturbance. If the interlude is short-lived and the disruption does not overwhelm the patient, the therapist's error creates an important traumatic adaptive context and trigger for the patient's inner responses. The latter is characterized by a series of sound unconscious perceptions communicated to the therapist in encoded form. The patient will then respond to these perceptions with adaptive behaviors and fantasies, and often with the mobilization of memories consonant with the traumatic experience. Under these circumstances, the present situation with the therapist is on some level an actual version of a past pathogenic experience with a hurtful parental figure. In essence, this is in no way the condition for a transference response, but instead entails an unconscious, sound reaction that is nontransference in nature.

Still, the proper understanding and analysis of experiences of this kind provides a great deal that is constructive to the patient. To carry out such work, the therapist must either rectify his or her error or desist in its expression, doing so with the help of the patient's encoded communications, which are a guide in these directions. The therapist must then prove capable of interpreting the unconscious meanings of the experience for the patient, with full but implicit acknowledgment of the latter's veridical perceptions. Extensions into fantasy and into deviant responses may also be interpreted. The total experience will, as a rule, considerably illuminate the unconscious basis of the patient's emotional disturbance. This type of work can be called truth therapy stimulated by errors and deviations by the therapist.

A CLINICAL VIGNETTE

Mr. Gregory was in psychotherapy with Dr. Henry. He began one session with a bitter attack against his boss. The man is greedy and underpays. When business was going poorly, he cut back everyone's salary. Suddenly realizing he was speaking of money, he took out a check for the therapist and paid his last month's bill, which he had received the previous session. He had meant to pay at the beginning of the hour, but had forgotten.

Mr. Gregory had had a dream the previous night. There was a man with a moustache coming at him with a scooper, intending to scoop out the contents of his abdominal cavity. Then Mr. Gregory was on a street and there was a derelict begging for coins. When Mr. Gregory refused to give him money for drink, the man ripped his pocket open and stole his wallet.

Oddly enough, the man had a moustache, not unlike the one that Dr. Henry sported. Mr. Gregory's father had also had a moustache. His father had been a coin collector, but when he died, he left the collection to charity. Since his estate was small, both his wife and children had been furious. That was typical of father, selfish and greedy and insensitive to the needs of his children. His underlying hatred of his family had been covered over by a kind of sleazy seductiveness. Besides, he'd walk around the apartment nude and never bothered to close the bedroom door when he had relations with Mr. Gregory's mother. It was puzzling: if Mr. Gregory hated his father so much, why did he become involved in sporadic homosexual escapades? Anyhow, he could never get a nickel from his father, but as soon as his son went to work, the old man demanded every penny he earned.

Puzzled by what he was hearing, and sensing an important issue, Dr. Henry pointed out to his patient that he seemed concerned about money and about being robbed and exploited. Some of these concerns actually had a bodily quality, as if Mr. Gregory felt someone was trying to take from him his vital inner organs. This someone was clearly connected to his father in the past, and to himself—Dr. Henry—in the present. Mr. Gregory had forgotten to offer his check at the beginning of the hour, suggesting that all of these images had something to do with his fee for therapy.

Mr. Gregory suddenly remembered his vague impression that Dr. Henry had charged him for one session more than they had actually had in the previous month. He figured he must be mistaken, since Dr. Henry was, in his eyes, someone who never made a mistake. Now that Mr. Gregory thought of it, he took out a calendar and made a quick check. There had indeed been an overcharge.

Mr. Gregory now remembered an incident from his early adolescence that he had not recalled in years. While still in junior high school, he had gotten a job delivering newspapers. Determined to have his own bike, and unable to induce his father to buy one for him, he began to save his money. He had gathered over a hundred dollars when he came home one day to discover that the money was missing. After much denial and hemming and hawing, his father admitted that he had taken the cash in order to pay some overdue bills. He promised to pay back his son as soon as he could. He never returned a penny. The exploitation was infuriating. Strangely, Mr. Henry now connected it to the way in which, with some of his passing homosexual affairs, he would find an opportunity to steal small amounts from the wallets of his companions. The previous night, he had gone to a bar and picked up a man because he had experienced an insatiable homosexual lust. He had tried to take a hundred dollar bill from the man's wallet later that night, but he did it in an awkward way so that he was caught and castigated soundly. It had been a terrible mess.

Dr. Henry apologized for his error. It was now clear, he went on, that Mr. Gregory had experienced his mistake as an exploitation, a robbery. The incident had reminded him of his father and of the ways in which his father had stolen from him. On some level, the overcharge was also experienced as a physical assault. Still, with all of this understood, it was well for Mr. Henry to realize that his response to the overcharge was distinctly divided. On the one hand, he set aside his own sense that a mistake had been made. He then made use of Dr. Henry's mistake to justify unconsciously his own destructive sexual exploits and dishonest pursuits. It seemed now that the awkward fashion in which he attempted to steal and arrange to be caught was a self-destructive way of living out his belief that Dr. Henry was trying to steal from him and that the error should be caught and punished. The overcharge seems also to have been seen as some type of homosexual seduction that Mr. Gregory hoped to use to justify his own exploitative sexual pursuits. It was likely that the homosexuality had its origins in part in comparable experiences with his father. Through the homosexuality, Mr. Gregory was living out his father's seductiveness and exploitiveness: he was seemingly loving of men on the surface, while in some fantasied and behavioral fashion scooping out their insides and robbing them of their money. Dr. Henry's error had been misappropriated as a way of reinforcing Mr. Gregory's need to live out these kinds of destructive perceptions and fantasies.

In the following session, Mr. Gregory reported that he had overcome his year-long reluctance to approach his boss for a raise, and had handled the situation so well that he got an increase far beyond his expectations. He had received a call from a highly seductive homosexual lover but experienced no interest whatsoever in seeing him. There then followed a further reworking of the fee incident with Dr. Henry and Mr. Gregory's earlier experiences with his father.

Dr. Henry's inadvertent error created an unexpected therapeutic opportunity and moment for his patient. While some residual of uncertainty and mistrust is likely to linger within the patient, Dr. Henry's capacity to pick up the area of Mr. Gregory's concern proved quite salutary. At the patient's direct and encoded behest, he returned the check and wrote out a new bill. He was also able to very sensitively interpret the meanings of the experience for his patient. The incident had a highly positive immediate effect on the patient, though much additional working through had to follow.

Mr. Gregory had picked up the error in his bill on a conscious level, but quickly set the realization aside and subjected it to a splitting and fragmentizing process. He therefore maintained no certain conscious awareness that he had been overcharged. Instead, he had ignored his own warning signals and had proceeded to pay the amount for which he had been charged. Nonetheless, the excessive fee continued to be perceived quite clearly on an unconscious level and served as a stimulus for this patient's subsequent behaviors and dream.

It is evident how trigger decoding fostered a highly perceptive understanding of this patient. The stimulus of the overcharge was experienced as a homosexual bodily assault, as a form of stealing, and as a reflection of impoverished need in Dr. Henry. These were all quite valid perceptions. Upon private self-analysis, Dr. Henry discovered a latent homosexual wish toward his patient, which he had not resolved. Mr. Gregory was quite well off, while Dr. Henry was suffering from the pressure of a number of large financial commitments. He soon realized that he had entertained an unconscious fantasy of seducing Mr. Gregory and being paid as a homosexual prostitute. The error he had made had not only provided his patient with a significant moment of insight, but himself as well.

With these painful conscious realizations, Dr. Henry was able to get under control his underlying homosexual and financial needs and to assure that they did not significantly further influence his interaction with this patient. Dr. Henry felt a special sense of relief that he had resolved these conflicts and pathological needs, especially when he realized that Mr. Gregory's raise would make him all the more inviting. In this kind of secondary fashion, therapists can benefit from the unconscious therapeutic ministrations of their patients.

Mr. Gregory's communications to Dr. Henry were a sensitive working over of his therapist's error. Dr. Henry was able to make good use of his patient's endeavors and responded in part by bringing his countertransferences under control. His ability to correct his mistake and to offer sound interpretations not only provided insight to his patient, but also a constructive unconscious image that Mr. Gregory could take in (introject) psychologically. It involved someone who might unwittingly make a mistake, but who would then be capable of correcting it and understanding its implications. Thus, on one level, Dr. Henry's interpretations provided meaningful insight for his patient, who was able to use his new understanding in order to function better at work and control the disturbing aspects of his homosexual impulses. Mr. Gregory was also able to incorporate an image of a therapist capable of excellent ego functioning, a positive introject that would help to reinforce the best aspects of the patient's own capabilities. Implicitly, Dr. Henry provided Mr. Gregory with an unconscious model of conflict management and resolution not available to the patient on the basis of his earlier life relationships.

These are some of the ways in which truth therapy accomplishes its curative effects. It does so cognitively in terms of the mastery of specific activated unconscious perceptions, fantasies, and conflicts. It also cures interpersonally through the incorporation or introjection of a well-functioning therapist who serves as an internal object that reinforces the more adaptive aspects of the patient's own functioning. Simultaneously, this kind of introject serves to neutralize highly pathological and destructive introjects (inner objects) derived from earlier pathological interactions with parental and other figures. The battle against neurosis actually takes place on many levels, cognitive and interpersonal. Truth therapy is curative in all of these spheres.

The truth therapy paradigm provides the patient with an opportunity to respond fully and both consciously and unconsciously to a therapist's interventions. Once an intervention is made, the truth therapist will listen to the patient's response for both direct and encoded reactions. True insight and growth are signaled by the recall of a distinctly new memory or fantasy that extends and uniquely illuminates the therapist's intervention. This is a sign of new mastery. A previously unconscious constellation, which has contributed to the patient's pathological behaviors entirely without his conscious awareness, has entered consciousness and can now be understood in perspective.

In this particular clinical interlude, the contributions of Mr. Gregory's exploitation and seduction by his father to his own unwanted homosexual behaviors were understood in a manner never before available to either patient or therapist. Still, one must pause and realize the great pain inherent to recognizing how one's own father helped push oneself into homosexual encounters. Highly disturbing conscious and unconscious perceptions of the father were involved. Beyond these were the patient's own fantasied and behavioral reactions, themselves rather primitive and frightening.

Mr. Gregory experienced a sense of accomplishment after the session described here. He was able to make rather uncanny connections between his present life and his past experiences. Consciously, he had a distinct appreciation for the efforts of Dr. Henry, though he remained a bit perturbed over his having made a mistake in the first place. Still, he experienced a sense of inner calmness that was quite unfamiliar to him. In these seemingly small ways, Mr. Gregory had benefitted from a moment of truth in psychotherapy.

There are many other ways therapists might have responded to this particular interlude. Many psychoanalysts would have interpreted this material as reflecting aggressive homosexual *fantasies* in this patient, and would have suggested that they were entirely derived from earlier experiences with his father. If they had connected this material in any way to the therapeutic relationship and to themselves, they would have suggested a pathological *transference* reaction in which Mr. Gregory was attempting to demean Dr. Henry and to mistakenly attribute to him homosexual wishes and impulses. In the main, they would have proposed the presence of a distorted and transference-based homosexual fantasy toward the therapist as a means of accounting for the acting out, homosexual encounter of the previous night. It would be the rare psychoanalyst indeed who would have suspected that he or she had provided some measure of impetus for these behaviors. Rarer still is the therapist capable of acknowledging the actual homosexual implications of the billing error. The patient's valid unconscious perceptions would be interpreted as unconscious fantasies, and experienced reality would be treated as the patient's distorted and sick imagination.

Many other psychotherapists would be so actively engaged in deconditioning or directing Mr. Gregory that they would not even get to hear his dream. Still others, upon hearing the dream, would dissect it as a reflection of the inner problems of the patient. They would ask him to live out the scooping activity and being scooped. He would be pressed to play the beggar as well as his own role in refusing the coins. He would then be asked to imagine himself as victim and victimizer in the theft. All of this would be used to show Mr. Gregory split-off aspects of himself, fantasies and impulses of which it would be proposed he had been unaware. No attention whatsoever would be paid to the therapeutic interaction or to Mr. Gregory's responses to these existential pressures. If Mr. Gregory grew more and more enraged and concentrated on images of being raped and robbed, these would be attributed to impulses of his own to rob and rape others. Some connection might be made to Mr. Gregory's father, but it would be of little consequence. Only the here-and-now impulse and image would matter—and this only as long as the here-and-now between patient and therapist, and especially their unconscious interaction, was deleted (split off) from the present moment.

Some therapists would allow group members to interpret this dream, again largely in terms of Mr. Gregory's demeaned self-image and disturbing fantasy systems. Some, instead, would place Mr. Gregory in a tub, nude with other men, as a way of getting him to accept his homosexuality or to totally repudiate it. The dream, the therapeutic experience, the actual overcharge, all would be treated as nonexistent. Mr. Gregory would then either suddenly realize that he had been overcharged and treated unfairly, and question the entire treatment experience, or readily succumb to the implicit abuse to which he was being unwittingly subjected. This could serve as a means of unconsciously punishing himself for what he perceived as his own homosexual misdeeds. On this level, the overcharge would also be experienced unconsciously by Mr. Gregory as an expression of his therapist's own aggression and homosexuality, and used as unconscious justification for the continuation of the patient's own pathological behaviors. Remarkably, the human mind can find some relief in almost any so-called therapeutic measure, no matter how evidently hurtful to the recipient and self-serving to the perpetrator.

CHAPTER 23
TRUTH AND THE SECURE FRAME

The basic form of truth therapy is quite rare in present-day practice. Still, there are therapists who today attempt to work within an essentially ideal and secure therapeutic framework. They offer the patient an entirely private and confidential treatment experience, with clearly established sessions. They respond interpretively and with framework-management (frame-securing) responses to the patients' material, always with a keen sensitivity to the critical encoded messages it contains. To the greatest extent humanly possible, they do not impose their own pathological and inappropriate needs on the patient, but remain committed to sound responses to the therapeutic needs of their clients.

Under these conditions, it is the implications of the therapist's capacity to secure and maintain the frame that evoke anxiety and disturbance. However, in contrast to situations where the therapist is in error and the patient responds primarily with valid and disappointing unconscious perceptions, under these conditions the therapist is functioning in sound fashion and the patient's reactions tend to be distorted and transference-based (i.e., inappropriate to present reality and derived from past relationships). This communicative and dynamic correlation appears to be rather consistent: the errors and pathology of the therapist evoke mainly unconscious but valid and sound communications and responses from the patient; in contrast, the effective functioning of the therapist leads on an encoded level to expressions of distortion and pathology in the client. However, in terms of actual behavior and functioning, poor interventions by the therapist often lead to a direct deterioration in the patient's functioning, though at times, quite paradoxically, they elicit a mobilization response with a notable measure of adaptive value; on the other hand, sound and validated interventions generally produce an enhancement of the patient's immediate coping capacities.

Truth therapy, it should be emphasized, is a natural extension of classical psychoanalysis and psychoanalytic psychotherapy. It owes to this classical paradigm its appreciation of a secure and stable set of ground rules and boundaries for the therapeutic setting and relationship. It derives as well from this approach a deep and abiding interest in the patient's communications and a commitment to the search for their true meanings and implications. It incorporates the theory of neurosis that locates the sources of these problems in the patient's unconscious mental life, replete with both disturbing fantasies and disruptive perceptions. It accepts the principle that analysis and resolution of these inner struggles are undoubtedly the best means through which most individuals can be offered relief from their emotional suffering.

The truth therapy approach elaborates the fundamental appreciation in classical psychoanalysis of the patient's relationship to the therapist, but does so by taking into full account the therapist's relationship to the patient. The resultant extension of the present focus on the patient promotes a distinction between pathological and transference-based reactions in patients and those that are healthy and founded on nontransference qualities. It also extends the usual psychoanalytic approach by taking into full account the spiraling conscious and especially unconscious communicative exchanges between the patient and therapist, affording full consideration to the manifest and latent implications of the inputs and messages from both participants to treatment. The truth therapy approach is thus concerned with both unconscious intrapsychic and unconscious interpersonal processes. As such, it is more comprehensive than previous psychoanalytic approaches, an aspect that leads to propositions, techniques, and understanding that are at times at variance with usual psychoanalytic efforts and thought.

In many ways, then, truth therapy appears to be a natural extension and completion of the psychoanalytic method initiated by Breuer and Freud almost 100 years ago. It is clear too that truth therapy could not be based on any of the other psychotherapeutic paradigms. In a major sense, truth therapy has arisen out of the specific recognition and resolution of the psychoanalytic psycho-therapeutic conspiracy. It is therefore more readily integrated into the psychoanalytic approach and would be far more difficult for therapists of other persuasions to accept without a period of violent and catastrophic working over.

A CLINICAL VIGNETTE

Mr. Jackson was in psychotherapy with Dr. King. Treatment had been arranged with a secure frame, including full responsibility for sessions and payment by Mr. Jackson through his own funds. The patient had entered treatment because of a sense of dissatisfaction and depression, which he experienced because of his inability to stop having affairs and his need for occasional interludes with prostitutes. His wife had become quite suspicious of his escapades and this had led to frequent quarrels, many of which had been overheard by his son, who was now in early adolescence. Despite all conscious resolve to desist from these activities, Mr. Jackson continued to see other women.

This patient showed a determination to stick with the therapy and his twice-weekly sessions despite a considerable degree of skepticism. He was a successful professional man who felt a deep commitment to pursue the goals he set for himself. Nonetheless, he made several attempts to have the therapist alter the ground rules by providing make-up sessions when he went off to professional meetings and by changing hours when he became interested in another professional activity that would interfere with his sessions.

On one occasion, after making such a request, Mr. Jackson went on to allude to his feeling that he was trapped in his marriage. He recalled the sense of safety he felt when involved with women other than his wife. Only at home did he feel the discomfort of being closed in. He recalled a dream of entrapment, which he felt was set off because his search for an affair was thwarted. He thought now of conscious fantasies and beliefs that his wife wished in some terrible way to control him and to ruin his professional career. He was unable to cite any hard evidence for these feelings, but they remained with him. He commented too that his wife had plenty of evidence of his involvement with other women, and that long ago she should have taken a firm stand against his sexual promiscuity.

On the basis of this encoded directive, Dr. King pointed out that Mr. Jackson himself saw make-up sessions and changes in their schedule as a form of laxity and promiscuity that only encouraged his involvement with extramarital relationships. While the manifest request was for flexibility and kindness, the hidden plea was for some kind of support for the very symptoms he hoped to resolve through the therapy. Thus, while the conscious request was to change his hour or to make up a particular session, his indirect message was quite the opposite: maintain the stated conditions of treatment and help him to control his impulsive sexuality.

Mr. Jackson responded with a new piece to the puzzle that needed completing as a full statement of the unconscious basis for his neurotic behavior. He suddenly recognized unwitting ways in which his mother had encouraged her husband's affairs, often ignoring blatant signs of their existence. There then followed a period of relative noncommunication, of lying fallow.

Some sessions later, Mr. Jackson slipped again and sought out and engaged a prostitute. In a session soon after this incident, Mr. Jackson requested a change in the time of one of his sessions. Once again, he provided Dr. King with the material to maintain the frame as arranged. Following a series of interpretations not unlike those already summarized, Mr. Jackson began the next hour by reporting a dream in which he was cornered in a cage by a lion or a tiger. Somewhere, he sensed the presence of a lion tamer. Nonetheless, while he felt a bit more secure, he remained fearful of being bitten to pieces.

The scene of the dream reminded Mr. Jackson of a recent trip to the zoo with his wife and son. They had had a marvelous time together and yet, the following night, he went out and met with a prostitute. He was annoyed with himself because his wife had been quite warm and loving. Despite those perceptions, and possibly because of them, he also had the feeling again that she was trying to entrap and suffocate him. His affairs were something like breaking out of the cage before he was devoured and destroyed.

Somehow, the images brought him back to the early years of his life when he slept in his parents' bedroom. The dream reminded him of early childhood nightmares which had often involved lions and tigers tearing men to pieces and devouring their flesh. He then recalled an overwhelming experience of an abortion that his mother had had at home, a memory filled with images of terrifying screams and bloody bedding. He had never felt safe in his mother's arms or in her care. When she fought with Mr. Jackson's father, he sometimes thought she would tear him to pieces.

When Mr. Jackson again asked if Dr. King wouldn't change his mind and shift one of his hours for the following week, the therapist intervened. He pointed out that his patient seemed to be struggling still with the conditions of treatment and his responsibility for fixed hours. But perhaps he could now see that in therapy he felt trapped in a cage and was fearful of being annihilated or devoured. This particular image and anxiety seemed to derive from experiences in his parents' bedroom, which conjured up images of lions eating men. This must in some way be connected with his image of his mother as capable of destroying his father. It must also relate to his memories of his mother's abortion, which seemed to be connected to fantasies and images on his part of her destructiveness. As a result, Mr. Jackson seemed terrified of a relationship with established fixed conditions and boundaries, fearful of his annihilation. Just as he felt entrapped when he got close to his wife, he felt entrapped and endangered when he—Dr. King—worked effectively and maintained the agreed-upon conditions of therapy. Clearly, the underlying fear in both of these relationships was that of entrapment and annihilation, fears that derived in part from his early experiences with and images of his mother.

Mr. Jackson now suddenly remembered an odd fantasy that he had prior to coming to the session, in which he imagined placing a stick of dynamite against the wall of the therapist's consultation room and setting off an explosion. He realized now that the image implied a destruction of the enclosure of the office and an attempt, through violence, to solve his anxieties about entrapment. He now recalled for the first time in years that his mother locked him in the bedroom closet when she felt that he had misbehaved. He was terrified of ghosts and goblins at the time, and was convinced that he would suffocate to death. He had set up an appointment with a prostitute that night and had forgotten to mention it to Dr. King. He decided to cancel it and to spend the night giving the session some further thought.

Within the secure frame, both patient and therapist fear persecution by the psychotic parts of each of their personalities, parts that are likely to find expression under such conditions. The therapist is often fearful as well of some type of harm based on the renunciations and restraints that he must accept in order to be an effective holding figure. The patient is worried, consciously and unconsciously, about entrapment and annihilation, and about a therapist who is so powerful and capable as to secure the therapeutic situation.

While there is a background of basic trust, revealed in Mr. Jackson's dream through the presence of a lion tamer in the cage, patients consistently fear therapists who are on some level more capable than they are of both understanding and control. While patients make use of the wisdom of such therapists, they remain in mortal fear that the therapist's knowledge will ultimately be used to destroy them. These concerns are, or should be, quite unfounded, and yet they are quite intense and persistent. Such fears are distortions of the image of the therapist and not justified in his or her sound and sensitive interventions and behaviors. It is in this way that transference and distortion emerge in treatment as a response to the therapist's sound functioning. These responses are mainly a reflection of the patient's own pathological inner mental world, introjects, memories, fantasies, and perceptions.

The unconscious bases of the patient's emotional disturbance under these secure-frame conditions are (1) earlier experiences with his mother, which generated a mixture of pathological fantasy and perception and then required the acting out symptoms used by the patient as a means of protecting himself from this constellation; and (2) fears that the enclosure created by the ground rules of therapy implied that the therapist would soon attack and destroy him as had his mother in the past. It is here that the patient's earlier experiences are inappropriately imposed upon the present situation with the therapist. It must be stressed, however, that they are inappropriate only when the therapist has in no way behaved in a manner that would justify this kind of perception. For Dr. King, this seemed to be the case.

At the behest of the patient's encoded communications, Dr. King maintained the frame and interpreted the underlying anxieties and fantasies that helped to account for the hidden basis of Mr. Jackson's repetitive affairs and his fears of treatment. The truths involved were confirmed by the unique fantasy and memory recalled by the patient after Dr. King's interpretation. This material clearly provided new insight into the underlying factors in Mr. Jackson's disturbance. Their comprehension and working through led to symptom alleviation and growth.

Moments of this kind in truth therapy are almost unobtrusive. They bring together some of the terrifying aspects of a patient's earlier life and present thinking and feeling. When the therapist has erred, they involve sensitive perceptions that are highly disturbing to both patient and therapist alike. They ask of the therapist an ability to recognize that images of incompetence, of being ineffectual, of being vicious and seductive, of being attacking and devouring, and of many other highly charged and negative attributes, are at times sound and fair readings of the implications of his or her own interventions.

All of this requires that therapists who usually enter the profession with idealized beliefs in their own mental health must face their own unanalyzed residuals of disturbance. It requires that they recognize the failings of their own analyses or therapy and of their own therapeutic efforts. It even asks that therapists recognize that at times their patients function directly and especially on an unconscious level in a far more healthy fashion than they themselves. It requires not only a renunciation of omnipotent fantasies and beliefs regarding oneself as a therapist, but also an ability to forego highly satisfying or pathological modes of relatedness, which tend to infantilize patients and exploit them. It also asks the therapist to make a full investment in cure through truth and insight, rather than through some more immediate though tainted means.

The truth is a unique and precious commodity. It alone can form the basis for genuine growth and the development of new and highly flexible adaptive resources. It alone can provide lasting conflict resolution and the modification of pathological fantasies and perceptions. Its use by the therapist is the only means through which the patient can experience and take in (introject) a truly sound, relatively unconflicted, unsplit (integrated), nondumping, healthy figure as a way of supporting the patient's own ego functioning. The truth is also a priceless basis for creativity and maturation, even though it requires the surrender of previously held fictions and lies. While always initially chaotic, the truth is the only foundation for sound identity and individuation.

There are many patients and therapists who believe that they are unable to tolerate and endure the temporary period of disorganization and seeming catastrophe that is always a part of discovery and growth. For them, the possibility of truth therapy is abhorrent. For them, lie therapy must prevail. Given that at present there are no more than a handful of effectively functioning truth therapists, the lure of some other means of cure must be quite enormous. The following chapters examine some of the reasons why this is so.

CHAPTER 24
THE ATTRACTION TO LIE THERAPY

Allowed the play of their natural instincts, most human beings seek both immediate gratification and immediate relief. The ability to simultaneously think abstractly, delay response, and anticipate consequences—and thus to fully utilize what Freud called the reality principle—is a difficult accomplishment. While many individuals give lip service to these capacities or appear to possess them, they show little ability to use such resources when under stress.

This may appear to be a pessimistic view of humankind, but it is nonetheless a realistic one. It contains within it seeds of great optimism, in that a full confrontation with these almost instinctive human tendencies is one of the few means by which they can be modified. As people, we require repeated reminders of the disadvantages of selfish actions, action-discharge modes of relief, blind instinctual-drive gratification, and impulsive acts of revenge. Maturity can come only from a mastery of our infantile selves.

Given these tendencies, it is small wonder we are attracted under emotional stress to lies and lie-barrier systems, like iron filings drawn to a magnet. Since the truth tends to be momentarily unbearable and difficult to utilize for immediate adaptation, we are all prone to make use of fictions when under pressure. We shift to thoughtless action or to a form of thinking that is actually mindless, a way of using ideas to discharge and dump into others the anxiety, perceptions, and fantasies that plague us. We substitute lies and lie-barrier formations for the chaotic truths that disturb us, whether they are perceived within ourselves or in others. If we are able to tolerate encoded representations of these truths, we may eventually discover their meanings. If instead we seek to build impenetrable barriers against their expression, we remain bound to lie-barrier systems, sometimes for our entire lives.

When it comes to emotional disturbance, the advantage of lies and lie-barrier systems is evident in their immediate utility, the promise of immediate relief, and the avoidance of the nightmarish qualities of the truths that they supplant. Lies permit a rather malignant shift from victim to victimizer and provide a false sense of mastery through illusion and delusion. As products of our imagination, they are inherently gratifying. Their protective and blindly defensive qualities endear them to us and lead us away from contemplating their flaws and liabilities.

In some ways, one of the most compelling lessons in the development of psychoanalysis and the many forms of psychotherapy entails the realization of the human attraction to unconscious lie-barrier systems. With these, we may believe we possess immortality and omnipotence. We may defeat our most powerful enemies, within and without. We may create images of sanity that belie our present or impending sense of fragmentation.

The gains are not simply personal. While a case can be made for a view of present-day society as founded on conscious and deliberate lies, the emphasis here is on the collective use of *unconscious* lies and fictions as a way of coping with emotional stress. With our tendency to reduce situations into simplistic elements and to act quickly and thoughtlessly, lie-barrier formations are extremely handy. We are ready to share with others socially approved systems of this kind. Many cultural institutions, such as marriage, schooling, and government, are based in part upon unconscious lie collusion. Virtually every form of psychotherapy in existence is founded on one or another lie-barrier system. Through a process that is largely unconscious, though consciously rationalized, all a potential patient (an emotional sufferer) need do is seek out the lie therapy that best suits him or her. If a mistake is made, one need only move on to another system.

All of this is based on entirely human tendencies that we are loathe to modify. It is only the realization of the liabilities of each and every lie-barrier system that motivates some of us to find another way of coping. Even then, we must be on a constant alert against slipping back, falling prey to the lure of one or another lie system.

Prior to psychoanalysis, the underlying truths of a patient's emotional disturbance were considered so entirely overwhelming that their very existence was denied. Lie-barrier and avoidance techniques were all that existed—hydrotherapy, massages, electric shock, and direct suggestion. Each met with some success, each failed abysmally with many.

It was Josef Breuer who found these particular lie-barrier systems useless in his work with Anna O. With her help, a new, somewhat less burdensome, though still troublesome, form of lie-barrier therapy was created. With it, the patient would be heard and the therapist would probe. However, the lie-barrier quality was assured through the requisite that all that was involved was a tracing out of the recent roots of the patient's emotional disturbance—a search for genetic origins. Even then, the therapeutic process was so unsettling that both patient and therapist abandoned its use. Breuer never treated another patient completely through the cathartic method, while Anna O. sought further help in a sanatarium and eventually denounced psychoanalysis as a treatment procedure.

Freud had the wisdom to create psychoanalysis out of the ashes of the cathartic method. He had the courage to probe deeper into the origins and underlying truths of his patients' emotional disorders. Nonetheless, he too required a series of tenets that would assure a maintenance of lie-barrier qualities to psychoanalytic work. These involved the belief that the patient's associations reflected conscious and unconscious fantasies and were entirely devoid of valid unconscious perceptions. They entailed the use of the concept of transference as a means of denying the therapist's contributions to the therapeutic interaction and to the patient's communications. They therefore involved the denial of important aspects of reality as they pertained to the therapeutic experience, and often to the early life experiences of his patients as well.

Psychoanalysis is a form of lie-barrier therapy in which the therapist's own psychopathology and erroneous technical measures are denied through an overriding focus on the postulated psychodynamics and genetics of the patient.

It seems likely that psychoanalysis itself, and the development of psychotherapy into an extended array of treatment measures, was humanly possible only because lie-barrier systems were woven into their basic tenets and techniques. Given the monstrosities that dwell within each of us, and granted our uncertainties regarding their mastery, few therapists would have dared to venture into psychoanalysis without some form of lie-protection. The personal confrontation and risk, and the required self-knowledge and control, are of such inordinant magnitude that few, if any, could have survived the ordeal. One can easily imagine thousands of therapists taking flight from psychotherapy in a manner fashioned by Breuer. Perhaps only the foolhardy and psychotic would stay on—hardly the basis for an effective treatment modality.

Only now, having gathered strength from the last 100 years, partly through lie-barrier formations and partly through glimpses of the truth, does there seem to be genuine hope of developing a breed of truth therapists capable of analyzing and working through the actual meanings of their patient's emotional disorders. In this evolutionary process, therapists initially needed lies for their survival; as we have gained strength and insight into mental functioning and adaptation, it is now possible to forego such protective measures to a very large extent. Still, it is sobering to realize that in all likelihood the history of psychotherapy could not have unfolded in any other way.

Psychoanalysis alone has given us a basis for a discovery of the actual truth. In some way, the lie-barrier systems developed by psychoanalysts have been supplemented by a growing number of truthful propositions. Until now, only a few analysts have acquired insight into these problems to a point where they have stated accurate truths as they pertain to the therapeutic interaction and the nature of emotional illness. However, it is quite clear that there are a growing number of therapists who are now prepared to experience the upheaval contained in these new realizations and insights and to carry psychoanalysis to a new and highly unique plane. The evolutionary process has been so gradual and so strongly derived from psychoanalytic propositions, the new treatment form might well not require a new name. It would not be surprising to find it some day referred to simply as psychoanalysis or psycho-analytic therapy.

As far as one can tell, there are no significant signs of this type of evolution in any other treatment modality. Since most of these approaches preclude open communication from patients, it is highly unlikely that this situation will change. By and large, the greatest impetus for the shift within psychoanalysis from lie to truth therapy comes from the *unconscious* needs of patients and, to some extent, their therapists. It can be shown that all patients on an unconscious level have a sense of, and wish for, some form of truth therapy. The problem lies in the inability of most patients to translate these unconscious needs and realizations into consciously directed actions and wishes.

Similarly, as with Freud himself, some truth-loving therapists are also split and struggling to become aware directly of the source of their dissatisfaction with the treatment modality they presently use. However, there is a critical distinction here between patient and therapist. It is inevitable that patients will express most of their wishes for truth therapy on an encoded and unconscious level. This is their only communicative responsibility and, when they do so, they are indeed functioning as truth patients. In contrast, the situation requires of therapists a *conscious* awareness of these strivings and their translation into sound interventions and man-agements of the ground rules for them to function as truth thera-pists. They must be knowingly aware of the disadvantages and flaws in present-day technique. Lacking the possibility of offering their own free associations to their patients, therapists must arrive at these realizations through self-analysis. Therapists are also more restricted in the means through which they can translate their unconscious wisdom into truth therapy and into conscious realiza-tions and behavioral actualizations. They must express themselves directly and without internal contradiction, while patients may do so either directly or indirectly. This is, for the therapist, an arduous but great accomplishment, hard-won and difficult to main-tain. To sum up, then, there are only natural-born patients (we are all capable of conveying the necessary mixture of direct and encoded communication), but there are no natural-born therapists (it takes painful knowledge and sacrifice to work consciously and consistently with the interactionally evoked truths of a patient's neurosis).

Most nonanalytic therapists impose a set of procedures and beliefs on their patients without any substantial regard for the patient's own needs and communications. Instead of permitting the patient consciously and unconsciously to orchestrate and guide the treatment process, these therapists impose their own preordained ideas onto their clients with little regard for their responses. They offer powerful lie-barrier systems, which the patient can either accept or reject. All of this, as stated earlier, is agreeable to many patients and therapists alike.

Eventually the specific assets and liabilities of each and every major treatment modality must be studied. Here, however, the focus is on the pressing question of just how lie-barrier therapies can bring relief to individuals who are suffering from emotional disorders. Along the way, the risks of lie-barrier therapies must be identified as well. In light of their pervasive use and enormously variable attributes, there must nonetheless be a number of basic means through which lie-barrier treatment procedures produce their results. How does not knowing, fabricating, and avoiding seem to have curative effects? Are there other attributes of lie-barrier treatment forms that also bring relief to their patients?

CHAPTER 25

THERAPEUTIC CHOICES

A neurosis or emotional disturbance is a complex psycho-physiological, psychosomatic, interpersonal, sociocultural entity. The intrapsychic and interpersonal contributions to neurosis, and especially those unconscious processes and contents that contribute to its development and sustenance, have been reviewed. Social and cultural factors also play a significant role in symptom formation. The family constellation is pivotal in this regard, in that it provides the individual with his or her basic interpersonal interactions, while simultaneously incorporating cultural influences. In general, the societal and cultural factors in emotional illness tend to be broad and general, while interpersonal and intra-psychic elements prove to be rather definitive.

With factors in five basic areas (somatic, intrapsychic, interpersonal, familial, and sociocultural), it seems evident that an emotional disturbance can be influenced and modi-fied through experiences and interventions whose main effects take place on quite different levels and in rather distinctive spheres. Theoretically, it should be possible to influence a neurotic symptom through somatic means such as medication and electric shock; through intrapsychic means by an analysis of unconscious fantasy and memory formations; through interpersonal means by modifying the nature of specific core relationships and interactions; through familial means by altering family dynamics; and through sociocultural means by changing such factors as the individual's immediate environment, relationship with society, economic status, or other comparable measures. A series of clinical investigations is still necessary to define the positive attributes, limitations, and distinctive liabilities of therapeutic interventions on each of these levels.

Whatever the area of intervention, intrapsychic and interpersonal dynamics always come into play. In some interpersonal and familial treatment paradigms, these dynamics are given some small measure of attention, though the unconscious inputs from the therapist are typically ignored. In this type of therapy, and with the use of sociocultural manipulations, no attention whatsoever is paid to the intrapsychic and interpersonal responses in the patient consequent to the therapist's interventions. The unconscious implications of the therapist's techniques are also afforded no consideration.

Because of the splitting involved, many of the interventional measures used by therapists today reflect manifest constructive attentions accompanied by latent (encoded) messages of a highly destructive and infantilizing nature. At times these messages are quite seductive and, as a rule, they reflect some unmanaged difficulty within the therapist—some measure of countertransference. Confronted with a mixed message, the patient's response is often unpredictable and similarly divided. At times, the investment is made in the surface communication, and the unconscious messages are obliterated or ignored. At other times, little attention is paid to the surface effort, and the patient's reaction, which is usually highly critical and mistrustful, is geared mainly to the therapist's unconscious expression. Having paid no attention to unconscious communication, a therapist who obtains this kind of reaction is at a loss to understand its meaning. It is usually attributed to the patient's ingratitude and paranoid tendencies.

It seems self-evident that all therapists, though they intervene at different levels of experience and interaction, would benefit from an understanding of unconscious dynamics, intrapsychic and interpersonal. On this basis, they might revise their techniques so that their multi-leveled messages to their clients were more integrated and offered them direct and encoded communications that tended to be relatively consonant with each other. While awareness of unconscious meanings and transactions can indeed be obliterated on both sides of the therapeutic dyad, their influence is ever-present.

It seems likely that a treatment approach that takes into full account these unconscious processes, whatever the level of intervention, has a greater chance of providing the patient with a flexible and adaptive resolution to his or her neurosis than an approach that attempts to obliterate and evade the unconscious factors. Thus, while unconscious dynamics are but one determinant of a neurosis, they are perhaps the most significant factor of all. Of course, there are situations where familial and sociocultural elements are so powerful that a full illumination of unconscious intrapsychic and interpersonal dynamics has little effect on the patient's emotional disturbance. Similarly, there are neuroses so deeply founded on pathological intrapsychic and interpersonal elements that no measure of familial and sociocultural change will significantly alter the patient's symptoms.

By and large, naive logic dictates a comprehensive approach to emotional illness. Nonetheless, a careful reading of unconscious expressions indicates that there is an optimal means through which changes at all levels should be effected. Such an approach affords the patient a maximal opportunity for communicative expression, is founded upon a basically healthy mode of relatedness between patient and therapist, and fully respects the patient's need for relative autonomy, individuation, and growth. The specific paradigm that best meets these requirements is that of valid psychoanalytic psychotherapy. Clinical studies confirm this proposition. They indicate that, virtually without exception, patients unconsciously have an exquisite sense of their need for insight-oriented therapy—for truth therapy in its best and ideal form.

The same investigations have shown that, consciously, patients (split as they are) wish for some form of lie-barrier therapy rather different from their own unconscious prescription. They will therefore clamor directly for a deviant mode of treatment, while unconsciously attempting to guide the therapist toward a secure frame contract and therapy. Since therapists have, until now, remained focused on their patients' manifest communications and wishes, they have tended to comply with these surface pressures and to ignore the contradictory encoded communications. In keeping with the demands of the market place, they have attempted to fulfill the conscious requests of their clients. The special qualities and requisites of sound psychotherapy have been ignored. The underlying detrimental consequences of this type of collusion have been set to the side. As a reward, some patients under some circumstances have indeed seemed to function better as a result.

On a basic psychophysiological level, the human organism appears to be designed for immediate coping with little foresight and only a small measure of afterthought. We tend to function defensively and pragmatically, to move toward immediate relief with only a minimal consideration for others. As a rule, it is only when those around us repeatedly respond negatively or fail to satisfy our needs that we consider such measures as delay, anticipation, the feelings and needs of others, and the development of an adaptation useful not only in the present but in the future. In essence, then, we are lie-oriented individuals who are capable of investing in the truth only after an extraordinarily difficult period of disappointment, hurt, and unfulfilled need. In general, patients do not represent the truths of their neurosis unless they are suffering greatly and acutely. Then too, they maintain this kind of expression only for limited periods of time. Efforts geared toward some form of action-discharge symptom relief are interspersed with thrusts toward truthful communication and insight.

Lie-barrier therapies are designed, then, to meet and reinforce the usual ways of coping for most individuals. They are designed also to interfere or destroy the natural but restricted human tendency to seek out emotional truths and understanding in limited doses. The lies and fictions and defensive lie-barrier systems that are offered to patients in this way may sometimes prove serviceable. They may offer modes of relatedness, defenses, sanctions, and pathological forms of gratification that may somehow be more effective and satisfying to the patient than his or her current means of adapting. They do, however, limit the possibilities for growth and flexible coping, and tend to create a need within the client for further reinforcement of this kind. Beyond these general effects, there are a number of specific and interrelated means through which lie-barrier therapy can provide patients with symptom relief. An understanding of these basic mechanisms is necessary for a conceptualization of the curative factors in the plethora of treatment modalities described in the first section of this volume.

CHAPTER 26
THE CURATIVE VALUE OF LIES

The first curative dynamic in lie-barrier therapy is the *avoidance of the truth effect*. The truths that underly neurosis are disturbing, terrifying, and difficult to handle. Many treatment modalities that avoid these truths, falsify the causes of emotional disturbance, and offer barriers to the realizations of these causes can provide some measure of symptomatic relief to their clients.

Neurotic symptoms tend to have their onset after some form of trauma. The patient's previous equilibrium, maintained by a delicate balance between pathological unconscious pressures and necessary defenses, is disrupted by some internal or external circumstance. From within, the disturbing factor may be the onset of puberty or of middle age. Externally, it may involve the loss of a loved one, a significant change in the environment, or an interpersonal conflict. In some form, the trauma often resembles earlier traumas that left the individual vulnerable. Defenses are mobilized but fail. A new adaptive compromise is effected, though now with symptoms that express the underlying struggle. At such moments, the unconscious constellations find less and less disguised expressions in symptoms, behaviors, dreams, and other forms of communication. The patient then seeks out either some means of reinforcing his or her defenses or some way of lessening the effects of the underlying unconscious constellation.

The disturbing truths of neurosis are encoded in the patient's symptoms, behaviors, and other forms of communicative expression. Virtually every form of therapy in existence today intervenes by offering patients false substitutes for the truths that they are struggling to express. The psychoanalyst does so through fanciful dynamic formulations. The gestalt therapist and existentialist carries this out through a series of maneuvers that concentrate the patient in the here and now and on his or her own immediate and conscious experience. The primal scream therapist does so by seeming to probe deep into the patient's past. The learning therapist carries this out through deconditioning.

Whatever the means, the truth is either avoided, attacked and destroyed, or falsified. In principle, by ignoring the conscious and unconscious communicative interaction between patient and therapist—the means by which these truths are mobilized in the treatment experience—the actual underlying basis of the patient's emotional disturbance is subjected to obliteration.

There are several additional facets to this basic avoidance of the truth of the patient's neurosis. Among the more general is the reassuring (superego- or conscience-appeasing) need in patients to convince themselves that they are trying to discover the underlying truth of their sickness, while in reality no such effort is taking place. This is the *I-am-trying-(but-not-really)* aspect of lie-barrier therapy.

Often, when an individual is suffering emotionally, his or her pain is compounded by self-condemnation based on inevitable efforts to avoid situations in which the symptoms seem to be intensified, and by related efforts to avoid self-exploration and self-understanding designed to clarify the source of the disturbance. While the need to take flight on various levels is common and almost instinctive, there is a tendency in many patients to turn against themselves because of their seeming cowardice. Pressures build up from within, and often from without, to do something about the emotional disturbance. For the moment, the prospect of determining the truths on which it is founded appears terrifying. A compromise is worked out, usually quite unconsciously, in which the patient seems to be seeking help through insight, engages the services of a therapist, and yet accepts a set of conditions for treatment under which the true basis of the emotional disturbance is not likely to be detected. Unconsciously, the patient has some sense that this is the case, though consciously he or she attempts to assuage his or her conscience (superego) by making an apparent effort to obtain professional help and symptomatic relief.

On an unconscious level, our deepest investment is in the truth no matter how painful. Because of splitting, on a conscious level and quite to the contrary, our deepest investment is in lie-barrier systems. Patients are therefore able to ease their own inner sense of pressure by seeking out a treatment experience in which they appear to be consciously trying to get at the roots of their neurosis (or to find symptom relief through some other means justified by the therapist's investment in the techniques involved), while unconsciously (entirely outside of awareness) they are involved in a procedure that will avoid the truths involved.

At times, this kind of split message (a type of self-deception) does indeed provide a patient with some immediate sense of relief from his or her symptoms. At the very least, aspects of guilt and self-condemnation (pressures from the conscience or superego) are lessened. Given the delicate state of the dynamics of an emotional disorder, this change may indeed prove salutory.

However, the patient in lie-barrier therapy is never quite at peace. There is a buildup of a lie-barrier system, a set of fictions that is substituted for a truthful understanding of his or her neurosis. At times, this conscious structure may solidify and sufficiently defend against the underlying truths so as to bring about full symptom remission. Nonetheless, the truth itself, based on ineradicable unconscious perceptions, fantasies, memories, and introjects, will continue to seek expression. Often, there are reality traumas or other types of experiences that mobilize these truths. At such times, the patient will either require a reinforcement of his or her defenses, or will suffer again from a symptomatic disturbance. Nonetheless, under more favorable conditions, avoidance and obliteration of the truths of a neurosis may bring some measure of symptom relief to a patient.

CLINICAL VIGNETTES

Mrs. Lerner sought therapy for episodes of anxiety and depression. A young housewife, she wished to get pregnant but had been unable to do so. She accepted a referral to Dr. Marks, whose secretary made the first appointment. During the consultation, it was agreed that Dr. Marks would complete insurance forms that would enable Mrs. Lerner to be reimbursed for 80 percent of the fee. The insurance company would pay Dr. Marks directly. In addition, because of insurance company policy, there would be no charge for missed sessions, and Mrs. Lerner could take vacations whenever she wished.

In the sessions, exploration was soon directed to Mrs. Lerner's hostility toward her husband. Her failure to conceive was conceptualized as an attack on his masculinity. It was traced out to an abortion suffered by Mrs. Lerner's mother when the patient was three years of age. The patient's sense of triumph, and yet guilt, in being the only child of her parents was also viewed as a factor in her psychological need not to conceive.

While no pregnancy ensued, Mrs. Lerner found the therapy fascinating and stimulating. Her sense of depression lifted, though the episodes of anxiety continued. She felt especially well after missing a session in order to join her husband on a business trip. Upon her return, she inquired in some detail as to how the therapist had spent his time while she was away. Dr. Marks described a small vacation of his own, which he had taken with his wife. Mrs. Lerner then reported that while away, her husband had seen a urologist. His sperm count was quite low and there was no doubt that this had contributed to her sterility. She had never wanted to mention it before, but he was often impotent. On their very first date, he had been unable to perform sexually.

On her trip, she had visited her father. He was still working, but he was not "really functioning," she said. "He goes to his job but does nothing. He is a fraud and they should fire him. They are afraid to do it because he knows too much and is liable to spill the beans." When she visited the plant, they laid it on thick about how great a worker he was. It was a farce, but she loved it.

Dr. Marks suggested to Mrs. Lerner that she had a demeaning attitude toward the men in her life, her father and her husband. She had a need to see them as inadequate and, certainly with her husband, there was evidence from earlier sessions of her need to cut him down. On the other hand, if her husband really was impotent, she need no longer attack herself or her own sterility. It was clearly his problem, not hers. Perhaps it was he who needed therapy. Then too, they should explore Mrs. Lerner's need to marry an impotent man.

After a bit of silence, Mrs. Lerner commented that she had always been attracted to ineffectual men. She found them highly stimulating, though she knew not why. Oddly enough, she was feeling aroused at that very moment. Certainly, it could have nothing to do with Dr. Marks. It was indeed a great relief to realize how much of all of this was her husband's problem. She now felt furious at her gynecologist, who had blamed her for the sterility and clearly failed to understand what was really going on. Dr. Marks commented that gynecologists often make mistakes of that kind, and Mrs. Marks joined in, suggesting that maybe she should sue him for malpractice.

Mrs. Lerner was manifestly seeking to understand the basis for her depression and anxiety, and for her inability to conceive. For the moment, any psychological contribution to her sterility is a moot point in light of her husband's low sperm count. Her anxiety and depression can be viewed on a sociocultural level as responses to her failure to achieve motherhood. Within the context of familial and interpersonal dynamics, they may well have had sources in hostility toward her husband and in earlier feelings toward her father. Reactions toward her mother, in part based on the early miscarriage, may also be seen as a factor.

Intrapsychically, Mrs. Lerner consciously and unconsciously perceived the sense of impotence and helplessness in both herself and her husband. These perceptions were depressing and a source of anxiety, though the specific conflicts involved were not defined. There is evidence too that the patient entertained unconscious fantasies of having masculine attributes and of being stronger than her husband, who was viewed unconsciously as castrated and feminine. Her preference for impotent men reflected these underlying fantasy systems. Her choice served too as a defense against sexual fantasies toward her father, who was quite seductive in her childhood, and yet it provided a gratifying link with him in light of his past and present inadequacies. There was a strong incestuous element in her selection of men.

Once Mrs. Lerner sought out and entered therapy, all of these dynamics became concentrated in her relationship with her therapist. Any interpretation that failed to begin with this central deter-

minant would circumvent what had become the most critical
stimulus and basis for her immediate neurotic adjustment. On the
other hand, once the communicative interaction between herself
and Dr. Marks had been defined, its connections to her outside
relationships could be meaningfully understood.

If this session is examined for encoded messages in light of the
conditions of treatment (the triggers), some important discoveries
may be made. By virtue of the presence of a secretary and the
inclusion of an insurance company in this therapy, Dr. Marks had
modified the basic conditions of the ideal treatment relationship
and experience. In this hour, which took place after a missed
session for which the patient was not charged, Mrs. Lerner spoke
of the impotency in her husband for which she now had proof. She
conveyed the realization that she knew on some level of his impotency from the very first date. Organized around the adaptive
context of the therapist's deviant ground rules, this material conveys a telling unconscious perception of the ways in which they
reflected the impotency of Dr. Marks. Quite unconsciously, Mrs.
Lerner had selected a therapist who would satisfy her need to
relate to impotent men. Dr. Marks had readily, however unconsciously, complied.

On the surface, the therapy seemed to be moving along quite
well. Mrs. Lerner was cooperative and often found reason to praise
her therapist. She welcomed the opportunity to travel with her
husband and was grateful that she would not be charged for the
missed sessions. She felt less depressed, but remained anxious. The
massive direct and pathological gratification that she obtained
from Dr. Marks through his deviation had provided her with some
measure of symptom relief. However, his impotency may well have
contributed to the continuation of the anxiety symptoms.

The split in Mrs. Lerner is quite evident. While consciously
praising her therapist, she communicated her unconscious perceptions of his failings through encoded messages. These perceptions
were extended and elaborated upon in the allusions to her father,
who went to work but did nothing. Unconsciously, Mrs. Lerner
fully appreciated the treatment conditions that surrounded her.
She indicated a fear of leaving treatment because of concerns that
Dr. Marks, who had already released information regarding her
treatment to the insurance company, might further betray her. She

also described through an encoded derivative the false praise that she bestowed upon her therapist, which he unwittingly accepted.

The theme of incompetence and not understanding is further elaborated in the allusion to the gynecologist. Here, Mrs. Lerner's underlying rage at her therapist found expression. Still, nothing was done to express this hostility directly or to terminate the therapy. Avoiding the truth of her communications and their connection to her emotional illness, and maintaining a relationship with another impotent man, had helped to reassure her, and to reduce her sense of depression and anxiety. Consciously, she felt quite satisfied, though unconsciously she was rather condemning and angry. Treatment of this kind can continue on for many months in this vein.

Mr. Norman was in gestalt group therapy with Dr. Olin. Placed in the hot seat where he must work with his therapist, he recalled a dream in which there was a dog barking at him and threatening to bite him. Dr. Olin told him to be the dog, and Mr. Norman said that he wanted to bite someone. Dr. Olin asked whom. Mr. Norman joked, "You."

DR. OLIN: Be me being bitten by the dog.

MR. NORMAN: Dumb dog. Bites and barks, but doesn't know a damn thing.

DR. OLIN: There's a part of you which feels ferocious and ignorant.

MR. NORMAN: At times I feel utterly stupid. I say a lot of things at work and they turn out to be meaningless. Now I want the dog to bite me, I want to let him do it.

DR. OLIN: Sometimes you attack the group members here like a mad dog. You're now trying to fight against the mad dog part of yourself. In that way, you could change ignorance into knowledge. Your attack on yourself interferes with your use of your own capabilities.

MR. NORMAN: I still haven't worked it out. I feel hopelessly confused and angry. But now I feel my body relaxing, so maybe there is some hope. I think it should come together by and by.

The group setting and the concentration on the here and now, and on the immediate experiences of the patient, were designed to obliterate the interactional truths that fueled this patient's neurosis.

His current feelings of inadequacy were based in part on a valid unconscious perception of Dr. Olin's inability to understand the true underlying meanings of his patient's communications. The image of the dog is in keeping with the therapist's relentless biting barbs at his patients. Mr. Norman hinted that some type of self-punitive need was being satisfied in the treatment situation when he spoke of wishing that the dog would continue to bite him. The promise of understanding is a lie-barrier cliché designed to deny and split off the total lack of true insight in this treatment experience. Mr. Norman unconsciously recognized the stupidity of it all, but he stayed with the treatment because he felt he was at least trying to seek a cure for his own inner sickness.

Psychotherapists of all kinds make extensive use of *clichés* in the lie-barrier treatments that they offer to patients. The psychoanalyst makes use of theoretical formulations such as penis envy, Oedipus complex, separation anxiety, and such, doing so in a manner totally devoid of interactional and unconscious meaning. Non-analytic therapists fill their patients with clichés and slogans. Transactional analysis, with its games and slogans (e.g., I'm okay, you're okay) is a prime example of the effort to *cure through cliché*. Inherently devoid of active meaning, these slogans and bits of jargon are an ideal vehicle for pretending to seek and discover meaning, while maintaining a state of mindlessness in which meaning is dynamically absent.

The vignettes used in this chapter hint at other dynamisms for the effectiveness of lie-barrier therapy. Far more takes place in these treatment experiences than the avoidance of truth and the substitute of meaningless or dead fictions. It is therefore necessary to probe deeper.

CHAPTER 27

THE DANGERS
OF LIE THERAPY

Quite a few of the salutory effects of lie-barrier therapy derive from the clinical fact that whenever a therapist deviates from the ideal and necessary conditions for insight therapy and the use of its basic techniques, he or she is expressing, on some level, an aspect of his or her own psychopathology. This particular postulate is based on extensive clinical observations of patients' encoded responses to these departures from the norm and from extensive clinical work by a number of therapists and analysts with members of the healing professions.

The introduction of the therapist's pathology into the therapeutic interaction must be understood in full perspective. On the one hand, such a measure consistently produces a disturbed and disturbing image of the therapist. It generates in the patient a negative or hurtful (aggressive, seductive, insensitive and/or narcissistically invested) unconscious introject (i.e., the psychic incorporation and internalization of the hurtful qualities of the therapist and his or her intervention). On the other hand, an unconsciously pathological response from a therapist, especially if it occurs infrequently, may create an important therapeutic opportunity for the patient. In terms of unconscious truths, this is possible, however, only if the therapist understands the unconscious implications of his or her error and responds to the patient's material accordingly.

Beyond that, the introduction of some kind of psychopathology, however blatant or subtle, through deviations in the conditions of treatment and noninterpretive interventions, promises the patient a form of lie-barrier therapy for his or her use. It also offers an opportunity on some level for the patient to concentrate his or her attention and unconscious therapeutic efforts on the cure of the therapist. Thus a *therapist-pathology lie-barrier system* serves functionally to introduce the therapist's difficulties into the therapeutic interaction and to reduce correspondingly the expression of the patient's own psychopathology. This factor has a number of consequences and implications, each of which may have a positive effect on the patient's symptoms.

First, there is the unconscious realization in the patient that the therapist is every bit as sick as he or she, and perhaps even more disturbed and riddled with pathology. This type of *cure by nefarious comparison* can be highly reassuring to the patient. It is especially satisfying in that the therapist in some way represents himself or herself not only as an expert, but as a model of mental health. Realizations that give lie to this image are, in part, quite reassuring to patients. There is a lessening of self-condemnations and other superego pressures that tend to intensify when patients consistently experience their own sickness as uniquely bad and unpardonable and as making them different from everyone else.

The unconscious perceptions of the therapist convey a message to the effect that being emotionally sick and filled with disturbing impulses, wishes, and fantasies is not all that bad since the therapist suffers in kind. As a bonus, the therapist becomes less of a threat to the patient. How comforting indeed, even if it occurs unconsciously and through encoded realizations about other persons, for the patient to realize on some level that his or her therapist is, in these significant ways, no better off than himself or herself. It takes the sting out of being emotionally ill. It forms the basis for an unconscious kinship and collusion, which can also prove to be symptom alleviating.

Of course, the therapist may go too far in expressing his or her emotional disturbance. He or she may make use of interventions that are blatantly disruptive and crazy, and which flagrantly violate the rights and feelings of the patient. Nonetheless, while some patients will leave a therapist of this kind, others will stay on, reassured that their therapist really is far more insane than they. There is the added challenge to contain the dumping of the therapist and to cure the blatant sickness he or she has expressed. There is also the most welcome opportunity to allow the therapist's illness (unconsciously) to dominate the therapeutic work.

An additional curative factor under these conditions lies in finding that the pathology expressed by the therapist in some way constitutes a version of the psychopathology not only of the patient, but also of his or her parental figures. Because of this latter factor, the sick therapist becomes a basis for forgiving or coming to some kind of terms with the sick parent. The patient has a fresh opportunity to cure through displacement onto the therapist the parent whom he or she failed to cure in the past. In addition, the patient's internal conflicts with parental introjects (the internalized parents) are somewhat lessened by the realization that the therapist is not unlike the parental figure. Even actual interpersonal conflict between a patient and his or her parents may be mollified because of the realization that the therapist is sick in ways similar to them.

Thus there are many unique advantages in having an emotionally ill therapist despite any detrimental consequences. Patients are spared the envy and dread of the well-functioning therapist and the contrast between such a therapist and the sick part of themselves and their parents. Further, the therapist's psychopathology implicitly sanctions and gives approval to the sickness in the patient, as well as in his or her parents. With the introduction of the implied acceptance of sick modes of functioning and relating, the patient often feels a strong sense of relief.

A CLINICAL VIGNETTE

Ms. Petre was a young woman in her early twenties being seen in eclectic therapy with Dr. Rusk. As the material from the patient appeared to permit, the therapist would offer directives, advice, personal opinions, and even describe his own fantasies and dreams to Ms. Petre. While at times the patient responded with a sense of confusion, she also repeatedly told Dr. Rusk how helpful this therapy was for her. At times she experienced intense sexual fantasies about her therapist, and these were traced to early experiences in her parents' bed, during which she was required to massage her father's back and was otherwise exposed to him sexually.

Dr. Rusk came to his waiting room to escort Ms. Petre into his office. With a titter, she informed him that his fly was open. With a nervous laugh, Dr. Rusk zippered up his fly and assured the patient that he had no intention of seducing her. He had gone to the bathroom to urinate and had simply forgotten to close his fly.

Once in the consultation room, Ms. Petre said that she felt somewhat aroused. It really had nothing to do with Dr. Rusk's fly being open. Instead, it involved a neighbor who lived across from her apartment. He had a habit of leaving his blinds open and of parading around his apartment naked. Ms. Petre had reacted with a mixture of revulsion and stimulation.

Now that she thought about it, she could remember her father walking around their apartment naked until she was well into her teens. He even did it when her girlfriends were around. She used to hate him for it, but now she felt only pity. Somehow, he simply didn't know better. His own mother had been very exhibitionistic and seductive, and he must have been overstimulated himself. Ms. Petre couldn't blame him, since he had never been taught to set limits and maintain decorum. For him, it was perfectly innocent, as if it would have no effect on his daughter—the patient. At least Ms. Petre herself tried to understand things and not hide from them. She felt good rising above her father's foibles.

Somehow, Ms. Petre now thought of a party that she had attended on the week-end. Everyone got drugged out and started to disrobe. It was crude and impersonal; her own problem in smoking pot seemed insignificant in light of the states of the others. She kept her own clothes on and, when one of the men came after her, she put him down. He backed off and she felt pretty strong in her stand. It was like she was surrounded by a bunch of mad people and was the only sane one in sight. She felt strange thinking so well of herself, but there it was.

Now she was thinking of her college roommate. She was a promiscuous woman who could never keep her pants on. She was always out of control and helpless. Ms. Petre remembered many rap sessions in which she tried to help her with her problems.

Despite her best efforts, the roommate's promiscuity only got worse. There were times Ms. Petre wanted to give up on her, but she wouldn't have been able to live with herself if she did. Someone had to try to help the poor girl.

Dr. Rusk had been extremely seductive and exhibitionistic in his verbal approach to this patient. In earlier sessions, Ms. Petre, through encoded messages, had made repeated efforts to call to his attention the problems reflected in this kind of so-called therapeutic work. She had tried unconsciously (via encoded messages about herself) to trace these difficulties to his poor training and to traumatic experiences with his own parents, some of which he had actually revealed to her. Dr. Rusk listened only to his patient's manifest communications. Instead of offering interpretations, he would tend to stress the way in which the patient consciously felt about herself for the moment.

In the present session, Dr. Rusk had fallen silent because he had been upset over his fly having been open. Were this not the case, he would have spent time asking the patient how she felt when her father exhibited himself and would have probed her mixed feelings toward him in the present. He would have questioned her behavior at the party and probably castigated her for her inhibitions. He would have prodded her to loosen up and to let herself go.

Fortunately, he did not make these interventions in the actual session. It then proved possible for Ms. Petre to express in encoded form some rather telling unconscious perceptions of her therapist. It also afforded her an opportunity for some active *unconscious interpretations* on his behalf. Sad to say, they went unheeded, though for us, Ms. Petre revealed rather cogently some of the motives that moved her to continue in this treatment experience.

Dr. Rusk was, as already indicated, a highly exhibitionistic, aggressive, and seductive therapist. Not infrequently, these problems with impulse control spill over into gross behaviors in the interaction with patients. This is what transpired on this occasion.

Dr. Rusk's failure to zip up his fly served as an important adaptation-evoking stimulus (trigger) for Ms. Petre. It was especially powerful in light of Dr. Rusk's usual propensities. After the session, Ms. Petre had felt a strong sense of relief, though some of it was derived from Dr. Rusk's uncharacteristic silence in this hour. Paradoxically, some of it also stemmed from the uncontrolled behavior of the therapist. This is revealed in the material extracted here.

Dr. Rusk in some way expressed himself as a therapist in a manner not unlike the distinctly pathological behaviors of Ms. Petre's father. He exposed himself sexually to his patient on a verbal level and through innuendo with the open fly, just as Ms. Petre's father exposed himself physically. In a way, Dr. Rusk's behavior proved reassuring to Ms. Petre, who had, prior to treatment, experienced only uncontrolled rage toward her father. In part because of her unconscious realization that her therapist was little different from her father, she had begun to feel pity toward her parent—a pity that she also felt unconsciously toward her therapist.

Ms. Petre also felt reassured by the realization that she was able to handle her impulses better than her father or therapist. She understood on some level that she was in some way emotionally more healthy than both of these figures. She felt less angry with herself for her sexual frigidity and anxiety symptoms, which had brought her to treatment. In light of what she was exposed to by her father and, without her conscious recognition, by her therapist as well, her symptoms seemed understandable and tolerable. They also seemed less distressing because of the failings in her father and therapist.

The expression by Dr. Rusk of his own seductive-exhibitionistic psychopathology in his relationship with Ms. Petre proved to be more than a basis for relief through nefarious comparison. It provided Ms. Petre with an opportunity to function unconsciously in a therapeutic fashion. In this session, she made an attempt at an unconscious interpretation. Through encoded derivatives manifestly related to her father (and therefore in latent fashion), she attempted to help Dr. Rusk understand that his need to exhibit himself inappropriately to his patient derived in some way from seductive interactions with his mother. In this instance, this was not simply a matter of unconscious speculation. Dr. Rusk had reported sexual dreams to Ms. Petre about both herself and his mother. While the patient had not consciously put these pieces together, she had been able to work them out on an unconscious level. She responded now to the evident acute disturbance in her therapist by offering in derivative fashion the insights she had gained into his emotional problems.

The communicative segment regarding the party reiterated the theme of reassurance for Ms. Petre in light of the flagrant pathology of others. Of course, it appears again in the memories of the college roommate. If a patient is unable to master the unconscious basis of his or her own inner disturbance and the fantasy-memories and perceptions involved, it is not surprising to find that he or she will resort to reassurance measures of this kind. Sometimes, these patients will seek out rather disturbed individuals as friends and lovers. At other times, usually quite unconsciously, they will also seek out therapists who are quite evidently unable to manage their own inner disorders. The craziness in these other individuals, including their therapists, is highly reassuring and enables the patient to better tolerate his or her own emotional failings. In addition, the patient is often able to defensively seal off his or her own craziness by concentrating on the madness in those who surround him or her. In this treatment situation, by remaining unconsciously focused on the evident disturbances in Dr. Rusk, Ms. Petre found considerable relief from the pressures of her own inner turmoil.

Ms. Petre also attempted to be curative by offering herself to her therapist, again on an unconscious and encoded level, as a model of mental health and control. At the party, she kept her clothes on and did not become involved in the orgy. With her roommate, she maintained a semblance of decorum and showed her how to relate to others in mature fashion. In that relationship, she attempted to be directly therapeutic. This particular allusion represents Ms. Petre's own unconscious awareness that functionally, she had become therapist to her therapist—largely in response to his need to become patient to his patient.

It was Ms. Petre's unconscious hope that she could cure the therapist where she had failed to cure her father. Dr. Rusk's continued insensitivities to these therapeutic ministrations had of late led to a sense of disillusionment and hopelessness in his patient. Quite frequently, it is because a therapist has failed to benefit and change on the basis of his or her patient's unconscious therapeutic efforts that a patient will eventually leave a treatment situation of this kind. Conspiracy of this type is satisfying only up to a point; beyond that, it becomes a source of disappointment, anger, and regret.

Unfortunately for Ms. Petre, when her unconscious therapeutic work with Dr. Rusk failed, she acted out aspects of her problem by going that night to an open sex club. Whereas in the past, she had felt considerable guilt after an interlude of this kind, she plunged herself wildly into the situation on this occasion. She felt high and elated, even though there was something hollow about the sexual experience.

Unconsciously, Dr. Rusk had provided Ms. Petre with sanction for this kind of behavior. Because he had failed to interpret and clearly rectify his error and the damage he had done, his patient identified with him and acted out sexually in her own form. The following hour, Dr. Rusk filled Ms. Petre with praise for her ability to be so open and comfortable with her sexual self. This served to reinforce the earlier license provided unconsciously by Dr. Rusk for this kind of sexual acting out. The momentary diminution of superego-conscience pressures had led Ms. Petre to feel elated by her sexual behaviors.

Sad to say, a week later Ms. Petre had a nightmare in which she lost control and began to murder people randomly on the street. Of the men, she demanded sex, and if they hesitated, she killed them. The dream prompted such a powerful sense of anxiety and guilt that Ms. Petre inadvertently took an overdose of sleeping pills. Although she became quite toxic and ill, she survived the episode. Dr. Rusk attributed the implied suicide attempt to her inordinately primitive and punitive superego, which he believed he had been trying to modify with his reassuring interventions. Soon after, for reasons unknown even to herself, Ms. Petre left treatment.

While this particular patient eventually suffered considerably because of the destructive qualities of the lie-barrier systems offered to her by Dr. Rusk, she had for a long time felt considerably better under these conditions. Lie therapy can go awry and sometimes prove quite destructive for a particular patient. At times it is even destructive for the therapist, who on some level is also aware of the failings in this kind of approach. It is this type of disillusionment that contributes in part to the relatively high suicide rate in psychiatrists and psychotherapists.

CHAPTER 28
MODES OF RELATEDNESS

Clinical study has shown that the ideal therapeutic mode of relatedness is possible only under truth therapy conditions. This particular form of relatedness has been termed a *healthy symbiosis*. This implies a mode of relatedness in which one person, the symbiotic recipient, obtains the major share of appropriate gratification, while the other individual, the symbiotic donor, also finds satisfaction, though to a lesser extent.

In a healthy symbiosis, there is nurturing and caring, though at a reasonable distance. The instinctual drive satisfactions involved are sound and growth-promoting. While protective, the constructive symbiosis is designed mainly for growth, development and individuation in the symbiotic recipient, though secondarily in the symbiotic donor as well. The specific attributes of a healthy form of symbiosis vary in keeping with the nature of the relationship—mother–child, patient–therapist, or whatever. In the psychotherapeutic relationship, the healthy symbiosis requires a therapist capable of interpretation and of creating the ideal therapeutic contract and setting, and further requires a patient who will basically accept these conditions of treatment and relatedness.

In general, deviations from the basic contract and intervention errors by the therapist shift the mode of relationship between himself or herself and the patient from a healthy symbiosis to some pathological form. There are three possibilities:

1. *Pathological autism*, in which the therapist's interventions are essentially the product of his or her own inner fantasies and needs. They have no *meaningful* connection to the patient's material and, in particular, to the unconscious and interpersonally activated implications involved. The therapist is either silent when he or she should intervene, or he or she speaks without relevant meaning. This critical relationship-link (through knowledge or meaning) between patient and therapist is virtually absent.
2. *Pathological symbiosis*, in which the therapist's errors and deviations tend to invite inappropriate forms of fusion or merger between himself or herself and the patient. This type of caring involves pathological instinctual drive satisfactions and has corrupt and corrupting qualities that reflect disturbances in the superego. The relationship is unconsciously geared toward inappropriate and infantilizing forms of interaction and is inimical to growth and individuation. Instead, it pathologically binds the symbiotic donor and the symbiotic recipient in extremely needy and destructive ways, while nonetheless offering an abundance of unhealthy satisfactions.
3. The *parasitic* mode of relatedness, which is always pathological and highly exploitative. The therapist's deviations and errors have a destructive thrust that is devoid of nurturing attributes. The therapist's interventions reflect his or her needs to gratify himself or herself at the expense of the patient with little concern for the patient's own needs and requirements.

The healthy symbiosis implies a measure of reasonable separateness between the patient and therapist that can be extremely threatening for both. On an object relationship level, the central aspect of virtually all pathological syndromes is the maintenance of some type of sick mode of relatedness that secretly binds the two individuals involved. Often, the pattern is set in the early relationship between the future patient and his or her mother. For both patients and therapists alike there is a history of a notable pathological symbiosis (or some other pathological mode of relatedness) in which the mother used the child narcissistically as an extension of herself and as a way of gratifying her own needs without due consideration for those of the child. Nonetheless, the child (and the patient), weakened in his or her functioning and capacity to relate because of the pathological inputs from the mother, gladly accepts the merger and other pathological gratifications afforded to him or her in this way. These are seen as a reasonable alternative to isolation and regression and to the imagined possibility of annihilation. Pathological symbiosis also enables both symbiotic partners to preclude separation and other morbid anxieties. However, growth and maturation are sacrificed in favor of infantilization and pseudo-maturation, and true individuation is not achieved.

The separation anxieties that underlie a relationship of this kind are often quite extreme. They are experienced by the child (patient) in terms of fears of annihilation or death, which they believe will transpire without the sick protective merger with the mother (therapist) figure. The mother's (therapist's) own dread of separateness is communicated to and dumped into the child, who then tends to suffer from comparable fears and anxieties. The outcome is usually a highly ambivalent, infantilizing mode of relatedness overflowing with pathological forms of satisfaction on which the young child (patient) becomes inordinately dependent. The damage to his or her inner and outer functioning reinforces fantasy-beliefs that, without merger with the maternal figure and the satisfactions therein, there will be no survival.

A pathological mode of object relatedness is a concomitant of all types of psychopathology. Because of this, all patients who enter treatment wish on some level for a pathological mode of relatedness (autistic, symbiotic, or parasitic) with their therapists. As it happens, all lie therapies entail some gratification of this wish, in that they are essentially, on an object relationship level, forms of pathological relatedness.

As previously noted, many patients seek a pathological symbiotic mode of relatedness with their therapists. This is perhaps the most common form of interaction in present-day society. The therapist who is unwilling to comply is experienced as threatening and persecutory. As noted, the patient fears that he or she will not survive without the pathological link. Nonetheless, such pressures are an avenue for sound framework management and interpretations of a kind that can eventually provide the patient with both a healthy interpersonal experience and a sound mode of relatedness, as well as insight into his or her own pathological needs. As such, they afford the patient (and secondarily the therapist) an important type of therapeutic opportunity.

Here too, there is an important difference between patient and therapist. With the former, the thrust toward pathological relatedness is inevitable and is an expression of his or her object relationship pathology, which requires therapeutic work. Such efforts are not essentially collusive, and become so only when the therapist gratifies the patient's sick needs. In contrast, the therapist's basic position should involve the offer of a healthy therapeutic symbiosis. There is no appropriate basis for pathological thrusts from the therapist. Once again, it is the responsibility of the therapist to be aware of such tendencies and to analyze and control them so that they are of little influence on the therapeutic work.

Each lie-barrier system involves a form of pathological relatedness. Those lie barriers that involve autistic (idiosyncratic rather than shared) fantasies suit therapists who wish to impose their own sick imagination on their patients, and patients who wish to have no meaningful relationship with their therapists. Pathologically symbiotic lie-barrier systems satisfy those patients and therapists who wish to engage in pathological mergers and thereby magically undo separation and other anxieties. Whenever a therapist shifts from his or her role as functional therapist to that of functional patient, he or she is attempting to become a symbiotic recipient. In many forms of psychotherapeutic conspiracy, especially those in which the patient becomes the functional therapist on an unconscious level, this type of role reversal is characteristic. In its sick or inappropriate way, patients find considerable satisfaction in recognizing the interpersonal vulnerabilities of their therapists and in adopting a nurturing role even though it is essentially unconscious and pathological.

Rather typically, the pathological symbiotic mode of relatedness is invaded with highly primitive sexual and aggressive impulses. It therefore affords both participants considerable sadomasochistic satisfaction, again in collusive fashion. The destructive and undermining qualities of this type of lie-barrier relatedness mar its utilization.

Finally, there are those patients who enter therapy with the wish only to parasitize and dump sickness into their therapists. They have no interest in truly understanding themselves, and they wish only to exploit and malign. While they obtain some degree of relief in this fashion, they are extremely trying for truth therapists who attempt to contain their pathological projective identifications and to help them understand the unconscious nature of their behaviors and associations. On the other hand, lie therapists with intense self-punitive and masochistic needs are often quite unconsciously the willing victims of this type of parasitizing patient. Still, it is even more common to find patients who are willing to be parasitized by their therapists. In all, then, pathological relationship satisfactions are another means through which lie-barrier therapies provide relief to their participants.

A CLINICAL VIGNETTE (CONTINUED)

In the course of her work with Dr. Rusk, Ms. Petre experienced many interludes in which he plied her with pathological symbiotic gratifications. Dr. Rusk virtually took over her life during one period of crisis when Ms. Petre was unable to extricate herself from an extremely self-destructive relationship with a man—modeled unconsciously, however, on her relationship with Dr. Rusk.

Since growth-promoting insight was not the medium of this treatment process, Dr. Rusk actually saw the young man and scared him off with a series of direct threats. Ms. Petre was deeply gratified by his protective behaviors, unaware that her responsive associations to Dr. Rusk's behavior centered on ways in which her mother controlled, manipulated, and smothered her with an utter disregard for Ms. Petre's own needs. She also had a dream of being held so tightly that her chest was crushed.

Typically, Ms. Petre was consciously appreciative of Dr. Rusk's intervention, while quite unappreciative and fearful on an unconscious level. Still, the lure of a return to the pathological symbiosis that she had experienced with her mother, who had provided enormous tainted rewards in food, clothing, and such, led to a period of good feeling on her part. Eventually, when Dr. Rusk was unable to maintain such an inordinately high level of pathological symbiotic gratification, Ms. Petre became profoundly depressed and angry.

A strikingly large number of patients who enter treatment are seeking some form of pathological symbiosis with their therapists.

Therapists themselves, with needs of this kind unresolved and often a major factor in their choice of profession, unconsciously offer a vast array of pathological symbiotic modes of relatedness in return. The gestalt therapist who controls and manipulates his patient, the encounter therapist who works in a group and with directives, the nude marathon therapist available at the patient's beck and call, the primal scream therapist who offers himself or herself as an exclusive figure, all offer versions of pathological symbiosis and parasiticism to their patients.

Because of the underlying destructiveness and hostility, and the inevitable qualities of seduction and infantilization, virtually all pathological symbioses have some measure of parasiticism as well. Many of these techniques are designed unconsciously to exploit the patient and to inappropriately gratify the therapist. The stated goal of assisting the patient to resolve his or her emotional disturbance is belied by the destructive qualities of the mode of relatedness offered by the therapist.

In Ms. Petre's treatment with Dr. Rusk, there were interludes when he was directly attacking of his patient, such as when she failed to follow his advice or to otherwise handle a situation well after he had detailed the steps involved. In many sessions, Dr. Rusk pressured his patient to surrender all sexual restraints. Unconsciously, these interventions were designed to gratify Dr. Rusk's own promiscuous tendencies at the expense of his patient. Sad to say, quite unconsciously, many therapists parasitize their patients in this way, even though consciously they do not wish to be harmful.

Of course, pathological modes of relatedness may produce symptom relief, but there are also self-punitive and masochistic gratifications inherent to the victim in this form of relationship. Virtually without exception, every patient enters psychotherapy with some measure of guilt and some consequent need for punishment. Plagued by their own internal consciences or superegos, patients hope to alleviate some of their internal pain and suffering through a measure of sacrifice and self-hurt. In their outside lives, these individuals likewise often select persons for relationships who have and who will hurt and punish them. In choosing their therapists, such individuals unconsciously have a similar goal in mind.

Freud saw masochism as the greatest obstacle to successful treatment. Fresh studies have indicated that masochism is as well a major unconscious motive for the perpetuation of lie-barrier therapies of the kind so rampant today. By paying a price to the superego and hostile parent, and by placating their incessant demands for punishment, patients of this kind find momentary relief from their symptoms and anguish. In this first 100 years of psychotherapy, unwittingly sadistic therapists have unknowingly fulfilled this function again and again.

This type of victimization and masochistic satisfaction was more than evident in Ms. Petre's therapy. Whenever she seemed to falter, Dr. Rusk would be there to confront and attack her, justifying his interventions with a belief that in this way he was toughening up her ego. On an interactional and unconscious level, whenever Ms. Petre regressed or developed a symptom, it was attributed to her own masochism or sadism and to her sick fantasies.

This kind of criticism and sadistic attack on a patient, through which the therapist exonerates himself or herself from any contribution to the patient's sickness, and through which the patient is held entirely accountable for the disturbance, exists in virtually every form of psychotherapy. The patient is sick; the patient is bad; the patient is entirely accountable (rather than partly); the patient is wrong; the patient is distorting; the patient needs to be confronted—and many comparable attitudes—are qualities that are rampant in present-day therapeutic work. The sickness, and thereby the badness, in the therapeutic interaction is located almost exclusively in the client. Often, the punishment is unbearable. Still, the more intense the attack, the greater the relief from internal superego pressures. At times, the level of symptom alleviation is nothing short of miraculous.

The attempts by therapists to engage their patients in pathological symbiotic, autistic, and parasitic modes of interaction and relatedness also involve a measure of seductiveness. Unconsciously, Ms. Petre was secretly stimulated and gratified by Dr. Rusk's seductive interactions with her. She was flattered that he would want to leave his fly open as a sexual message to her. Implied here was a sense that he was attracted to his patient, and this delighted Ms. Petre. The utterly inappropriate and pathological qualities of these behaviors were quickly set to the side, split off.

Although quite sick, a therapist's seductiveness toward a patient will sometimes lead to symptom alleviation based on factors of this kind. This helps to account for the reported satisfactory results in those psychotherapies where the therapist actually has sexual contact with his patients, petting and intercourse. The patient attempts to extract some relief from the flattery and from the inherent and unconsciously perceived sickness in the therapist who proposes to cure a neurosis in this manner. He or she also gains some relief from superego pressures, which comes about because the burden of guilt is shifted to the therapist who is behaving in a destructive fashion. The patient's inevitable unconscious outrage goes underground and is communicated through encoded messages, which both patient and therapist then ignore.

In the autistic mode of relatedness between patient and therapist, therapists intervene in a functionally meaningless fashion. They make use of everyday and psychoanalytic clichés, of interventions that pop into their minds as a result of their own fantasy life, and of comments essentially unrelated to the conscious and especially unconscious meanings of their patients' communications. Some patients dread meaningful relatedness with their therapists since it will lead to the unfolding of the primitive and psychotic fantasies and perceptions that exist within their minds on an unconscious level. They will therefore obtain some relief with a therapist whose communications have virtually nothing to do with their inner disturbance and its implications—and instead reflect the sickness in the therapist.

Another version of pathological autism in therapists is seen with the silent therapist or analyst who fails to intervene even in the presence of abundant material for interpretation. Apparently, this type of autism is confined to selected psychoanalytic psychotherapists. Virtually all of the other treatment modalities give license to the more active form of nonmeaningful communicative autism, and to parasitism and pathological symbiosis based on extended self-serving interventions.

Among the most important splits within human beings are divided wishes in regard to the basic mode of relating to others. Unconsciously, there is a powerful need for a healthy mode of relatedness and for the consequent growth and autonomy that it brings. Through encoded messages, patients will criticize efforts by therapists directed toward pathological ways of relating. They will make unconscious interpretations and attempt to help the therapist create a mutually satisfying healthy symbiosis.

Unfortunately, on a conscious level, most patients clamor for a pathological mode of relatedness and the inappropriate defenses and gratifications that it provides. They will attempt in actuality in one way or another to engage the therapist in this fashion. In general, they have little difficulty in doing so, since virtually all present-day therapists are prepared to relate in this fashion. Once a pathological mode of relatedness has been secured, efforts toward understanding are impossible. The basic mode of relief and gratification is embodied in the manner of relating itself. Exploratory efforts are a sham and a pretense designed to assuage guilt within both parties to treatment regarding the secret and pathological satisfactions that they are sharing. So-called interpretations and efforts to generate insight under these conditions are functionally useless and meaningless, and totally contradicted by the actual nature of the ongoing therapeutic interaction. Truth therapy is precluded, and relief is provided in deviant fashion. Action-discharge is the mode of cure even when it comes to the use of words. The pain and threat of insight and growth are avoided.

There are many other nuances to the ways in which lie-barrier therapy can provide patients with a measure of symptom relief. To touch upon the most important of the remaining factors, one must consider the basic attributes of modes of cure as applied to emotional problems. There is a continuum that creates a polarity, with genuine insight and understanding at one end and action-discharge at the other. The former is most effective when the ground rules and framework of treatment are secure. Under these conditions, the exploration of the patient's neurosis unfolds in terms of the patient's anxieties about the therapist in light of his or her capacity to offer a healthy symbiosis and a sound holding environment and relationship. In contrast, the action-discharge evacuatory mode of cure (the search for immediate and blind relief) is founded upon one or more deviations in the ideal therapeutic contract and on other forms of pathological self-gratification expressed by the therapist in his or her work with the patient.

Action-discharge cure implies pathological satisfaction, corruption of the superego, and the use of pathological defenses and modes of relief in which blind immediate action predominates. Delay is felt to be hurtful. Words are used as vehicles of discharge and evacuation rather than for understanding. The individual is essentially mindless despite the use of language.

There is an action quality to all that is carried out and a relative disregard for others.

Most neurotic individuals opt for action-discharge modes of cure in their daily lives. They therefore seek out a therapist who will create a treatment situation and relationship in which their own needs for action-discharge will find sanction and be allowed expression. There is then a commonality in regard to the use of pathological means of symptom alleviation and implicit support for the patient's own pathological solutions. Patients then intensify their own action-discharge efforts, often through blatant forms of acting out. They soon feel considerably less distress than before, much of it because of the conscious and unconscious sanctions from the therapist. If the therapist can solve his or her emotional problems in this way, so can the patient.

Among the most common forms of action-discharge solutions to emotional problems, modification in the usual ground rules and boundaries of relationships stands high. These are termed *framework deviation cures* to emphasize that symptomatic relief arises mainly from the deviation from the basic rules of relatedness that have been agreed upon or which would be ideal between patient and therapist. In life itself, prior to all dynamic and genetic considerations, each person must decide whether or not he will cope and adapt within the given rules of relatedness, social interaction, and such. There is a great deal of sacrifice made by the person who accepts constructive rules of family, society, and personal interaction, and who attempts to cope within that framework. Such a person stands in contrast with one who initiates his or her coping efforts by breaking the constructive framework of rules and laws.

In the first instance, the possibility for true understanding and insight is considerable. Acceptance of sound rules and regulations implies a capacity for frustration tolerance and an acceptance of one's own limits and limitations. It provides the possibility of a healthy form of coping that does little to harm others. It can form the basis for internal change and inner conflict resolution as a means of symptom relief, rather than a search for cure through the manipulation and exploitation of others.

Sound emotional health and growth is possible only on the basis of adaptation within accepted and sound covenants. Still, to attempt to cope in this way requires a strong capacity for delay and an ability to tolerate the experience of anxiety and conflict as a prelude to resolution. Both momentary chaos and helplessness may occur, though the eventual mastery of the underlying difficulties proves to be highly satisfying and rewarding. This is, of course, a consistent factor in all truth therapy situations.

In sharp contrast, the breaking of a rule or regulation can provide the perpetrator with an immediate sense of power and satisfaction. There is a feeling of omnipotence and immortality, much of this because the ultimate rule of life is the inevitability of death. The rule-breaker may tend to adapt by exploiting others and by disregarding their needs—needs that are reflected in appropriate compacts. The investment is in acting and doing; both delay and understanding are disregarded.

Lie-barrier therapies strongly favor action-discharge and framework-deviation modes of cure. There is conscious and unconscious sanction and even pressures on the patient in this type of treatment experience to break the rules, to selfishly gratify himself or herself, and to disregard restraints and regulations. Because actions of this kind are in general highly gratifying, manic-like, and especially popular, treatment modalities of this kind are in strong favor. The inner voice of need for restraint and realization of detrimental consequences is usually but an encoded whisper. For a large number of individuals, there is much relief in finding someone who will consciously or unconsciously, implicitly or explicitly, take over a significant measure of responsibility for their maladaptive actions. Therapists are providing such relief by the bucketful.

CHAPTER 29
A SOBERING PERSPECTIVE

Solving an emotional problem through an understanding of its underlying basis and through genuine internal change is an arduous and painful process. Every patient who enters psychotherapy wishes on some level, more or less, to find peace through some other means. In this quest for immediate relief, the liabilities and difficulties that accompany these maladaptive solutions tend to be denied and set to the side. Suicide attempts are dismissed as a reflection of the incurable masochism of the patient. The break-up of relatively sound family structures is justified by long pronouncements regarding family pathology. Highly destructive episodes of acting out, hurtful to many others, are rationalized as expressions of independence.

Every form of psychotherapy has created a theory of emotional illness as a way of justifying its technical procedures. Similarly, every treatment modality has a series of built-in rationalizations designed to protect the therapist when treatment fails. These are self-fulfilling systems fraught with circular reasoning and with lie-barrier fortifications of their own that are virtually impossible to penetrate.

Patients are deeply attracted to lie-barrier therapists. When the underlying nature of the therapeutic transactions in which they are involved are pointed out to them, these patients vary in their responses. Some will hear nothing in the way of criticism or evaluation. They remain blindly invested in a therapeutic experience that they themselves soundly criticize through encoded derivatives. Others will listen and be concerned, and some of these will even terminate obviously destructive treatment experiences. Paradoxically, they then often seek out a new form of lie-barrier therapy in the unconscious hope that it will support them or suit them in some better fashion that the first experience.

Such needs are intensely and characteristically human. For those who have the courage and insight to prefer truth therapy, there is now a growing number of such therapists available in the United States. They are easily recognized by their adherence to the ground rules and boundaries of the psychotherapeutic situation and by their almost exclusive use of interpretations organized around the ongoing therapeutic experience with themselves. They show a fierce dedication to the total truth which they know their patients will often not appreciate consciously, though it is enough that they will do so on an unconscious level.

There are so many near-instinctive and defensive needs to avoid the truth therapy situation that a constant attitude of vigilance is required not only to find such a treatment experience, but to be mindful of its maintenance. In time, as psychotherapists invest more and more in this means of therapy, the responsibility for the basic adherence to this treatment paradigm will fall largely to their patients. Only an informed, motivated, dedicated public and profession can coordinate the movement toward the widening use of the truth therapy approach.

On the other side, it is possible to develop safeguards against becoming unwittingly involved in a lie-therapy situation. Any treatment situation that is not established with specific ground rules regarding fee, frequency of sessions, responsibility for hours, and the absence of physical contact is a form of lie-barrier therapy. Any therapist who does not afford the patient an opportunity for free association and full communicative expression, and who does not provide the patient with total confidentiality and privacy, must perforce be a lie-therapist. Any treatment situation in which the therapist responds noninterpretively with personal reactions, suggestions, beliefs, manipulations, and such is also a form of lie treatment. Any deviation in true neutrality and any alteration in the basic ideal ground rules of treatment shift the therapeutic interplay into the lie-barrier realm. Change in mode of treatment is possible only if the therapist is capable of recognizing the true nature of what is taking place, and of rectifying and interpreting as well.

Sad to say, by these standards, virtually every type of therapeutic experience available to patients today is some form of lie-barrier therapy. The enormity of this need must be recognized. By identifying the true nature of the therapeutic interaction and experience, it is hoped that not only will many therapists shift to the basic truth therapy modality, but also that lie therapists will understand their techniques better and improve them accordingly.

There can be little doubt that lie therapy, because of its powerful immediate attraction, will be with us for many decades to come. It seems necessary, then, to understand and improve these approaches, and to eliminate those that are entirely destructive and dangerous. There are some patients and some therapists who cannot deal with emotional truths, and the former certainly deserve an opportunity for therapeutic relief. Nonetheless, it is often quite difficult to identify such persons, and it may well be that everyone deserves an attempt at truth therapy before shifting to the other mode.

The very recognition of truth and lie therapy leads to a fundamental realization regarding the nature of humankind. Psychologically we have been engineered for immediate action and for the search for immediate relief when dealing with emotional disturbance—for flight rather than fight. Superimposed upon this core discharge system is another group of functions devoted to delay and understanding, which can, if mobilized, take over and direct us to a more thoughtful and constructive mode of adaptation.

It seems likely that we are split psychophysiologically at a most basic biological level. The direct response system serves us well in the way of protection, defense, and adaptation in the immediate situation, though there may be many penalties in the long run. The second level of adaptation serves us and those around us in highly effective fashion, with little disadvantage except for the necessary pain of insight and growth. However, only through mastery of the more immediate lie-barrier system does it become feasible to make use of the more lasting truth-insight mode.

That collusion and conspiracy is rampant within the field of psychotherapy is a staggering and disturbing realization. Psychoanalysis and many other forms of psychotherapy are manifestly committed to the unrelenting pursuit of truth, which, as Freud indicated, cannot in any way be set aside or falsified when it comes to emotional illness. It is therefore only by discovering the existence of untruths and the false use of true statements that further growth can unfold. One does not deliberately set out to find lies and deceptions in the work of psychotherapists. Instead, these emerge only gradually in the face of enormous internal resistance arising from our need to idealize and believe in those who are entrusted to heal our pain and suffering. These are, indeed, disturbing realizations. And yet, as we now know, true growth and development, personal and professional, can take place only with this type of painful honesty.

REFERENCES

Berne, E. (1961). *Transactional Analysis in Psychotherapy*. New York: Grove Press.

Bion, W. (1962). Learning from experience. In *Seven Servants: Four Works by Wilfred R. Bion*. New York: Jason Aronson, 1977.

Bird, B. (1972). Notes on transference: universal phenomenon and hardest part of analysis. *Journal of the American Psychoanalytic Association* 20:267–301.

Breuer, J. and Freud, S. (1893–95). Studies on hysteria. *Standard Edition* 2:1–305.

Chertok, L. (1968). The discovery of transference. *International Journal of Psycho-Analysis* 49:560–575.

Chertok, L., and de Saussure, R. (1973). *The Therapeutic Revolution: From Mesmer to Freud.* New York: Brunner/Mazel, 1979.

Cranefield, P. (1958). Josef Breuer's evaluaton of his contribution to psycho-analysis. *International Journal of Psycho-Analysis* 39: 319–322.

Ellenberger, H. (1970). *The Discovery of the Unconscious.* New York: Basic Books.

Ellis, A., and Harper, R. (1961). *A Guide to Rational Living.* New York: Institute for Rational Living.

Elms, A. (1980). Freud, Irma, Martha: sex and marriage in the "dream of Irma's injection." *Psychoanalytic Review* 67:83–109.

Enright, J. (1975). An introduction to gestalt therapy. In *Gestalt Therapy Primer,* ed. F. Stephenson, pp. 13–33. New York: Jason Aronson, 1978.

Freud, S. (1894). The neuro-psychoses of defence. *Standard Edition* 3:43–61.

—— (1900). The interpretation of dreams. *Standard Edition* 4–5: 1–627.

—— (1905). A fragment of an analysis of a case of hysteria. *Standard Edition* 7:3–122.

—— (1910). The future prospects of psycho-analytic therapy. *Standard Edition* 11:139–152.

—— (1914). On the history of the psycho-analytic movement. *Standard Edition* 14:3–66.

—— (1918). From the history of an infantile neurosis. *Standard Edition* 17:3–122.

—— (1920). The psycho-genesis of a case of female homosexuality. *Standard Edition* 18:147–172.

—— (1925). An autobiographical study. *Standard Edition* 20:3–74.

—— (1926). Inhibitions, symptoms, and anxiety. *Standard Edition* 20:77–174.

—— (1927). Fetishism. *Standard Edition* 21:149–158.

—— (1937). Constructions in analysis. *Standard Edition* 13:255–270.

—— (1940). Splitting of the ego and the process of defense. *Standard Edition* 23:271–278.

Grotstein, J. (1981). *Splitting and Projective Identification*. New York: Jason Aronson.

Herink, R. (1980). *The Psychotherapy Handbook*. New York: New American Library, Meridian Books.

Howard, J. (1970). *Please Touch*. New York: Dell Publishing.

Janov, A. (1970). *The Primal Scream*. New York: G. P. Putnam's Sons.

Jones, E. (1953). *The Life and Work of Sigmund Freud, Vol. 1*. New York: Basic Books.

Klein, M. (1952). Note on some schizoid mechanisms. In *Developments in Psychoanalysis*, eds. M. Klein, P. Heimann, J. Riviere, pp. 292–320. London: Hogarth Press.

Langs, R. (1976a). *The Bipersonal Field*. New York: Jason Aronson.

—— (1976b). *The Therapeutic Interaction*. New York: Jason Aronson.

—— (1978). *The Listening Process*. New York: Jason Aronson.

—— (1979). *The Therapeutic Environment*. New York: Jason Aronson.

—— (1980). *Interactions: The Realm of Transference and Countertransference*. New York: Jason Aronson.

——, ed. (1981a). *Classics in Psychoanalytic Technique*. New York: Jason Aronson.

———— (1981b). *Resistances and Interventions.* New York: Jason Aronson.

———— (1982). *Psychotherapy: A Basic Text.* New York: Jason Aronson.

Little, M. (1951). Counter-transference and the patient's response to it. *International Journal of Psycho-Analysis* 32:32–40.

McCartney, J. (1966). Overt transference. *Journal of Sexual Research* 2:227–237.

Perls, F. (1969). *Gestalt Therapy Verbatim.* Lafayette, California: Real People Press.

Pollock, G. (1968). A possible significance of childhood object loss in the Josef Breuer–Bertha Pappenheim (Anna O.)–Sigmund Freud relationship: I. Joseph Breuer. *Journal of the American Psychoanalytic Association* 16:711–739.

Spotnitz, H., and Meadow, P. (1976). *Treatment of the Narcissistic Neuroses.* New York: The Manhattan Center for Advanced Psychoanalytic Studies.

Sulloway, F. (1979). *Freud, Biologist of the Mind.* New York: Basic Books.

Waldhorn, H., ed. (1967). The place of the dream in clinical psychoanalysis. *Monograph II: The Kris Study Group of the New York Psychoanalytic Institute*, pp. 52–106. New York: International Universities Press.

INDEX

Abreaction, 14, 67
  discovery of, 65
  in human potential movement,
    23–25
  in primal scream therapy, 68
Action-discharge
  projective identification in,
    245–246
  relief through, 241, 313–314
Adaptive context, 301
  traumatic, 263
Affect
  conversion of, 68
  strangulated, 67
    in primal scream therapy, 151
Analysis
  historical, 59
  of origins, 60–61
Analyst
  critical of psychotherapy, 41–42
  myth of uninvolvement of, 112
  passive and silent, 31
  transference beliefs of, 108,
    140–141
Anna O. (Bertha Pappenheim), 43,
  60

"absences" of, 67
acquaintance with Freud's wife,
  85
Breuer's countertransference
  difficulties with, 85–87
Breuer's reluctance to discuss,
  78–83
Breuer's treatment of, 61–65
career of, 65–66, 95
collusion with Breuer, 69, 75–76,
  92–98
cure of, 66
defenses of, 121–122
evaluation of case by Breuer, 100
exposure of sexual nature of
  therapy by, 122–123
and failed therapeutic efforts, 74
at father's death, 88–89
hallucinations of, 71–74, 161
hysterical childbirth (pseudocyesis) of, 81–82
  encoded message of, 90–91, 95
  as nontransference, 93, 114
  transference aspects of, 113
institutionalization of, 65
lie-barriers created by, 281